Intellectual Trends in the Ch'ing Period

HARVARD EAST ASIAN STUDIES

The Center for East Asian Studies at Harvard University administers postgraduate training programs and research projects designed to further scholarly understanding of China, Korea, Japan, and adjacent areas.

1. China's Early Industrialization: Sheng Hsuan-huai (1844–1916) and Mandarin Enterprise. *By Albert Feuerwerker.*
2. Intellectual Trends in the Ch'ing Period. *By Liang Ch'i-ch'ao. Translation by Immanuel C. Y. Hsü.*

INTELLECTUAL TRENDS IN THE CH'ING PERIOD

(*Ch'ing-tai hsüeh-shu kai-lun*)

清代學術概論

By

Liang Ch'i-ch'ao

梁啟超

Translated with Introduction and Notes by

Immanuel C. Y. Hsü

Foreword by

Benjamin I. Schwartz

HARVARD UNIVERSITY PRESS
Cambridge, Massachusetts
1 9 5 9

Distributed in Great Britain by Oxford University Press, London

This volume was prepared in part under a grant from the Carnegie Corporation of New York. That Corporation is not, however, the author, owner, publisher, or proprietor of this publication and is not to be understood as approving by virtue of its grant any of the statements made or views expressed therein.

Library of Congress Catalog Card Number 59–6158

Printed in the United States of America

To

SERGE ELISSÉEFF

in appreciation of his kindness

Preface

This work of Liang Ch'i-ch'ao presents a balanced impression, in brief compass, of the major intellectual currents of the Ch'ing period (1644–1911) in China. Part I deals with the reaction of early Ch'ing scholars against the abstract, metaphysical, and meditative intellectual climate of the preceding Sung and Ming periods. Their primary aim was to shift scholarly attention from philosophical discourse to practical action, from the individual to the public. Part II deals with the unprecedented rise of textual research on ancient works during the middle Ch'ing period. It was commonly known as the *k'ao-cheng hsüeh*, and through it the rich cultural heritage of China's past was re-ordered and made accessible to modern scholars. Part III considers the rise of the Modern Text Movement during the late Ch'ing. Throughout these three parts the discussion clearly shows the interlocking nature of scholarship and politics in the Confucian society.

This translation also presents for the first time in English the inner world of the Chinese intellectuals during the Ch'ing period. The author was a prominent figure in modern China and held several high ministerial posts after the birth of the Republic in 1912. His early training in the School of Empirical Research and his later participation in the Modern Text Movement gave him incomparable authority to write this book, which has achieved something of the fame of a modern classic in China. It has been re-issued repeatedly and has been in wide use as a standard textbook in the Chinese schools.

In preparing this translation I have received helpful advice from several able scholars. Numerous obscure concepts and difficult sentences in the Chinese text would have eluded my understanding but for Professor Lien-sheng Yang's illuminating explanations. These concepts, having no ready English equivalents, presented a formidable terminological problem, which has been surmounted, even if imperfectly, only through the penetrating suggestions of English expressions by Professors Benjamin I. Schwartz and John K. Fairbank. To these three professors I am also indebted for their patient editing of the manuscript, and Professor Schwartz has in addition favored me with a foreword. Thanks are due also to Professor William Hung and Mr. Chaoying Fang for correcting the renditions of book titles in the three bibliographical sections. My colleague Ch'ü T'ung-tsu has always kindly placed his extensive knowledge at my disposal.

The combined efforts of these scholars have materially assisted me in completing the translation and avoiding many mistakes, but I remain responsible, of course, for all the inadequacies of this work. My sincere thanks also go to Miss Mary Miller of Radcliffe College for stylistic improvement, to Mr. Charles P. Barnes of the Harvard University Press for editorial assistance, and to Mrs. Mary Yates for typing the manuscript.

I.C.Y.H.

Cambridge, Massachusetts
October, 1957

Contents

Reference Matter

Foreword

by Benjamin I. Schwartz

In recent years there has been a growing interest among students of modern China in the political and social setting of China on the eve of the so-called "Western impact." Little attention has been devoted so far to what might be called the intellectual setting. What was the intellectual situation in China on the eve of the Opium War? There is, of course, a ready and obvious answer to this question. China was Confucian. Presumably, in order to understand Confucianism all we have to do is to peruse the available translations (most of them still highly unsatisfactory) of the Confucian classics. Presumably, no historic distance separates the eighteenth- or nineteenth-century literatus from Confucius and his disciples.

Such a view is, of course, entirely in keeping with the stereotype of Changeless China and is in striking contrast to the Western intellectual historian's view of the West. To the Western intellectual historian, a word like "Christianity" suggests infinite complexities, all sorts of polarities and tensions and, above all, change over time. Few would argue that one can understand Thomas Aquinas simply by reading the gospels. So sensitive, indeed, have Western intellectual historians been to changes in the *Zeitgeist* that they tend to measure such changes in terms of decades and years rather than in terms of centuries.

It is, of course, conceivable that even a close and profound study of the intellectual history of China will not reveal the range of possibilities and the diversity of elements which we find in the intellectual history of the West. For one thing, Western intellectual history is fed from such highly diverse streams as Greece, Judea, Rome, and the barbarian north. Is it conceivable, however, that China was dominated for centuries by a completely unproblematic, unchanging something called Confucianism? Or is it possible that the monochromatic appearance of the Chinese intellectual historic landscape is, in part, a function of our distance from it, of our feeble grasp of the language, and of the conceptual categories in terms of which issues are discussed?

Those who are at all close to Chinese studies are by now fully aware that there is much more life and movement here than had been suspected. We know that Han dynasty Confucianism had its own characteristics. We know that during the centuries which stretched from the end of the

Latter Han dynasty to the middle of the T'ang dynasty Confucianism ceased to exercise a dominant hold even on those strata whose class interests it presumably represented; we know that Confucianism recaptured its hold only in the quite novel form of Neo-Confucian philosophy. We know about Chu Hsi and Wang Yang-ming and finally we are dimly aware of a reaction against Neo-Confucianism during the Ch'ing period. In short, we know that the mind of the eighteenth-century scholar cannot be understood simply by reading the *Analects* of Confucius. We must see him in his own eighteenth-century environment and in terms of the generations which immediately preceded him.

We know all these things, but we know them only dimly, as through a dark glass. The issues involved in the trends and counter-trends which sweep over the landscape came through to us in a rather muted, muffled way and since it is difficult for us to grasp the urgency of the issues, it is difficult for us to feel the passions which may have underlain them. The major effort to achieve understanding still lies ahead of us.

There may, of course, be those who doubt the value of the whole enterprise. If there has been intellectual change in China, such change, they may contend, has had no socio-political consequences. The social system remained basically the same. Wang Yang-ming and Juan Yüan may have been miles apart in their intellectual outlook, but they were both bureaucrats in the same bureaucratic, despotic system.

In the first place, it should be pointed out that the historian of ideas has every right to be interested in the history of ideas, whether such ideas have or do not have consequences for the social system. Secondly, ideas may have consequences of great human significance quite apart from their effect on the formal social structure. Thirdly, our knowledge of the development of the social system of China is still as rudimentary as our knowledge of the intellectual history of China. We are, as yet, really not in a position to determine whether such changes may or may not have had socio-political consequences. If they did not have such consequences, this fact in itself raises interesting problems for further inquiry.

One of the least known periods of China's obscure intellectual history is precisely that period which stretches from the middle of the seventeenth century (the period of Manchu conquest) until the end of the nineteenth century, and in some subtle ways well into the twentieth. The trends and counter-trends of this thoroughly "Confucian" period are not only of intrinsic interest in themselves. They also form the background of the thought of those nineteenth-century scholar-officials who were forced to meet the challenges of that century, both foreign and domestic. It is only in terms of these trends that we can ever achieve an understanding of their mental world: that the outlook of such active figures as Wei Yüan, Tseng Kuo-fan, and even of transitional figures such as Chang

Ping-lin, K'ang Yu-wei, T'an Ssu-t'ung, and Liang Ch'i-ch'ao himself can ever be fully understood.

It is considerations such as these which have prompted the following translation of Liang Ch'i-ch'ao's short work on the intellectual trends of the Ch'ing period. The work has not been chosen because it is regarded as, in any sense, a definitive or even very profound work. By the author's own admission, it was a work written in extreme haste. It cannot compare in weight of scholarship with Ch'ien Mu's "History of Intellectual Trends in China during the last Three Hundred Years" (*Chung-kuo chin san-pai-nien hsüeh-shu shih*) (1937), or even with Liang's later, more detailed work on the same subject (*Chung-kuo chin san-pai-nien hsüeh-shu shih*) (1923). Its treatment of many leading figures is highly sketchy. Some highly interesting figures are dismissed with a bare mention or are not mentioned at all. At times it reads like a catalogue of book titles. The sustained and forced analogy between the European Renaissance and the Ch'ing period, which presumably prompted the writing of the book, is questionable on all counts as are many of the sententious judgments scattered throughout the book.

However, the book clearly reflects the author's current preoccupations as of 1920 — for a more detailed discussion of Liang's thought, see Joseph R. Levenson's *Liang Ch'i-ch'ao and the Mind of Modern China* (Cambridge, Mass., 1953). While this personal outlook undoubtedly gives it a tendentious character, it nevertheless lends the book a certain interest of its own as a document. Liang considers himself — quite correctly — to be one of the characters in the story he is recounting and goes so far as to treat himself in the third person in a remarkably detached manner. The fact that he himself had been one of the last representatives of the famous Modern Text school, that he had then become an all-out Westernizer, and that he was now, in his later years, much more reserved in his attitude toward Western values lends a certain living immediacy to his essential message — that there could and ought to be a degree of organic continuity between the China of the twentieth century and the China of the preceding three centuries. Not only did this earlier China contain values (such as those of Buddhist philosophy which had once more been brought to the fore by the Buddhist revival of the end of the nineteenth and beginning of the twentieth century) which can be used to correct and supplement the values of the West, but it even contained values which are ostensibly equivalent to the Western — the values of "scientific method," of "practical statesmanship," and of "socialism" can be found within the stream of Chinese culture. It was eminently desirable that Chinese youth be encouraged to find Chinese roots for these values. We find commingled here both nationalist and genuinely traditionalist motives.

Apart from its interest as a contemporary document, however, Liang's book, at the very minimum, constitutes a sort of convenient handbook of bibliographic and personal information. It is not, however, a mere catalogue, for it furnishes us with a succinct — if not particularly profound — delineation of the main trends of the period. Liang familiarizes us with some of the basic issues and with the language in terms of which these issues are discussed. The book can thus serve as a brief, introductory guide to those interested in further explorations.

It may be appropriate at this point to speculate on some of the interesting problems raised in Liang's work.

One of Liang's main aims is to drive home the realization that the Ch'ing period constitutes a distinct period in China's intellectual history. The early sections stress the spiritual reaction which takes place during the tragic and turbulent years of the mid-seventeenth century against the Sung and Ming schools of Neo-Confucian philosophy. He is, of course, aware that the leading figures of the transitional generation — Ku Yen-wu, Huang Tsung-hsi, Wang Fu-chih, Yen Yüan, and others — have by no means cut all ties with their immediate past, but he is inclined to stress the elements of discontinuity, the fact that a genuinely new "tide of thought" emerges from the crisis of these years. One might argue that Liang exaggerates the distinctness of this period — its discontinuity with the past.

David Nivison in his excellent, unpublished thesis, "The Literary and Historical Thought of Chang Hsüeh-ch'eng (1738–1801)" (Harvard University, 1953), discusses the Ch'ing "school of empirical research" (*k'ao-cheng hsüeh*), the leading school of thought during the Ch'ing period, which is extensively discussed in Liang's text. It is characterized by its emphasis on positive, factual knowledge of the classics and of the historical record. (See footnote 1 of Section I of translation.) Nivison maintains that in its deep suspicion of all general concepts, this school was actually in the tradition of both Wang Yang-ming (1472–1528) and Chu Hsi (1130–1200). Now while this generalization may be correct when applied to the strikingly original and many-sided figure of Chang Hsüeh-ch'eng (1738–1801), I am inclined to doubt its complete validity as applied to the "school of empirical research" in general. Nivison argues that Wang Yang-ming's insistence that moral law or principle cannot be isolated "from the action of one's own mind in given situations" was given a new application by the scholars of the Ch'ing. It was used to "throw doubt on the validity of any general statements in metaphysics." The mere fact that Wang's metaphysics stresses the concrete individual situation while Ch'ing positivism stresses the concrete individual fact does not, to my mind, prove a very strong filiation between the two. Wang himself freely engaged in metaphysical discussion, and the bookish scholasticism of the

Ch'ing scholars would probably have been more alien to him than the intellectualism of the followers of Chu Hsi in his own day.

On the other hand, it can be argued that Chu Hsi was the legitimate father of the "school of empirical research." It was he who insisted that "principles" be derived from an "investigation of things," and he was himself a great classical scholar and historian. Nevertheless, Chu Hsi and his disciples were quite willing to devote considerable time and energy to the philosophic analysis of abstract concepts. To the leaders of the "school of empirical research" this willingness to turn aside from the empirical data to such abstract discussion of "empty words" leads to the dark suspicion that Chu Hsi — or at least his followers — believed that "principles" constitute an autonomous reality apart from the "things" in which they are embedded.

Thus, while the Ch'ing developments cannot, of course, be understood apart from the whole "Problematik" of Neo-Confucianism, it seems to me that Liang is justified in speaking of a new "tide of thought." Whatever the figures of the mid-seventeenth-century spiritual reaction may have owed to Chu Hsi and Wang Yang-ming, however, there can be no doubt of their genuine revulsion against what they regarded as the latter-day epigones of Neo-Confucian thought. They depict the literati of the late Ming period as philosophic scholiasts who had, on the one hand, lost contact with the basic concerns of their own Masters and who were, on the other hand, profoundly ignorant of the classics and of the historic record. In their "lectures" they simply split hairs on fine points of doctrine based on a few concepts derived from the *Great Learning* and *Doctrine of the Mean.* They had strayed far from "pure" Confucian doctrine.

What are the more fundamental issues which underlie this reaction? This writer has found it helpful to think of these trends and counter-trends in terms of a basic polarity which can already be found in the earliest texts of Confucianism — the polarity between the aim of self-realization (*hsiu-shen*) and the aim of "setting the world in order" (*p'ing-t'ien-hsia*). It is, of course, the *chün-tzu* (the superior man) who is fundamentally concerned with both aims. In the *Analects* both aims form part of an inseparable whole. The *chün-tzu* can realize himself fully only in the political vocation. On the other hand, only he who has engaged in extensive self-cultivation can be a good servant of society. There may be a polarity here, but there is certainly no contradiction.

It is only after the Master's death that the problems involved in this polarity come to the fore. They become particularly acute after Confucianism becomes the state philosophy of a highly bureaucratized state. Is it indeed possible to pursue both aims with equal vigor or must the accent inevitably fall on one rather than the other? Does the moral self-cultivation of the *chün-tzu*, based on his conscientious adherence to the prescriptions of proper behavior (*li*), provide a sufficient foundation for his vocation as an official, or does the aim of "ordering of society" call for a concentration on the techniques of professional statecraft? Wang An-shih (the famous Sung statesman, 1021–1086), argued that if the Confucian aim of "ordering society" was to be achieved, a concentration on professional statecraft – on "policy-making" – was essential. His opponents argued that the overwhelming concentration on professional statecraft was not only detrimental to the moral self-cultivation of the individual, but also ran directly counter to Confucius' teaching that it was the self-cultivation of the *chün-tzu* which itself provided the main means of perfecting human society. The concentration on the external manipulation of institutions was foreign to the spirit of Confucianism.

I would here suggest that, in large measure, it was considerations of this sort rather than any fascination with metaphysical problems per se which lay behind the spectacular development of Neo-Confucian philosophy. In their opposition to Wang An-shih's program, the fathers of Neo-Confucian philosophy stressed the aim of self-realization more strongly than ever. The *chün-tzu* can realize himself, however, only to the extent that he knows his own nature. To know his own nature he must know the nature of the total reality of which man is a part. It is at this point, perhaps, that the Neo-Confucian thinkers were influenced by the grand systems of Mahayana Buddhism, which could not conceive of treating the problem of human salvation in isolation from a consideration of the nature of reality. Nevertheless, the underlying concern with individual self-realization remains authentically Confucian. Furthermore, one can certainly not say that either Chu Hsi or Wang Yang-ming is indifferent to the political vocation of the *chün-tzu*. They simply conceive of this vocation mainly in terms of moral self-cultivation. The charge was indeed later made that they had actually abandoned the aim of "ordering the state" entirely: that even in their official pursuits they were mainly interested in the effects of their experience on their own moral progress. Their latter day followers were also attacked for becoming interested in philosophic dialectic as an end in itself.

When we turn to the transitional figures of the seventeenth century, we find that, however much they may differ from each other, they all seem to share the burning conviction that one of the main causes of the Ming collapse was the fact that its intellectual leaders had somehow lost touch with reality. To the Westerner, it is, of course, striking that in their ardent desire to get back to "reality" they all tacitly assume that such reality is to be found exclusively within a Confucian framework. Indeed, they are convinced that they are rescuing pure Confucianism from the perversions of their predecessors, but there is, of course, a ready explanation for this tenacious loyalty to Confucianism. Confucianism was by now the inalienable class philosophy of the scholar-bureaucrats. (Whether this explanation is entirely adequate is a question I shall not attempt to consider at this point.)

If we turn our attention to Ku Yen-wu, who is one of the most important figures of this generation (in terms of subsequent influence), we find that in his search for reality he by no means renounces the Neo-Confucian stress on moral self-cultivation. Both he and Huang Tsung-hsi, however, again stress what they regard as the long-neglected aim of ordering human society. They are both advocates of "practical statesmanship" (*ching-shih chih-yung*). However, while Ku is thus seemingly aligned with Wang Anshih, it is interesting to note that the direction of his reform program is quite antithetical to the highly centralizing, interventionist policies of the great Sung statesman.

Furthermore, in the thought of Ku Yen-wu the neglect of "practical statesmanship" among the latter day Neo-Confucian thinkers is closely linked with their passion for abstract thought divorced from any "solid" knowledge of either the classical canon, history, or even their own environment. The classics contain the principles of practical statesmanship, and such principles can be extracted only by a systematic and scientific study of the classics. The historical record provides the laboratory in which these principles are tested. Hence only a comprehensive and accurate knowledge of the classics and of the historic record can provide the key to "practical statesmanship" as well as to self-realization. The attainment of such knowledge was still a task of the future.

Now, in stressing the importance of empirical scholarship, Ku Yen-wu was not introducing an entirely new principle into Confucianism. Here again one can discern the roots in the *Analects* themselves.

Confucius' concept of the good society was not like Plato's republic — an ideal structure constructed by a step-by-step process of deductive reasoning and then contrasted with all "conventional" societies which had actually existed. His good society had actually existed in the past. To know the essential facts about the culture and social order of the early Chou was, in effect, to know the "Way." The acquisition of learning was thus an integral part of Confucius' whole program. To know history was to know the norms which had in the past actually been realized in history.

What is more, with Confucius — as with Ku Yen-wu — one has the feeling that learning has almost become an autonomous value above and beyond the instrumental role it plays in the whole Confucian program. The great tragedy of the Master's life was his failure to fulfill his public vocation. This tragedy led him to seek consolation in his role as teacher and "transmitter" of the knowledge of the past. "Is it not pleasant to learn with a constant perseverance and application?" — these are the opening words of the *Analects*. With Ku Yen-wu also (who refused to accept office under the Manchus), one again feels that while learning is a means to the end of practical statesmanship, it is also to some degree a value in itself.

It is, however, only in the generation which succeeds the transitional generation of the late-Ming, early Ch'ing period that learning comes to occupy the center of the stage as a supreme end in itself. Many modern Chinese scholars have deplored this shift from the promising "practicality" of Ku Yen-wu and Huang Tsung-hsi to the "escapist" scholasticism of the "school of empirical research," which preoccupied itself so exclusively with the delights of textual criticism, bibliography, epigraphy, and other such closeted pursuits. A variety of explanations have been offered. Mr. Nivison suggests as one factor that during the Manchu dynasty one witnesses an expansion of the social base of the literate class. The literati were becoming far too numerous to be absorbed into the civil service. On the other hand, there were numerous patrons – including the government itself – willing to employ these literati on learned projects. An even more popular explanation is that which stresses the peculiar repressiveness of the Manchu dynasty which forced the literati away from "practical statemanship" into the innocuous pursuit of pure scholarship.

While Mr. Nivison's explanation undoubtedly points to an important factor in the social situation of the time, neither explanation really accounts for the peculiar *form* of "escape." If learned projects commanded the support of so many patrons (including salt merchants), this would indicate that learning was already well established as a high prestige activity. It is true that the Ch'ing dynasty itself sponsored vast compilations and encyclopedic projects. (In doing this it was, of course, simply continuing, perhaps on a larger scale, a type of activity which was already highly developed in previous dynasties.) While such activities provided jobs, they by no means account for some of the most creative accomplishments of the leading figures of the "school of empirical research" – accomplishments which are obviously labors of love. Some of the most significant efforts of its methodology are to be found in what might be called the analysis in depth of given problems rather than in the type of hack mechanical compilation efforts supported by the government and the patrons.

Furthermore, while we do have during the Ch'ing dynasty the brutal persecutions associated wtih the Ch'ien-lung "Literary Inquisition," it is important to note that this persecution was concerned with the relatively specific question of attitudes toward barbarians. Is there any evidence that the dynasty was more repressive in the intellectual sphere than any of its predecessors? The dynasty itself was committed to the Sung philosophy, yet Tai Chen and others freely published their anti-Neo-Confucian tracts under its sway. On the matter of "practical statesmanship," the question is not whether the Ch'ing dynasty was open to all sorts of radical proposals for reform — the question is whether it was more repressive in this area than the dynasties which immediately preceded it.

Above all, the theory of Manchu repression overlooks the possibility of a logical progression from the outlook of Ku Yen-wu to the outlook of the "school of empirical research." As already indicated, Ku Yen-wu had himself exalted learning to a position of central importance and had himself been a pioneer in developing the inductive methods of scholarship which were to dominate the following generations. The ideal of comprehensive and accurate factual scholarship which he established was not an ideal to be quickly attained. If pursued consistently it could easily absorb the energies of entire generations. If his own writings are liberally interspersed with opinions on matters of "practical statesmanship," this is perhaps due to a certain laudable inconsistency on his part. Living in an age of crisis, he did not wait for the "facts to speak for themselves" but constantly confronted the facts with opinions which were certainly not simply induced from the facts themselves.

The fact is, that in China as elsewhere a purely inductive-empirical approach generally does not lead to larger general conclusions. The facts when confronted with a *tabula rasa* do not yield forth "answers" — particularly in the realm of human affairs. Even if such pioneers of "the school of empirical research" as Hui Tung and Yen Jo-chü continued to regard learning as a means to the achievement of ethical and political insights, their method led them elsewhere. It soon came to have a fascination all its own.

With many of the best minds of this period, rigorous scholarship became not merely a pleasure (as it already was to Confucius) but the supreme delight. Scholarship as a way of life has, of course, exercised its attractions in all times and places. The sense of mastery within a given field, the intimate acquaintance with all its ramifications and bypaths, the fascination of scholarly problems, the sense of triumph which derives from new discoveries no matter how small, and, finally, the sense of escape from the squalor and messiness of everyday existence — these are all delights which can compensate for much else.

As Liang indicates, the scholarly accomplishments of the "school of empirical research" are most impressive and still of vital concern to the student of Chinese studies. Whether the school marks the beginnings of "Science" in China as both Liang and Hu Shih maintain, is, of course, a question which hinges very much on the definition of that elusive concept. Its methods of research and verification do indeed remind us strongly of methods used by the philological scholarship of the latter half of the nineteenth century in the West, and the high prestige word "Science" has, of course, been appropriated for this scholarship. To the extent that a respect for accuracy, comprehensive factual knowledge, and inductive methods of verification are values of "Science," the school may be called scientific.

On the other hand, some of the weightiest figures in the philosophy of science insist that without the spectacular development of the deductive methods of logic and mathematics, the most spectacular achievements of the Western physical sciences would have been inconceivable. Yet, with such minor, questionable exceptions as Mei Wen-ting, the basic outlook of the "school of empirical research" was probably less favorable to growth in the disciplines of logic and mathematics than was the Neo-Confucian philosophy of the previous period. While the Neo-Confucian philosophers were quite willing to consider abstract concepts and their logical implications apart from any immediate reference to empirical data, the "school of empirical research" clung convulsively to the immediate fact. Its empiricism was by no means a "logical empiricism."

There is the further fact, which has been pointed out by others, that the "school of empirical research" (with some minor exceptions) was overwhelmingly concerned with the facts of human culture. There was, to be sure, some interest in astronomy, artifacts, and geography, but all as adjuncts of human studies. While Chu Hsi's definition of the phrase "the investigation of things" was potentially applicable to "things" of non-human nature, Ku Yen-wu, in his preoccupation with practical affairs, defines the phrase in such a way as to make it exclusively applicable to human relations (*jen-lun*) and not to "birds, beasts, plants and flowers." This does not, of course, constitute a conclusive argument against Liang's claim. It is noteworthy, however, that so far the most spectacular triumphs of "Science" have occurred in the natural sciences, while the most successful marriage of logical and mathematical method with empirical verification first occurred in the realm of the physical sciences.

Liang also points to the subversive implications of the critical attitude of such men as Yen Jo-chü toward various parts of the classical canon. While the skeptical attitude of various Ch'ing scholars concerning the authenticity of parts of the classical canon is one of the remarkable fruits of their methodology, there seems to be little evidence that it led to any immediate revolutionary implications for the whole complex of Confucian moral and social beliefs. The Confucian order as a whole was so much taken for granted that its validity did not depend on the question of the authenticity of this or that book. By the time twentieth-century scholars begin to draw subversive conclusions from the work of the Ch'ing scholars, the anti-Confucian tide had already set in. It is therefore doubtful whether one can speak of any spiritual continuity between Yen Jo-chü and the iconoclasts of the "May Fourth" period when Liang was writing.

Nevertheless, in the ultimate analysis the "school of empirical research" may have contributed to the final corrosion of Confucian faith. While scholarship was a traditional Confucian value, the fact that it had pushed the more ultimate values of self-realization and the perfection of society into the background, would argue for a striking diminution of faith in the higher hopes of Confucianism. Conventional Confucian attitudes persisted and were by no means shaken by doubts concerning the authenticity of sacred books, but they seem to have persisted more from habit than from any deep emotional conviction.

As a matter of fact, as Liang clearly indicates, by the latter half of the eighteenth century strong counter-currents against the "school of empirical research" had already set in. There is first of all the intriguing and little studied Modern Text school from which Liang himself drew youthful inspiration. As a result of the textual controversies of the Ch'ing scholars, the attention of certain individuals was suddenly drawn to some of the long neglected writings of the Han Modern Text school. These texts seemed to offer a new and fresh message which distinguishd them from both the arid, sterile scholasticism of the "school of empirical research" and the "empty" philosophizing of the Neo-Confucian philosophers.

When we examine some of the key texts of the school, such as Ho Hsiu's (second century A.D.) sub-commentary on the *Kung-yang Commentary*, we enter a rather unexpected world. Here we find a sort of apocalyptic vision which reminds us in its atmosphere of the book of Daniel or Revelation. We find a portrayal of Confucius as a sort of uncrowned Messiah-King. We find the germs of the notion of a redemptive history. This exotic strand within the Confucian tradition (the orthodox, in fact, questioned its right to the name Confucian) had been completely submerged ever since the latter Han dynasty.

If we examine the writings of some of the later nineteenth-century members of this school — Kung Tzu-chen, Wei Yüan and, above all, K'ang Yu-wei — we find that they claim to see in this strand of thought a new inspiration for positive activity in the political realm. It was not that the writings of Ho Hsiu and others provided concrete principles of "practical statesmanship." They rather provided a sort of religious inspiration for "practical statesmanship," for a positive concern with current affairs. It was, of course, only K'ang Yu-wei, already in touch with Western thought, who drew from these beliefs a full-blown theory of progress and a positive sanction for sweeping institutional changes.

There were, however, many literati in the late eighteenth and early nineteenth centuries who could never accept the visions of the Modern Text school, but who were nevertheless profoundly discontented with the fruitless scholasticism of the "school of empirical research." Living in a period of growing demoralization and crisis, they were seeking new inspiration and broader visions. There were many such as the illustrious

Tseng Kuo-fan who returned to a defense of Chu Hsi's ideas against the onslaughts of the Ch'ing empiricists. As a leader of the Confucian cause against the Taiping rebels, he could not but deplore the school's indifference to the value of moral self-cultivation. The T'ung-ch'eng literary school (which Tseng supported) on the one hand defended Neo-Confucian philosophy and on the other deplored the scholars' indifference to the aesthetic values of good style. Even some of the outstanding personalities who are often linked with the "school of empirical research" in some ways represent a reaction against it. Chang Hsüeh-ch'eng may support the school in its attack on Neo-Confucianism. This does not prevent him from attempting to construct a grandiose philosophy of history. Finally, during the nineteenth century and the beginning of the twentieth, we even have, as Liang indicates, a sudden revival of interest in Buddhist philosophy.

As a matter of fact, in order to recount the full story of the intellectual trends of the eighteenth and nineteenth centuries, one would have to devote considerable attention to the whole sphere of literature – a sphere which is very much neglected in Liang's study.

Nevertheless, the book does give us some rudimentary grasp of the intellectual setting of the period in which the "Western impact" takes place. It is primarily in terms of this setting that the most active minds of the nineteenth century must be understood. We in the West are, of course, naturally interested in their fragmentary "responses to the West," but their own outlook on the world which faced them was still basically conditioned by the intellectual trends of their own Chinese milieu.

Introduction
by the Translator

Introduction

by the Translator

Knowledge of the intellectual climate of an age is essential to understanding it. This was particularly true of the Chinese Confucian state, where scholarship and statesmanship were two sides of the same coin. The Master said, "He who excels in learning should serve in the government." Scholarship in traditional China, therefore, was the root of statecraft, and statesmanship, the fruit of learning. By reflecting the political climate of the time, scholarship was a political barometer.

Certainly this was true in the Ch'ing period, when China was ruled by a jealous foreign dynasty. In its early years great masters like Ku Yen-wu advocated the practical application of knowledge to public affairs as a way to restore Chinese rule, because they held the metaphysical speculations of the Ming philosophers to have been partially responsible for the decline and downfall of the dynasty. In the middle period of the Ch'ing, the rise of empirical research (*k'ao-cheng-hsüeh*) mirrored on the one hand the spontaneous growth of a proto-scientific spirit in historical research, and on the other, a sense of insecurity and frustration among scholars under foreign rulers.[1] In the late Ch'ing, scholars like K'ang Yu-wei openly used the Modern Text school of classical learning as a vehicle for programs of political reform, which culminated in the reform movement of 1898.

Important as is the nexus between politics and learning, our understanding of the Ch'ing period is marred by the lack of any serious work in English on its intellectual currents. The present translation goes far to fill this gap, being an inside and intimate account of the subject by a late Ch'ing intellectual and political leader, Liang Ch'i-ch'ao (1873–1929).

Although the name of Liang Ch'i-ch'ao is well known to students of Modern China,[2] a brief biographical sketch and an account of the conditions under which he wrote the present book are not out of place here. Born in 1873 in Hsin-hui near Canton, Liang was a precocious child. At eight he could already write well and at seventeen he achieved the *chü-jen*, the second highest literary degree in the nation. He studied under K'ang Yu-wei and later followed his teacher into politics. The *coup d'état* of 1898 drove him into exile in Japan, where he spent the next fourteen years writing prolifically in the cause of reform and constitutionalism. After the establishment of the Republic in 1912 he served as Minister of

Justice (1913) and Minister of Finance (1917) at Peking. At the end of World War I he traveled widely in Europe and was deeply affected by the ravages and devastation of the war. Materialistic Western civilization, which he had previously supported enthusiastically, clearly disappointed him, and in this disappointment he rediscovered the enduring value of the mellow, humanistic civilization of his native country. After his return to China he left politics to engage in writing and lecturing. He became a professor at Tsing Hua College in 1923, Director of the Peking Library in 1925, and died in 1929 at the age of 56.

It was in this period of revived interest in Chinese civilization that Liang wrote the present book. His training in the "school of empirical research" and his participation in the Modern Text Movement gave him incomparable authority to undertake this work. The first book on Ch'ing intellectual movements, it enjoyed great popularity in China and went through many editions after its appearance in 1921; the Chinese Communists reissued it in 1954 without editorial comment. The present translation is of the seventh edition of 1927, published by the Commercial Press in Shanghai.

For this choice of author and text, no apology is necessary, yet a word of explanation may be useful to put this work in its proper place. The book is admittedly not an intellectual history of the Ch'ing period, as the author himself clearly points out, but rather, an introductory work on the major intellectual currents of that period. It has been widely used in Chinese schools as a standard introductory work, not so much because of its depth of scholarship as because of its flashes of insight and its comprehensive grasp of those intellectual currents. The high regard it has received in Chinese intellectual circles may have been more than it deserved, but the fact remains that it has enjoyed a high place. This may have been due to Liang's tremendous popularity or to the pioneer nature of the work. Whatever the reason, nobody denies Liang's success in presenting in the present work a balanced impression of a vast subject in the briefest compass. It is primarily for this reason that it is considered an excellent introduction to the study of Ch'ing intellectual movements.

The shortcomings of this work are obvious. Liang himself pointed out that it was originally written as a preface to another book, but that it proved too long for that purpose and was published separately. As is true of most of Liang's writings, this work was written in an extremely rapid fashion and gives what Ch'en Tu-hsiu aptly called the impression of being a "flashing light and a fleeting shadow" (*fou-kuang lüeh-ying*); [3] over-simplification and over-generalization can be found in it here and there. I am not unaware of the two larger books on more or less the same subject, by Liang himself and by Professor Ch'ien Mu, as noted in Mr. Schwartz's Foreword. Yet Liang's later work of 1923 is three times as long as this earlier one, and it consists of his lectures, which are rather informal in presentation, colloquial in style, and loose in structure. It does not have the coherence and terseness of the present study. Ch'ien Mu's book of 1937 is definitely a superior piece of scholarship, benefiting as it does from Liang's pioneer works. Yet its much greater length — some five times longer than the text of my translation with a correspondingly greater degree of detail — has precluded any attempt to translate it for a Western audience in the present state of development of this neglected field of scholarship.

The difficulty of translating Chinese into English has been discussed by James Legge, Derk Bodde, and others, and I have nothing new to add.[4] To translate a writer of Liang's grasp makes one ever conscious of one's limitations and constantly fearful of doing him injustice. I have endeavored to make my translation literal and faithful even at the expense of what little literary grace happens to be at my disposal. The translation consequently follows the order of the Chinese text closely, except in a few cases where literal rendition is impossible or makes awkward reading in English.

Concepts that have no exact counterparts in English have presented the greatest problems, and it is extremely difficult, if not impossible, to standardize the translation of key terms. For instance, a simple term like *hsüeh* may be rendered in many ways — as learning, school of learning, studies, views, work, intellectual pursuit, etc. — depending on the context in which it appears, and it is by no means easy to select the right one. A basic term in the text, *k'ao-cheng-hsüeh,* which literally means research based on documentary evidence, has commonly been translated "textual criticism." But since its activities were not limited to textual research on ancient books but extended to include such work as identification of artifacts — ancient funeral gowns, hats, chariots, etc. — the rendition of "textual criticism" is too narrow to cover the entire meaning of the term. As textual criticism and identification of artifacts were all based on empirical research, a broader rendition of *k'ao-cheng-hsüeh* as the "school of empirical research" seems more accurate, despite its modern connotation. The term *chia-fa* is another difficult and even enigmatic concept. It denotes the method, traditions, intellectual outlook, and approach to learning of a school or a great master. In the absence of a ready and concrete English equivalent which can convey all these meanings, I have reluctantly translated it "methodology," in full consciousness of its inadequacy. *P'u-hsüeh,* rendered by someone as "unadorned learning," probably has a fuller meaning. *P'u* means something unassuming in bearing and unostentatious in appearance, yet solid in substance and wholesome in nature. "Solid scholarship" and "sound learning" are possible renditions for *p'u-hsüeh,* and it is the latter that has finally been kept. *Ching-shih chih-yung*, meaning something like the application of knowledge to public affairs, is here translated, for simplicity's sake, "practical statesmanship." These few examples suffice to indicate the hundreds of other difficult problems facing the translator, but further elaboration on this point is unnecessary since most of the terms are explained in notes upon their first appearance. Many of my renditions are admittedly unsatisfactory; they have been kept for no other reason than my inability to find better ones.

Book titles may sound very strange and even meaningless in an English form and are often not translated in other works. I am inclined, however, to the view that some form of translation is more useful to the English reader than none at all, although I am not sure that such an effort is appreciated by all. There are certainly many inadequacies in my renditions, and I hope my readers will sympathize with the difficulties faced by an inter-cultural interpreter and benefit him with their corrections.

Assuming the role of a translator for the informed reader, rather than an annotator for research scholars, I have chosen not to make extensive notes. A limited number of notes have been made in places where I believe such notes essential to a correct understanding of the text, or to my rendition of certain difficult key terms. Since Liang's original text also contains parenthetical references, his notations are referred to by starred (*) numerals, while my own are indicated by plain numerals. The page numbers of the Chinese text appear at the margins of the translation to facilitate textual comparison. For the reader's convenience, long paragraphs have been broken into shorter ones, and a table of contents, sectional headings, and a glossary-index have been supplied. I, of course, take responsibility for these minor re-arrangements which do not appear in the original text.

* * * * *

Early Ch'ing intellectual movements represent a reaction against the abstract, metaphysical, and meditative intellectual climate of the Sung and Ming, and a shift in emphasis from the individual to the public, from philosophical discourse to practical action. To appreciate the significance of these developments, a preliminary glimpse at the major pre-Ch'ing intellectual trends is desirable.

The material prosperity of the Sui-T'ang period had created a general moral laxity and social inertia, and the political disorder and military rebellions in the late T'ang generated a sense of weariness among the people. With the Sung came a desire among intellectuals to re-examine their inner selves, and this tendency toward inward searching paved the way for the development of a philosophy more metaphysical and introspective than practical Confucianism.[5] In this socio-intellectual milieu there evolved a new syncretic philosophy, known as the *li-hsüeh,* or Neo-Confucianism, which was a mixture of Buddhism, orthodox Confucianism, and Taoism.[6] This new philosophy dominated the intellectual world of the Sung and Ming, and discussion of the abstract idea of Mind (*hsin*) and (Human) Nature (*hsing*) became a vogue. Nevertheless, the Sung scholars and philosophers did not forsake the practical subjects in the original Confucianism, but continued to pay attention to the cultivation of self and the management of family relations in preparation for service to the state and the world at large.[7]

With the opening of the Ming period this practical aspect of Neo-Confucianism was greatly neglected, however. Students needed to study only the Yung-lo *Hsing-li ta-ch'üan* (Encyclopedia on Human Nature and Rational Principles) to pass the government examinations for the civil service, and the old classics went untouched.[8] Against this general drift toward metaphysical argumentation and abstract discourse, Wang Yang-ming (1472–1528) propounded his belief in the *liang-chih,* the intuitive knowledge of men. Although individual conscience and ethics were central in his thinking, politics and the general public also commanded his attention.[9] The general intellectual trend, however, still leaned toward introspective meditation and superficial conversation. Social ethics and consciousness reached a low ebb and latter-day epigones of the Wang school went so far as to proclaim that wine, women, and song were no obstacle to attaining Enlightenment. Some students even ingratiated themselves with powerful eunuchs like Wei Chung-hsien to win positions. Social degradation and political corruption having reached such extremes, a reaction was bound to arise.

A group of serious scholars formed a center in the Tung-lin (or so-called "Eastern Forest") Academy of Wusih, Kiangsu, to attack political corruption and attempt to turn the intellectual focus of the times from the abstract to the practical, from the individual to the public. Their criticism of the government and resistance to temptation and coercion led to their destruction by Wei Chung-hsien. They did succeed, however, in arousing a new intellectual interest in the practical affairs of the world.[10]

Meanwhile, several other currents against abstract and superficial discourse on Mind and Nature appeared in the late Ming.[11] For example, there was a reaction within the Wang Yang-ming school itself. Liu Tsung-chou (1578–1645), who admired Wang for a time, became very critical of the philosophy of "intuitive knowledge." He de-emphasized the metaphysical elements in the Wang school of learning, favored deeds over talk, and censured the powerful eunuch Wei Chung-hsien in 1621.[12] There was also a nationwide geographical survey conducted by Hsü Hung-tsu (1585–1641), better known as Hsü Hsia-k'e, who recorded his findings in his famous *Travelogue,* published posthumously in 1776.[13]

In the field of applied science, Sung Ying-hsing (born ca. 1600), compiled an encyclopedic work entitled *T'ien-kung k'ai-wu* (The Ingenious Creation of Things by Nature), published in 1637 in 18 sections, each devoted to a practical subject, with illustrations on tilling, weaving, hydraulics, coinage, gold-mining, and other subjects.[14] All this was in glaring contrast with the contemporary indulgence in abstract discourse. Western astronomy and mathematics also made their appearance in China about this time. Moreover, a growing interest in book collecting and publication gradually emerged, despite the general lack of interest in reading. Fan Ch'in of Ningpo established a library called *T'ien-i ko*, probably the largest private collection in the country. In line with this trend toward practical pursuits, three Buddhist masters, Lien-tz'u (d. 1615), Kan-shan (d. 1623), and Wan-i (d. 1655), appeared to reject the meditative Ch'an (Zen) Sect in favor of the Pure Land Sect and, unlike the Ch'an, promoted the study of the sutras.

Late Ming intellectual trends were thus already moving from introspective meditation and abstract discourse on Mind and Nature to a more serious type of learning and to practical subjects. Great scholars of the early Ch'ing – Ku Yen-wu, Huang Tsung-hsi, and Wang Fu-chih – were products of that environment, and their eagerness to pursue practical studies gained new impetus after the fall of the Ming. Examining the factors in the rise and fall of dynasties, they blamed the irresponsible intellectuals for the downfall of the Ming. By emphasizing serious scholarship and practical studies, the early Ch'ing scholars hoped to create a new and healthy intellectual atmosphere, which they intended to maintain after the overthrow of the Ch'ing.[15] When they realized the hopelessness of overthrowing the Manchu dynasty and the impossibility of making use of their practical studies under the foreign overlords, more and more of them resigned themselves to pure scholarship in hope of future usefulness. Their eager search for the true meaning of the classics and the various commentaries sowed the seed of textual research which came to full bloom in the middle Ch'ing period. Literary inquisitions and official persecution threatened the lives of those who dared to talk politics, and Emperor Ch'ien-lung explicitly stated that it was "especially not permissible" that scholars should consider it "their duty to govern the nation."[16] New generations had grown up under the Manchus and were naturally less resentful of their alien overlords. The now peaceful and orderly society was also conducive to serious scholarly work.[17] All these factors favored the growth of sound scholarship in ancient texts, which was both politically safe and intellectually rewarding.

During the height of empirical research on ancient texts in the middle Ch'ing period, the school of Han learning held sway over the nation. Although the Sung Neo-Confucianism of the Ch'eng brothers and Chu

Hsi was promoted by Emperors K'ang-hsi and Yung-cheng, it was still possible for scholars in the Kiangsu and Chekiang areas to counter it by advancing Han learning, which gained a new ascendency during the reign of Ch'ien-lung. This phenomenon itself intimated the possibility of comparative freedom in non-political, purely intellectual pursuits, even under a despotic, absolutist foreign rule. The bureau for the compilation of the *Ssu-k'u ch'üan-shu* (*The Complete Works of the Four Treasuries*) was established by the government at the request of Han scholars over the protest of the Sung school, and it became the headquarters of some three hundred Han scholars. They edited 3,457 works in 79,070 *chuan*; the synopsis of each entry represents the crystallization of the Han school approach to the subject.[18] The Han school's dominant position was not shaken until after the Taiping Rebellion, when influential officials like Tseng Kuo-fan and Lo Tse-nan took a new interest in Sung learning.[19]

The Chia-ch'ing (1796–1820) and Tao-kuang (1821–1850) periods saw a new trend in the intellectual world. The ideal of strict disassociation from politics became weakened, primarily because of the increasing relaxation of governmental vigilance and control. Scholars grew more daring in their ventures into politics; the great classical scholar Wang Nien-sun impeached the powerful and corrupt official Ho Shen[20] (1750–1799), and the great historian Hung Liang-chi (1746–1809) offered such candid, blunt advice, in response to an imperial call, that he was banished to the Northwest frontier.[21]

At about this time, Western missionaries and gunboats made their appearance in China, and the defeat of China in the Opium and Arrow Wars shocked the intelligentsia into seeking the source of China's weakness. Was it, they asked themselves, her lack of a religion such as the West had, or were there inherent defects in her political system?[22] A new intellectual movement was born, with the two-fold purpose of finding a force in China equivalent to Western religion and finding a way to strengthen her. The best way to achieve this was first to find sanctions for the new movement in the classics, which still had a strong hold on men's minds. The most useful school of classical learning was that of the Modern Texts, which canonized Confucius as an uncrowned king, a divine being, and founder of a religion, and which stressed his institutional reforms as well as the idea of political progress from "disorder" to "order" to "universal peace." The late Ch'ing reformers saw in these teachings a powerful support for their own program, and the new usefulness of Confucius was quickly seized upon by an ambitious scholar-thinker, K'ang Yu-wei. He was assisted in this bold venture by a famous pupil, Liang Ch'i-ch'ao, author of the work here translated.

This quick review of Ch'ing intellectual trends brings us to the crucial question of their significance in the history of Chinese thought. Any value judgment is by its very nature relative and not definitive, but there is little argument that it was largely through the Ch'ing endeavors that the rich heritage of China's past was re-ordered. Unintelligible ancient texts became intelligible, and lost or untransmitted texts were recovered. Had it not been for the textual research of the Ch'ing scholars, modern Chinese would not have such easy access to the treasury of their national ideas. Great as their accomplishments were, however, the Ch'ing scholars created no new strands of thought or new schools of philosophy. They may be said to have been proficient interpreters and devoted editors of Chinese civilization rather than its creative builders.

Intellectual Trends in the Ch'ing Period

(Ch'ing-tai hsüeh-shu kai-lun)

Translation

[*i] *Foreword*

When I finished composing my history of the European Renaissance, I asked Liang Ch'i-ch'ao for a preface and, since his preface was as long as the original book, it became in itself a separate, general account of Ch'ing learning. He then asked me for a preface. In view of the liberation that came about with the revival of antiquity and the transition from a subjective, deductive [method] to an objective, inductive one, I think the spirit of Ch'ing learning was virtually in harmony with that of the European Renaissance.[1] Nevertheless, time and again our material progress has been delayed, and although our contemporary scholars and high officials have been loudly advocating the promotion of science, there has been no marked success as yet. Why should this be so? In addition [to this question], I would like to raise a few more questions here concerning the history of the development of Ch'ing learning:

First, [members of] the Society of Jesus came with their science to the East during the transitional period between the Ming and the Ch'ing dynasties, and concentrated their attention on emperors and high-class people, such as the Ming empresses and the Ch'ing emperors.[2] Emperor K'ang-hsi, a founder of the Ch'ing dynasty, was particularly interested in their mathematics, [for the purpose of] geographical exploration and astronomical measurement, and gradually applied it to practical ends. In accordance with this train of development, European learning should have gradually been imported. Why then did [this interest] come to an abrupt halt after the K'ang-hsi period, leaving behind only mathematics and astronomy to hold the crumbling fort?

[*ii] Second, practical learning had become almost a fashion among the scholars during the interval from Ku Yen-wu (1613–1682) to Yen Yüan (1635–1704) and Li Kung (1659–1746). "Practical" actually meant "useful to people's livelihood," and normally [this learning] should have opened the gates to material development. Why was it then, that only the trend towards documentary research into the classical canon really prospered while all other [types of learning] simply did not develop, or at best, were only considered as side issues?

Third, Tai Chen's theory concerning "reason and desire" might have shocked men of the past and aroused those of the present; it was truly in the Renaissance spirit of the exaltation of the pleasure of the individual. His statement that "the evil that comes from suppressing desires is even greater than that which comes from holding back a flood" was indeed an extraordinary one to appear in China. But this theory was simply ignored in those days. There was neither approval nor overt opposition. Why was this so?

Fourth, when we come to recent times, aroused by the [West's] "strong ships and powerful guns," we established arsenals, translated Western works, and sent students abroad – demonstrating a lively tendency to progress. Why then did the "Modern Text Movement," which began some twenty years after the establishment of the [Kiangnan] Arsenal, not enjoy the participation of anyone conversant with Western languages? Furthermore, why did the rise of the theories of reform and restoration, constitutionalism, and revolution sway the nation and preempt the place of physics and chemistry, while pure science failed to develop?

Some of the causes may have had their origins in political circumstances. The Ch'ing had conquered China as an alien race; practical learning was bound to incur their suspicion, and thus [Chinese scholars] took up "sound learning" (*p'u-hsüeh*) to preserve themselves. This is the first point. Furthermore, during the last years of the K'ang-hsi period, various princes vied with each other [for succession], with the Jesuits on the side of the Heir Apparent and the Lamas on the side of Yung-cheng.[3] [*iii] (This was reported to me by Mr. Hsia Sui-ch'ing.) [The Jesuits] not only failed in this foreign [venture] but were also reprimanded by Rome, and missionary work thus unexpectedly became an obstacle to the introduction of Western learning [into China]. This is the second point.

There were also causes that had their origin in social customs: by nature our people are highly inclined to compromise. The revival of antiquity in Europe was highly combative, and while the revival of antiquity in the Ch'ing period attacked Sung learning, it relied on the sacred classics to defend itself. It sought traditional precedents and took a compromising turn. The lack of a definite character [in Ch'ing learning] was a great obstacle to scientific [development]. This is the third point. Our people had a taste for abstract discussion; society identified art with craftsmanship, whereas abstract and obscure discussion could, on the other hand, gain a man prestige. This is the fourth point.

Now times and circumstances have altered somewhat, and our nation is just beginning to talk enthusiastically about cultural undertakings. However, enough has remained of the social habits [of the past] to prove a great stumbling block to learning: under the economically-oriented influence of foreign circles, the doctrine of material profit is thriving – wealth is on top, social position comes next, and the attitude toward scholars is one suggesting remoteness and impracticality. On the other hand, the habit of abstract discussion remains unchanged. Democracy, socialism [?], reform and restoration, constitutionalism, and revolution are nothing but phrases. Is there any difference between the present situation and the past? I hope that my contemporaries will do their utmost to correct [these trends].

Chiang Fang-chen

January 2, 1921

[*i] ## *Author's First Preface*

(1) Two things prompted me to write this book. First, Hu Shih said to me, "The late Ch'ing 'Modern Text Movement' has had a great influence on our intellectual world; since you actually personally participated in it, it behooves you to record it." Second, Chiang Fang-chen had just completed his book, *Ou-chou wen-i fu-hsing shih-tai shih* [A History of the Renaissance Period in Europe], and had asked me for a preface. Feeling that a general preface would be no tribute to its high quality, I thought it preferable to take a similar period in our own history for a comparative study so that we could contrast the merits and failings of the two and give ourselves encouragement. Therefore, I [proposed and secured] his assent to substitute this piece of writing for the preface. However, when I started to write, I could not stop until I had written tens of thousand of words – a number almost equal to that of the book itself. There has never been such a preface anywhere in the world, and when the manuscript was finished, I could only declare it a work independent of Chiang's book.

(2) Eighteen years ago I wrote the "Basic Trends of Change in Chiness Thought," published in the *Hsin-min ts'ung-pao* [New People's Periodical]. Ch'ing learning was discussed in the eighth chapter, and I drew the following conclusions at the end of that chapter:

> [*ii] These two-hundred-odd years may be summed up as China's "Age of Renaissance," but its development was gradual, not sudden. Nevertheless, it was like a growing organism, which is now flourishing with an appearance of early spring. I have boundless expectations for the future of our intellectual world.

I said also:

> Ch'ing scholars took the seeking of truth in concrete facts as the aim of study and were generously endowed with scientific spirit, which was further enhanced by their organization of the division of labor [among themselves].

And again:

> Intellectual trends during the two-hundred-odd years of the Ch'ing were actually a reverse development of the intellectual trends of the previous two thousand or more years. It was like peeling a spring bamboo-shoot: the more it is peeled, the closer one gets to the core; or like chewing a piece of sugar cane: the more you chew, the more tasty it becomes. This development can be called most unusual, but if we ask what caused it, the answer is that it was caused by various conditions of the social environment.

[*iii] Today my fundamental views do not differ significantly from those of eighteen years ago, although my detailed observations now seem somewhat more exact than before. Furthermore, my words of those days were often for some set purpose and as a result, the conclusions often had a tendency toward unbalance. Now I have rewritten it completely, keeping only ten or twenty percent of the old material.

(3) The intellectual trends of the Ch'ing period contain much that is worth recording, but those trends that form the mainstream and that have the character of periodical movements were the "School of Empirical Research" [1] in the first half of the [Ch'ing] period and the "Modern Text Movement" in the second half. Actually the latter evolved out of the former, and therefore the present work features these two movements as its main theme, the rest being ancillary only.

(4) As an active participant in the "Modern Text Movement" myself, I could not but include myself in the narrative. The present work will discuss my person in a purely detached and objective spirit; that is, virtually as another Liang Ch'i-ch'ao, the present writer will criticize the Liang Ch'i-ch'ao of the past thirty years as an historical figure. Whether my criticisms are adequate or not, I cannot say; I have only striven to [*iv] do justice to the historical Liang Ch'i-ch'ao exactly as I have striven to do justice to the other historical personages.

(5) In this volume, I speak of all past men whom I revered greatly all my life and my highly honored teachers and friends directly by their names as a rule, and not by their other appellations, following the rule of simplicity in order to save the reader trouble.

(6) It took me fifteen days to write the manuscript from beginning to end and after finishing it, I sent it immediately to the *Kai-tsao tsa-chih* [La Rekonstruo] for publication in its current issues.[2] Since I had no time for revision and collation, there are doubtless quite a number of mistakes and omissions, which I hope my readers will correct.

Liang Ch'i-ch'ao

October 14, 1920

[*i]

Author's Second Preface

(1) After this book was completed, several of my friends read the original manuscript in advance, and three of them – Chiang Fang-chen, Lin Chih-chün, and Hu Shih – each suggested corrections. I accepted their views, added three sections, and made a number of corrections. I have not quoted these gentlemen's views in full, not in order to steal their contributions, but to avoid complications in the writing. Ting Ching-li[1] once said: "Who among posterity will ever know who corrects my writing?" I hereby record my thanks to these three men.

(2) For a long time I have nursed the aspiration of writing an "Intellectual History of China," but continually put it off, never carrying it out. When the manuscript of this book was completed, several of my good friends urged me on even more strongly, saying that I should also discuss pre-Ch'ing learning as a whole in order to conserve students' energies and to arouse interest in learning. As a result I resolved to write it [i.e., "An Intellectual History of China"] in five parts: (1) Pre-Ch'in Learning, (2) The Classical Learning of the Two Hans and Six Dynasties and the Neo-Taoism of the Wei and Chin Periods, (3) Buddhism of the Sui and T'ang Periods, (4) The Neo-Confucianism of the Sung and Ming Periods, and (5) Ch'ing Learning. I am now working on the section on Buddhism, under the title "A History of Chinese Buddhism," half of which has just [*ii] been drafted. I hope to complete these five volumes in a year, and although I dare not venture a guess as to whether I can or not, I [use this reckoning] merely to encourage and guide myself. Therefore, I have entitled the present volume *Intellectual History of China, Part Five.*

(3) The manuscript of this book was begun as a preface to another work, not as an independent work, and therefore much in its style and presentation seems to me unsatisfactory. However, since it is already completed, and as I am too lazy to make the effort to revise it, I have not called it "A History of Intellectual Trends during the Ch'ing Period" but "Intellectual Trends in the Ch'ing Period," because historical works cannot be so elementary and unfinished. When the five parts are all completed, I will revise [the present volume].

Liang Ch'i-ch'ao

November 29, 1920

PART I

The Early Ch'ing Period:

The School of "Practical Statesmanship" and Other Trends

[*1] *Section 1. Introduction*

A common term in current use, "periodic tides of thought," is an extremely fine descriptive phrase. In general, the people of a culturally advanced country, in a given period, because of environmental changes and psychological influence may unconsciously [find] the course of their thinking moving in a single common direction. Then a surge of interacting responses arises, like a tide that begins with a weak force, almost imperceptibly, but gradually mounts — mounts — and mounts — until it reaches its highest point, whereupon it ebbs and gradually disappears.

Not all "ideas" can become a "tide." To grow to a "tide," "ideas" must have considerable merit and, moreover, must be capable of meeting the needs of the time. Not all "periods" have such "tides of thought"; a period with its own tide of thought must be one of high cultural advancement. In our country since the Ch'in (255–207 B.C.), the [movements] that have truly developed into "periodic tides of thought" were the Classicism [*2] of the Han (206 B.C.–220 A.D.), the Buddhism of the Sui (590–617 A.D.) and T'ang (618–906 A.D.), the Neo-Confucianism of the Sung (960–1279 A.D.) and Ming (1368–1643 A.D.), and the School of Empirical Research of the Ch'ing (1644–1911 A.D.)[1] — only these four.

All these periodic tides of thought arise out of a "continuous mass movement." The so-called movement does not necessarily have consciousness, plan, and organization, and it is impossible to distinguish who are active [participants] and who are passive. Participants in the movement usually do not work out their strategy together nor do they know each other; the roles they fill while engaging in the movement are also distinctly different, as are the methods they adopt. A movement is frequently divided within itself into numerous small subcurrents which may even be invidious and hostile to each other, but they undoubtedly share one or more ideas in common as a point of departure for their thought. The force of such an idea is rather weak at first, but as the movement [expands] [the force] becomes greater, until finally [the idea] attains a kind of authority. This idea, within its own time, seems to "acquire a religious cast"; some men will even dedicate themselves to promulgating and defending it, often in the purest spirit of self-sacrifice. As its authority is gradually established, it acquires a kind of public esteem in society. [*3] Then people forget its *raison d'être* and savor it together. When it reaches this state, in modern parlance it is called "popular," and in the ancient term, "customary." A customary [mode of thought] is the faith of a given age; men hardly dare to contravene it, nor do they find pleasure in such contravention. It has a quasi-religious character. When a tide of thought becomes a custom, it reaches its time of maturity.

According to Buddhist doctrine, all transitory phenomena (*Samsāra*) can be divided as a rule into four periods: birth, life, old age, and death. The transformation of tides of thought can likewise be divided into four periods: (1) The Formative Period (Birth), (2) The High Period (Life), (3) The Period of Transformation (Old Age), and (4) The Period of Decline (Death). No matter what the country or the age, the development and metamorphosis of tides of thought generally follow this course.

The Formative Period is one of incipient reaction against the older tide of thought, which having passed its prime is like an overripe fruit that is beginning to rot, or a blood clot that is causing contusions. Therefore a reaction must set in. This reaction is in general a demand for the rise of a new tide of thought. But since construction must first be preceded by destruction, all important men of this period will devote their energies to destruction and have no leisure for creation. "No leisure" does not mean a setting aside [of the constructive task], for the essential creative spirit must already have come into being during this period – what the historian calls "the basic patterns for founding a nation" [must already [*4] be there]. Nevertheless, the details of the system are not yet established, and the methods of research are still in the trial and error stage, uncertain of adoption or rejection. Therefore, the works of this period are usually disparate and heterogeneous, yet in their very confusion and crudity there is an appearance of a full vital spirit. This is the characteristic of the Formative Period, comparable to the "birth" phase in Buddhism. From here it passes into the High Period.

Destructive activity is now at an end, and the old tide of thought is humbled into submission, no longer able to offer any competition, as indeed there is no need to waste energy in attacking or defending it. As a result of the ferment and cultivation in the previous period, the substance of thinking grows richer every day while research methods are also increasingly perfected. Schools of learning [lit., "portals and inner recesses"] gradually arise and continue to gain stature, glowing with "the beauties of the ancestral temples and the splendor of a hundred officials." [2] Contemporary men of talent and sagacity all consider them worth following and diligently urge each other on; even stupid men attach themselves [to these schools] in a chorus of conformity, because they consider it a disgrace not to gain a foothold within them. This is the characteristic of the High Period, comparable to the "life" phase in Buddhism; we then pass into the Period of Transformation.

The frontiers and areas [of study] have been exploited almost to the

limit by men of the previous period, but the intelligence and ability of scholars cannot be held in abeyance for long. All they can do is select re-
[*5] stricted problems for a "narrow but deep" study, or apply the research methods to other fields, thereby producing offshoots within a school.
restricted problems for a "narrow but deep" study, or apply the research methods to other fields, thereby producing offshoots within a school.
Furthermore, the contemporary environment certainly will differ from the previous one. The more recent branches are comparatively more aggressive and more adaptable under the new conditions; hence they often grow from subordinate to major schools. Thus the newly developed schools are in a position to stand opposed to the orthodox school or may even rapidly appropriate its place. This is the characteristic of the Period of Transformation, like the "old age" phase in Buddhism; at this point there begins the Period of Decline.

After a school of learning has reached its peak, an increasing number of opportunists emerge in the society who hope to associate themselves with it. This copying and recopying of a worn-out tradition goes on, and it is indeed disgusting. At this stage, the important and essential ideas of a school must already have been exhaustively expounded by previous masters, and their followers can only manipulate trivial points to show their ingenuity. Furthermore, the branches [of the school] are so diverse that mutual jealousy and intolerance are bound to grow up, and these expose its weakness all the more. Because the environment has already altered, the needs of the society have also changed direction. But [the school] still endeavors to exhibit the authority of the High Period. Naturally, men of any conviction are unwilling to accept this, and brilliant men, who know that renunciation of what is old must precede creation of what is new, consequently consider it an object for destruction. In this way the Formative Period of the second tide of thought has arrived and the demise of the [old] one with it. This is the inescapable destiny of the Period of Decline, like the "death" phase in Buddhism.

My observation is that the so-called "tides of thought" of both China and foreign countries during both ancient and modern times have all followed this course of transformation, and the three hundred years of the Ch'ing period are a most apt illustration of it.

[*6] *Section 2. General Setting*

What actually was the tide of thought of the Ch'ing period? Briefly speaking, it was a strong reaction against the Neo-Confucianism of the Sung and Ming, and its avowed purpose was "the revival of antiquity." Its motives and contents were entirely comparable to [those of] the European Renaissance, and the new forces that arose after the European Renaissance are just beginning to emerge in our country today. The characteristics of its rise and fall are exactly the same as those of the four periods discussed in the preceding section.

The representative figures of the Formative Period were Ku Yen-wu (1613–1682), Hu Wei (1633–1714), and Yen Jo-chü (1636–1704). It was a time when the Wang Yang-ming (1472–1529) school of learning of the late Ming had just passed its peak and had started to decline. Scholars were in the habit of "packing books away to avoid reading and drifted about conversing aimlessly." Neo-Confucian philosophers could [*7] no longer command the respect of the society. Ku Yen-wu and others rose to correct [the trend] with a forceful espousal of the theory that "without classical learning there can be no study of philosophic principles (*li hsüeh*)" [i.e., the latter must rest upon the former]. They called upon scholars to free themselves from the bondage of the Sung and Ming scholars and to seek [truth] directly from the old classics. Yen Jo-chü's examination of the forged classics stirred up the idea of "seeking after truth," and Hu Wei's attack on "River (chart) and Lo (writing)" [a kind of mystic art of divination] [1] swept away the foundation of "empty discussions," thus establishing the pattern of Ch'ing learning.

Meanwhile, the reaction against Ming learning took several other directions. First, the school of Yen Yüan (1635–1704) and Li Kung (1659–1746) advocated that "Knowledge should not be sought by introspection, nor from books, but from daily activities." The unique eminence of Liu Hsien-t'ing (1648–1695) had its basis in his [intellectual] proximity to this school.

Secondly, the school of Huang Tsung-hsi (1610–1695) and Wan Ssu-t'ung (1638–1702) had its basis in historical learning and extended [its scope to the consideration of] the practical affairs of the world. The teachings of Ku Yen-wu originally shared this spirit, but since [the learning of] men like Huang and Wan was not so extensive in scope as Ku's, they developed only in this [historical] field. Meanwhile, the learning of Ku Tsu-yü (1631–1692) also followed roughly the same path. Later, [this school] culminated with Ch'üan Tsu-wang (1705–1755) and Chang Hsüeh-ch'eng (1738–1801) into a separate school of Ch'ing learning.

Thirdly, the school of Wang Hsi-ch'an and Mei Wen-ting (1633–1721) specialized in astronomy and mathematics alone, initiating the beginning of natural sciences.

These various schools all espoused methods of learning fundamentally [*8] different from those of the Ming thinkers. Except for the school of Yen and Li which was cut short, all the rest were transmitted to later generations; Ku (Yen-wu), Yen (Jo-chü), and Hu (Wei) in particular were the undisputed great progenitors of "the Orthodox School." Those who stubbornly clung to the broken fortress of the older views [Neo-Confucianism] and would not leave in the face of destruction included Sun Ch'i-feng (1585–1675), Li Chung-fu, Lu Shih-i (1611–1672), and others, but even their intellectual tendency was to revert gradually from the Ming (1368–1643) to the Sung (960–1297). On the other hand, even the various "scholars of new learning" showed considerable traces of Sung influence in their thinking. Thus the revival of antiquity in this period may be called the return from the Ming to the Sung, and even gradually to the T'ang (618–906 A.D.) and Han (206 B.C.–220 A.D.).

The representative figures of the movement in the High Period were Hui Tung (1697–1758), Tai Chen (1723–1777), Tuan Yü-ts'ai (1735–1815), Wang Nien-sun (1744–1832), and Wang Yin-chih (1766–1834). These I call the Orthodox School, and I shall attempt to list the differences between the school of the Formative Period and the Orthodox School.

(1) While the schools of the Formative Period vehemently attacked part of Sung learning, they nevertheless accepted part of it. The Orthodox School, on the other hand, consolidated its own ramparts and relegated Sung learning to a position of complete neglect.

(2) The school of the Formative Period embraced the idea of the study of classics for practical ends and consequently preferred to discuss the fortunes and affairs of governments, whereas the Orthodox School carried on empirical research for the sake of empirical research and studied classics for the sake of classics.

The central core of the Orthodox School was Anhwei and Soochow, with Hui Tung originating the Soochow [branch] and Tai Chen the Anhwei. Hui Tung had studied with his father Shih-ch'i (1671–1741); his students included Chiang Sheng (1721–1799) and Yü Hsiao-k'e (1729–
[*9] 1777), although men like Wang Ming-sh'eng (1722–1798), Ch'ien Ta-hsin (1728–1804), Wang Chung (1744–1794), Liu T'ai-kung (1751–1805), and Chiang Fan (1761–1831) also came under his influence.

Tai Chen had studied with Chiang Yung (1681–1762) but he also regarded Hui Tung with the deference due a senior. In his birthplace his studies were carried on by Chin Pang (1735–1801), Ch'eng Yao-t'ien, Ling T'ing-k'an (1757–1809), the three Hus – K'uang-chung, P'ei-hui, and Ch'ün-ch'iao – and others. Among those who had studied with him in the capital, the prominent pupils were Jen Ta-ch'ün (1738–1789), Lu Wen-chao (1717–1796), K'ung Kuang-sen (1752–1786), Tuan Yü-tsai (1735–1815), and Wang Nien-sun (1744–1832), the last named transmitting [his learning] to his son Yin-chih (1766–1834). Tuan and the two Wangs [father and son] were thoroughly competent to illuminate Tai [Chen]'s learning; they were known in the country as Tai, Tuan, and the Two Wangs. Actually Ch'ing scholars loathed any creation of factions and frowned on playing up the teacher-pupil relationship. The great masters all regarded each other as teachers and friends and there were no factions to speak of.

Hui and Tai were equally renowned, with the former inclined to be inclusive and erudite and the latter, profound and incisive. Hui was only a "transmitter" [of knowledge], whereas Tai was a "creator"; this accounted for the difference in accomplishments of those who studied with them. Therefore, Tai [Chen] must be credited with the hegemony of the Orthodox School.

At that time, scholars who came under the influence of this school and made their contributions were innumerable. Men like Chi Yün (1724–1805), Wang Ch'ang (1725–1806), Pi Yüan (1730–1797), and Juan Yüan (1764–1849), all holding high and important positions [in government], honored and patronized [the school] wholeheartedly, as if they were upholding the Law. Thus this school reached what might be called its very pinnacle.

The basic method of learning [of the Orthodox School] was "to get at the truth through concrete facts" and [to hold] "no belief without evidence." Its area of study centered in the classics and extended to [*10] include traditional linguistics,[2] phonetics, history, astronomy and mathematics, water-works and geography, court regulations and institutions, stone and bronze inscriptions, collation of texts, assembling of lost texts, etc. Its citing of evidence and collection of material often reached back into the two Han periods and hence it won the title of "Han learning."

In those days, the intellectual trend was well nigh uniform. The remains of Sung learning of the Formative Period could no longer survive; only the so-called "Ancient Text scholars" [writers in the *Ku-wen* style], under the pretext of "demonstrating the way through good writing," attempted to carry on the "apostolic" succession and frequently found fault with the Han learning. But both their determination and their strength were insufficient to develop their forces.

The representative figures of the Period of Transformation were K'ang Yu-wei (1858–1927) and Liang Ch'i-ch'ao (1873–1929). During the all-flourishing stage of the Orthodox School, scholars distinguished themselves by studying certain classics alone. Chuang Ts'un-yü (1719–1788) began a study of the *Ch'un-ch'iu Kung-yang chuan* [The *Kung-yang Commentary* on the *Spring and Autumn Annals*] and achieved good results, and Liu Feng-lu (1776–1829) and Kung Tzu-chen (1792–1841) were very competent in transmitting his work.

The *Kung-yang Commentary* was a "Modern Text of classical learning."[3] During the Later Han (25–220 A.D.) there had been quite a violent conflict between the Modern Text school and the Ancient Text school. The *Mao Commentary* on the *Book of Odes*, the *Tso Commentary* on the *Spring and Autumn Annals* (*Tso-chuan*), and the *Officials of Chou* all appeared late and were known as the Ancient Texts. Scholars did not believe in [their authenticity], but toward the end of the Later Han, the Ancient Text school [who did believe them authentic] had flourished.

After Yen Jo-chü's (1636–1704) successful attack on the *Wei ku-wen Shang-shu* [The Forged *Book of History* in Ancient Text], a leaning toward skepticism about the classics gradually developed among the scholars. Hence Liu Feng-lu (1776–1829) seriously doubted the [authenticity of] the *Tso Commentary* on the *Spring and Autumn Annals* and Wei Yüan (1794–1856) felt extremely dubious about the *Mao Commen-*
[*11] *tary* on the *Book of Odes.* As to the *Officials of Chou*, it had been in doubt continuously since the Sung period. K'ang Yu-wei synthesized the doctrines of these various thinkers, drawing a strict line of separation between the Modern and Ancient Texts; he proclaimed that the Ancient Text classics and commentaries appearing late in the Later Han were all forgeries by Liu Hsin (ca. 46 B.C.–23 A.D.). Even Hsü Shen (1st–2nd century) and Cheng Hsüan (127–200 A.D.), who were most honored by the Orthodox School, were attacked [by him]. Thus the so-called "revival of antiquity" was extended back from the Later Han to the Former Han.

K'ang also used the *Kung-yang Commentary* to establish his doctrine of "Confucius as a reformer," in which he stated that the Six Classics were all created by Confucius, that both Yao and Shun were used by Confucius as disguises [for advocating reform], and that among the philosophers of the pre-Ch'in period there were none who did not "use antiquity as a pretext for advocating reform." This was certainly a very bold assertion which attempted to effect a sudden and profound liberation from the classical works of the previous few thousand years, in order to open the door to free learning.

Among K'ang's students, the most famous were Ch'en Ch'ien-ch'iu and Liang Ch'i-ch'ao (1873–1928). Ch'en died young, but Liang promulgated his learning widely by lecturing and writing. Yet because Liang had a comparatively closer kinship with the Orthodox School, he frequently could not bear his teacher's dogmatism; therefore, there were differences [between them] in the end. Both K'ang and Liang shared the idea of "practical application" of the Formative Period, using classical learning as a cloak for their political discussions. They departed from the original purpose of "studying classics for the sake of classics"; hence, their program did not prosper and became, in turn, a prelude to the introduction of European and Western thought.

The Period of Transformation in Ch'ing learning was at the same time its Period of Decline. Former masters like Ku, Yen, Hu, Hui, Tai, Tuan,

Sung & new school discuss fitly among adherents

and the two Wangs were not only erudite and eminent in knowledge, [*12] but also upright and spotless in character. As their approach to learning prospered, the whole nation followed in chorus; even vain and shallow people were anxious to associate with them. Surely this brought on the disdain of society. Moreover, the more important principles of this approach to learning had been almost exhausted by past scholars in their exposition, and all the novices could do was to follow with patchwork, having no longer any creative spirit themselves. Even if they could throw new light [on something], it was largely on trivia; this is, in the language of the Han people, to avoid difficulty by taking refuge in minor issues. Yet these people acted with such an air of self-importance that they assumed airs of an "oligarchy of learning."

With the rise of disputes, the [adherents of] Modern and Ancient texts attacked and belittled each other, exposing their shortcomings even more. Moreover, after the opening of oceanic communication and the introduction of foreign learning, scholars realized the folly of [adhering to] the old [learning], and renounced it one after another; its days were numbered. Yet in this period there still remained one or two great masters who guarded to the end the last outpost of the Orthodox School: Yü Yüeh (1821–1907) and Sun I-jang (1848–1908), both stemming from the [intellectual] line of Wang Nien-sun of Kaoyu. Yü had written only two or three works of special merit; all the rest were similar to those of the insignificant Yüan Mei (1716–1798) — a fact which symbolized the Period of Decline. Sun, on the other hand, was flawless and solid; it was indeed fortunate for Ch'ing learning to have this last support. Yü's pupil Chang Ping-lin surpassed his teacher in intelligence, yet because of his fondness for discussing politics he neglected his learning somewhat. Also, among the scions of the Hus of Chiki was one Hu Shih who employed the methodology of Ch'ing scholars in his pursuit of knowledge; in him [was evident] the residual influence of the Orthodox School.

[*13] In summing up the intellectual history of the past two hundred odd years with respect to its influence on the whole intellectual world, I can cover it in one phrase: "Liberation through the revival of antiquity." Its first step: the revival of Sung antiquity, [resulting in] liberation from the Wang [Yang-ming] learning. Its second step: the revival of T'ang and Han antiquity, [resulting in] liberation from the Ch'eng brothers [Hao (1302–1385), Yi (1033–1108)] and Chu Hsi (1130–1200) [i.e. Neo-Confucianism]. The third step: the revival of Former Han antiquity, which brought liberation from Hsü Shen (ca. 100 A.D.) and Cheng Hsüan (127–200 A.D.). The fourth step: the revival of pre-Ch'in antiquity, and freedom from all commentaries and sub-commentaries. With the revival of the pre-Ch'in antiquity, [the process] could not stop

until it brought forth a liberation from Confucius and Mencius. That it could obtain, step by step, the [final] result of liberation was made possible by its scientific spirit of research. Now that Ch'ing learning has truly declined — "The four seasons revolve; that which has accomplished its purpose withdraws." Its decline was inevitable, and was actually a beneficial occurrence; there is really no room for lingering regrets. If only we can apply its spirit of research to other ends, the demise of Ch'ing learning will not be a real demise.

After this general discussion I will now discuss the various periods in order.

[*14] *Section 3. Reaction to Sung-Ming Neo-Confucianism*

I have stated that "the point of departure of Ch'ing learning was a violent reaction against the Neo-Confucianism of the Sung and Ming," but what had the Neo-Confucianism of the Sung and Ming done to incur this reaction? There is frequently a cyclical alternation between doctrinal "emphasis on intellectualism" and "emphasis on voluntarism," between "materialism" and "idealism," and between "experimentalism" and "intuitive reasoning." In general, when a school reaches its zenith, it must also have spawned some errors. With errors come reactions, and another school may rise to replace it. That second school follows the same pattern from zenith to errors and reaction. But after each reaction and rejuvenation, the content of a school undoubtedly is renewed and becomes different from what it was before. The progress of human virtue, wisdom, intelligence, and arts is based entirely on this [process]. In the three thousand years of European intellectual history, the general outlines of this [process] were very clear; our country cannot be an exception to this rule, and during the transition of the Ming (1368–1643) to the Ch'ing (1644–1911), the traces of such a metamorphosis were particularly obvious.

After Buddhism had reached its heights in the T'ang dynasty, it was adopted by Sung scholars for the formulation of a new philosophy which was "Confucian externally and Buddhist internally." It reached an apex during the Ming, and it is hardly necessary to say that this new school of philosophy had great historic value. But what we most dislike about it are the following points: (1) Although it had adopted [certain aspects of] Buddhism after some modification, why did it hide their origin and even attack Buddhism bitterly? (2) Since the newly-created school bore [*15] the true face of neither Confucius nor Mencius, why should it borrow their names while subverting their substance? Thus, while admitting that the schools of the Sung and Ming really had a number of unique and useful aspects, I cannot pardon the way it was constituted and expressed. I say that by giving a false label to both Confucianism and Buddhism, it in fact even misrepresented itself. Wang Yang-ming (1472–1529) of the Ming was an outstanding, late proponent of that school, and he was even more greatly imbued with this habit. Take, for instance, his *Chu-tzu wan-nien ting-lun* [Doctrines Reached by the Master Chu in Later Life], where he forcefully asserted that Chu Hsi (1130–1200) and Lu Chiu-yüan (1139–1193) were similar, although in fact they were quite different. Actually he had adhered to Chu Hsi in name, yet he falsely charged Chu with having the same ideas as himself.[1] This habit proved to be a stumbling block to intellectual life in two ways: (1) It suppressed creativity: if a school was created by someone, why should he affiliate it to the ancients for the sake of prestige? If he must attach it to them, wouldn't it imply that men born later than the ancients ought not create? (2) It encouraged hypocrisy: when the sayings of ancient men were agreeable, it was all very well to esteem and transmit them, but when they were not, then to inform them with one's own views was no different from calling a deer a horse. Confusing the truth is dishonesty in learning; this was the basic trouble with the Sung and Ming schools.

When I went on to examine the substance of its thought, I found that [*16] the object of its study was simply too vague and intangible. A few outstanding and sincere scholars might have followed this path and achieved a state of repose for body and mind, but only rarely could ordinary mortals imitate them. It was too easy for superficial and pretentious men to pick up abstract phrases to brag about, and consequently there was a group in late Ming known as the *k'uang-ch'an* (wild dissemblers)[2] [who thought] that "every street is full of sages" and that "wine, women, wealth, and anger do not block the road to enlightenment." Their ethics hit rock bottom. Moreover, the civil service examinations and the students' curriculum to prepare for them engaged the attention of all the nation; students needed only to learn this kind of dubious and imitative language in order to be ready to jockey for position, wealth, and reputation. The whole nation indulged in it prodigally and one man after another neglected his learning and the use of his mind. Therefore, the defects of Neo-Confucianism in late Ming were just like those of Christianity in Europe during the Middle and Dark Ages. At its worst, it could completely block a man's ears, eyes, mind, and heart, making them useless, and dissipate his independent and creative spirit to the zero point. Since it is human nature to have a "desire for knowledge," when "hunger for knowledge" reaches such an extremity, how could reaction fail to set in?

Section 4. Ku Yen-wu (1613-1682)

During this period of reaction, the first man engaging in the "en-
[*17] lightenment movement" was Ku Yen-wu (1613–1682) of Kunshan, who launched his initial violent attack on the late Ming intellectual trends by censuring Wang Yang-ming (1472–1529) in these words:

Today's gentlemen assemble up to a hundred [lit., "several tens or a hundred"] guests and disciples to discuss "Mind" and "(Human) Nature," brushing aside the method of acquiring "knowledge through extensive learning" in seeking "consistency." They turn from the discussion "of the world [lit., "within the four seas"] troubles and poverty" in favor of discussions of "lofty and esoteric doctrines, and the excellence of single-mindedness." With this I cannot agree.[1*]

Again he said:

When present-day scholars happen to hit upon some new ideas, they want to abrogate all the pronouncements of previous scholars and rise above them. Unlettered men borrow accepted sayings to hide their ignorance, and men without character flee from their native place so that people cannot question [their origin].[2*]

He went on to say:

There have been men who could singlehandedly change the world, with their influence lasting as long as a hundred odd years: in ancient times, [for example], we have Wang Yen's (256–311 A.D.) *ch'ing-t'an* (pure discourses) [3] and Wang An-shih's (1021–1088) new doctrines. In modern times, Wang Yangming's (1472–1529) *liang-chih* (intuitive knowledge) was another case.[4] Mencius said: "A long time has elapsed since this world of men received its being, and there has been in the course of its history now a period of good order, and now a period of confusion." [5] Is it not for future sages to turn the world of disorder to order? [6*]

When a new school of learning is first established, unless it maintains a positively severe and aggressive attitude toward the old school of learning, it cannot blunt the edge of the old [school] and develop the forces of the new. Ku's rejection of late Ming intellectual trends was generally characterized by this kind of dazzling incisiveness. Thereafter, the Wang Yang-ming school gradually died out; those in the Ch'ing who still followed Neo-Confucianism as a means to high reputation all regarded themselves as disciples of the Ch'eng [brothers] and Chu Hsi [rather than of Wang]. Although it is said that Wang learning was very decadent in its last phase, tedious to the human mind, and that it was already withering by itself even without an attack from without, it was Ku Yen-wu who was most instrumental in loudly advocating [measures] to precipitate a change in patterns of thought.

Ku Yen-wu never attacked the Ch'eng [brothers] and Chu Hsi directly, refusing pointblank to recognize independence of Neo-Confusian philosophy. He said: "From ancient until modern times, how could there be a separate entity called the Philosophy of Rational Principle? Classical learning is itself a study of rational principle. Ever since men started to discuss the philosophy of rational principle apart from classical learning, heterodoxy has arisen." [7*]

[*19] The phrase "classical learning is the study of rational principle" was the new slogan of the school that Ku created. Whether it was correct or not need not be discussed in detail, but according to our present viewpoint this saying has two defects: 1) To substitute classical learning for Neo-Confucianism is to overthrow one species of idolatry in order to set up another. 2) Neo-Confucianism is a philosophy which should be divorced from classical learning as an independent subject. Nevertheless, [in spite of these shortcomings], the learning of the entire Ch'ing (1644–1911) period actually gained a new lease on life with this slogan. Formerly, there had been people who had ridiculed the classical masters of the Six Dynasties (221–589 A.D.) as men who "would rather say that the Duke of Chou and Confucius were wrong than admit that Cheng [Hsüan] and Fu [Ch'ien] were incorrect." So it was with the Neo-Confucianists after the Sung, Yüan, and Ming, who would rather affront Confucius and Mencius than criticize Chou Tun-yi (1017–1073), Ch'eng Hao (1032–1085), Ch'eng Yi (1033–1100), Chang Tsai (1020–1077), Shao Yung (1011–1077), Chu Hsi (1130–1200), Lu Chiu-yüan (1139–1193), and Wang Yang-ming (1472–1529). Criticizing them was almost equivalent to the crime of *lèse majesté* in a monarchy, and the so-called Neo-Confucianists had apparently become a most exalted intellectual oligarchy, looking scornfully down upon the multitude of scholars. When Ku's doctrine appeared, the sanctity of this intellectual oligarchy was completely destroyed by the "revolutionary army." This certainly marked a great liberation for the intellectual world of the last four or five hundred years.

In general, an outstanding scholar of the Formative Period did not have to make profound achievement but, as a rule, had to establish the scope of his work and create or revolutionize methods of research, in-
[*20] fusing into them a new driving spirit. Ku was such a man in the Ch'ing school of learning. Among his writings, only the *Yin-hsüeh wu-shu* [Five Books on Phonology] was systematically organized by himself into a finished work. His *T'ien-hsia chün-kuo li-ping shu* [On the (Strategic and Economic) Advantages and Disadvantages of the Countries and States of the Empire (120 *chüan*, 1662)] and *Chao-yü-chih* (Local Geography] both had great scope but were only rough drafts, not finished manuscripts. His *Jih-chih-lu* [Record of Daily Knowledge] was the crystallization of his life-long devotion, yet it was in the nature of a notebook or memorandum. He also left behind more than ten other works, which,

however, were merely monographs and not masterpieces. Why, then, did Ku still deserve the title of founding father of the Ch'ing school? Only because he constructed methods of research which may be listed in brief under three heads:

(1) To cherish creativity. Ku said: "The works by men of the entire Ming period (1368–1643) were nothing but plagiarism." [8*] On the difficulty of writing books, he said: "Only when the ancients have not touched upon [a subject] and when future generations find it indispensable, is it permissible to take it up." [9*] In his preface to the *Jih-chih-lu*, he said: "Since my childhood studies, I have always noted down what I perceived, and if it [turned out] to be incorrect, I revised it again and again, or if earlier men had said it before me, I omitted it entirely." It is therefore certain that the writings of Ku did not contain a single point repeated or borrowed from the ancients. This was also his view on essay-writing: [*21] "The trouble with modern writing lies entirely in its imitativeness; even if it is almost identical to that of the ancients, it does not make a great contribution." [10*] Again he said [to a friend]: "The trouble with your poem is that it contains Tu Fu, and the trouble with your essay is that it contains Han Yü and Ou-yang Hsiu. With these mental limitations in your heart, all through your life you can never be free from dependence." [11*] From this we know that Ku highly resented imitation and dependence.

(2) Extensive evidence. The synopsis of the *Jih-chih-lu* in the *Complete Works of the Four Treasuries* states: "Ku's learning had sound foundation and was broad and consistent. He would scrutinize every fact thoroughly and confirm it with supporting evidence; only then would he write it down in his book. Consequently, his citations were extensive and numerous, with only a few contradictions." This description can best express Ku's prescriptive methodology for learning.

Ch'üan Tsu-wan (1705–1755) said [of Ku]: "Whenever the Master traveled, he carried his books with him. At each ruined fortress he would ask old soldiers and retired veterans about the vicissitudes of its past history. When [answers] corresponded to what he had always known, he would open his books for confirmation." [12*] Herein lay the secret of Ku's learning. When he discussed a fact he had to produce evidence and was never satisfied with an isolated bit of evidence but required abundant evidence. Only when all the evidence was ready was he willing to voice his opinion. His own description of his study of phonology is this: [*22] ". . . I list the two terms primary evidence and secondary evidence; the former means cross reference within the *Book of Odes* and the latter, evidence supplied by other books. If both of them are absent, then I take a devious route to ascertain the sounds and arrange them in rhyme-categories. . ." [13*] The method employed here is that of modern scientific research and has been commonly used by scholars since the periods of Ch'ien-lung (1736–1795) and Chia-ch'ing (1796–1820), but at that time [early Ch'ing] Ku alone worked it out.

(3) Emphasis on utility. Ku said: "Confucius edited the Six Classics with the same intention as that of I Yin and Chiang T'ai-kung: to save people from trouble [lit., "from water and fire"]. Therefore, he states, 'Relying on empty words is not so good as putting them into practice' . . . In view of this, I decided not to do any writing unless it had a relation to the actual affairs of the contemporary world as indicated in the Six Classics."[14*] He carried this statement out faithfully, and everything he wrote for the rest of his life remained within this framework. Whether what he called "useful" was really useful or not is another question; the important thing is that he set up as the objective "the doctrine of utility," which necessarily brought knowledge and society into a closer relationship. This was certainly a good antidote to the late Ming partisans of abstract discussion and of the impractical, civil-service-examination type of literary composition.

The fact that Ch'ing scholars called [their work] "sound learning" in order to differentiate themselves from the stylistic formalists actually had its origin in Ku. Even in the recent decades it has been Ku's spirit that has [*23] inspired the influence of classical learning on the political structure.

Section 5. Yen Jo-chü (1636-1704) and Hu Wei (1633-1714)

Wang Chung (1744–1794) at one time drafted the *Kuo-ch'ao liu-ju sung* [A Tribute to Six Scholars of the Reigning (Ch'ing) Dynasty], these scholars being Ku Yen-wu (1613–1682) of Kunshan, Hu Wei (1633–1714) of Tehtsing, Mei Wen-ting (1632–1721) of Süancheng, Yen Jo-chü (1636–1704) of Taiyüan, Hui Tung (1697–1758) of Yüan-ho, and Tai Chen (1723–1777) of Siuning. Wang remarked:

> The revival of the ancient learning was first begun by Ku, and the pretentiousness and falsity of the "River Chart and Lo Writing"[1] were curbed by Hu. Chinese and Western astronomy became perfected in Mei's time, and the Ancient Texts [of classical learning][2] were strongly attacked by Yen. It was Hui who specialized in expounding the Han scholars' [version] of the *Book of Changes*. All these had been lost subjects of learning and not transmitted for more than a thousand years. When Tai Chen emerged he synthesized them all.[3*]

This tribute of Wang's was certainly very appropriate, as these six gentlemen were truly the leading Ch'ing scholars; however, in evaluating the extent of their influence on the intellectual world, I should like to single out Yen and Hu particularly, in addition to Ku and Tai.

The basis for Yen's greatness was his *Shang-shu ku-wen shu-cheng* [Commentary according to the Evidence on the *Book of History* in the Ancient Text], while Hu's was his *I-t'u ming-pien* [A Clarification of the Diagrams in the *Changes*]. To this Wang Chung had already testified, but since these two books studied only restricted subject matter, how [*24] could they influence the whole intellectual world? Furthermore, they were not free from defects of omission, over-simplification, and disorderliness – defects which have been exposed by later generations. Neither of the two was included in Juan Yüan's (1764–1849) edition of the *Hsüeh-hai-t'ang ching-chieh* [Explanations of the Classics in the *Hsüeh-hai-t'ang*], so why should I praise them so highly? The following are my reasons:

The *Shang-shu ku-wen shu-cheng* exposed as nothing but forgeries the sixteen chapters of the *Book of History* in ancient text which appeared late in the Eastern Chin period (317–419 A.D.), and also the Commentary on the *Book of History* attributed to K'ung An-kuo (ca. 165–74 B.C.) which appeared about the same time. The authenticity of these books had been suspect ever since Chu Hsi (1130–1200 A.D.) of the Sung period (960–1279 A.D.) and Wu Ch'eng of the Yüan period (1280–1367), but despite their growing doubt, [people] were terrified and hesitated to pass judgment on them. With the appearance of Yen's work, the case was closed once and for all.

What was the significance [of a work] which examined a forged book of ten odd chapters? It is not widely known that for the past thousand or more years this forged work had been studied by all the students of the country, that each was capable of reciting it even at the [early] age of seven or eight, and that they had always considered it in their hearts sacrosanct and inviolable. The emperors and kings of the various dynasties, in their frequent discussions of the classics with learned officials, as well as in formulating policies at critical moments, all revered it and relied on it. To depart [from this path] courageously and bluntly, exposing the book, required nothing less than the greatest courage.

Ever since the Emperor Wu (140–87 B.C.) of the Han apotheosized the Six Arts and suppressed the Hundred Schools, our countrymen had been allowed only citation and exegesis but no criticism of the Six Classics. Han Yü (768–824 A.D.) once said: "That which has passed through the hands of the sages is beyond the reach of discussion and [*25] criticism." If a man harbored even the slightest intention of doubting or criticizing a single word or sentence in a classical text, he felt instantly as if he had fallen into a position of "vilifying the saints and disregarding the law"; he would be uneasy and conscience-stricken, not only in dread of legal prosecution and irresponsible criticism.

As a rule, matters of a religious nature cannot be treated as a problem for scholarly research; once it has become a problem its sacrosanct position is already shaken. Now, not only had [the *Book of History* in Ancient Text] become a problem, but the results of the study had revealed that what had been previously honored as sacred was in part trash, and the [resulting] mental arousal, turmoil, and *volte-faces* are easy to imagine. From that time on, all classical texts could become problems for study, and to advance one step further, all classical tenets could also become problems for study. From the standpoint of the scholars of old learning, it might well be regarded as highly disturbing to human minds and to the prevailing world-order. At that time Mao Ch'i-ling (1623–1716) wrote the *Ku-wen Shang-shu yüan-tz'u* [Complaints on Behalf of the *Book of History* in Ancient Text] to argue with Yen, comparing himself to one who restrained a flood or drove away dangerous wild animals. Even during the Kuang-hsü period (1875–1908) there was a certain Hung Liang-p'in who also wrote several hundred thousand words, similarly aiming to reverse Yen's case. But from our standpoint today, [Yen's work] really [brought about] a general liberation of the intellectual world; from that time on, the Modern and Ancient Text classics stood side by side as problems to be studied; the Six Classics and the various philosophers stood side by side as problems for study; and Chinese classical canons and [*26] Western works of religion and philosophy stood side by side as problems for study. The earliest impetus toward all this was actually given here.

The general purpose of Hu Wei's *I-t'u ming-pien* [A Clarification of the Diagrams in the *Changes*] was to analyze what had been known since the Sung as the "River Chart and Lo Writing." [He proclaimed] that it was transmitted from Shao Yung (1011–1077 A.D.) who had received it from Li Chih-ts'ai (d. 1045) who in turn had received it from the Taoist priest Ch'en T'uan (ca. 906–989); [4] that it was not related at all to Fu Hsi, Wen Wang, Chou Kung, and Confucius, and was irrelevant to the tenets of the *Changes.*

Since this [statement] seems to pertain to an even more particularized and trivial problem, why should we consider it as equal in value to Yen's work? We must bear in mind that the so-called "Ultimateless" "Supreme Ultimate," and the "River Chart and Lo Writing" [5] were really the principal root and core of the structure of "Sung learning"; the discussions by Sung scholars of rational principle, ether, number, fate, mind, and nature all stemmed from them. Chou Tun-i (1017–1073 A.D.) himself spoke of "acquiring the untransmitted knowledge from the lost classics," and men like the Ch'eng brothers and Chu Hsi expressed the same idea in affirming that in this ["River Chart and Lo Writing"] could be found the Sequence of Orthodox Doctrine. Thus it held sway over the intellectual world for five or six hundred years with an authority almost comparable to [that of] the classical canons. Hu's work traced the *Book of Changes* back to Fu Hsi, Wen Wang, Chou Kung, and Confucius, as it also traced the "River Chart" to Ch'en T'uan and Shao Yung. It was not an unreasonable attack, but the Sung learning was thus dealt a "fatal blow"; thereafter, scholars became aware of the fact that Sung teachings were distinctly one thing and Confucian teachings were distinctly another. It was to their mutual advantage to be distinguished, as it was to their mutual disadvantage to be confounded.[6]* After that, scholars realized that the pur- [*27] suit of what Confucius called "truth" might be conducted in ways other than those of the Sung thinkers.

Moreover, our national predilection for expounding classics and philosophy in terms of "Yin-yang and the Five Elements" did not begin only with the Sung but actually with the Han, carrying with it all kinds of heretic doctrines and methods to deceive the world and dupe the people as well as to drown the spirit and block the intellect. Hu's book thoroughly exposed the origins of these heretic doctrines, making it impossible for them to gain prestige from their association with classical sayings. This was indeed a great intellectual revolution.

In mid-nineteenth-century Europe, the Englishman Darwin's *Origin of the Species* and the Frenchman Renan's *Life of Jesus* were published within two years of each other.[7] They shocked all the European intellectual circles profoundly, and had especially drastic effects on Christianity. Darwin simply enunciated his views on biology; how did they concern religion? Yet under their influence, the foundation of the church creeds collapsed. The *Life* by Renan apotheosized the Christ in the extreme, yet it hurt the cause of religion because Christ had never before been an academic problem but had now become one. If we understand this nexus we may readily infer the importance of the two books by Yen and Hu in Chinese intellectual history.

[*28] Speaking of the earliest revolutionaries in Ch'ing academic circles, there was still another man, Mao Ch'i-ling (1623–1716). His works, the *Ho-t'u yüan-ts'uan p'ien* [Basic Fallacies about the "River Chart"] and the *T'ai-chi-t'u-shuo i-i* [Supplementary Discussion on the Diagram of the Supreme Ultimate Explained] antedated Hu Wei's work, and the various studies undertaken by Ch'ing scholars later on often traced their origins to his work. However, since he criticized Ku Yen-wu in discussing ancient pronunciation, and Yen Jo-chü in discussing the *Book of History*, Han scholars respected him without according him the status of an authority. Ch'üan Tsu-wang (1705–1755) wrote *Mao Hsi-ho pi-chuan* [An Unofficial Biography of Mao Ch'i-ling] in which he said:

> Among Mao's works, some trumped up historical episodes to deceive people; some manufactured an orthodoxy of teaching [a kind of "apostolic succession"] to manifest his authenticity to others; some ignorantly repeated the mistakes of

past men which had already been corrected; some made irresponsible and flippant statements; some made senseless comments without investigating antiquity; some mistakenly refuted as groundless the words of the past which were in fact of sound origin; and some altered ancient books to suit themselves.

Ch'üan gave an example of each of these categories, and also wrote ten *chüan* of *Hsiao-shan Mao-shih chiu-miu* [Corrections of Mistakes of Mr. Mao of Hsiao-shan]. But speaking objectively, Mao did not fail to make a brave soldier of the Formative Period, who charged ahead and crushed his enemies, although he lacked "the integrity of a scholar." It is very fitting that no later scholars emulated him.

Meanwhile, there was a certain Yao Chi-heng who was imbued with an extraordinarily blatant, skeptical spirit. He questioned the *Book of History* in Ancient Text, the *Rites of Chou*, the *Preface to the Odes*, and even the *Classic of Filial Piety* and the *Ten Wings of the Commentary on the Book of Changes.* I have not seen his works on the general discus-
[*29] sions of the various classics, but his *Ku-chin wei-shu k'ao* [Examination of Ancient and Modern Forged Books] lists several tens of suspected forged works in the classics, history, and philosophy categories, and it contains a number of plausible and penetrating arguments.

Section 6. Huang Tsung-hsi (1610-1695) and Wang Fu-chih (1619-1692)

Of the great masters of the early Ch'ing, I have the highest regard for Ku [Yen-wu], Huang [Tsung-hsi], Wang [Fu-chih], and Yen [Yüan], all of whom were products of the reaction against Ming thought. It was from Ku that the [later] Orthodox School grew, as has already been indicated in the previous section; I shall now go on to consider the other three.

Huang Tsung-hsi (1610–1695) of Yüyao had studied with Liu Tsung-chou in childhood, [concentrating] solely on Ming thought. After middle age, however, he changed direction and stated: "The Ming scholars patched together their lectures from the dregs of [Sung] dialogues, with no roots in the Six Classics. They packed their books away and engaged in idle talk, giving rise to even more errors. Therefore, scholars must first exhaust the classics. However, to adhere exclusively to classical learning is impractical. To avoid pedantry, it is necessary to study history as well." [1*] He also states: "Without extensive reading it is impossible to verify the various manifestations of the Rational Principle. Wide reading without seeking out [the principle] in one's own mind makes for super-

ficial learning."[2*] Broadly speaking, Ku must be considered the father of classical learning in the Ch'ing period, and Huang, the father of historical learning. Huang's work, *Ming-ju hsüeh-an* [Comments on the Learning
[*30] of Ming Confucianists] marked the first "intellectual history" in China. He was also interested in astronomy and mathematics and had written eight books [about them]. Ch'üan Tsu-wang said: "Mei Wen-ting's discussion of astronomy on the basis of the *Chou 'Gnomon'* [a mathematical classic] overwhelmed the public as dealing with an untransmitted mystery; little did they realize that it was Huang who actually started it." His *Lü-lü hsin-i* [New Meaning of the Principle of Music] paved the way for the study of musical principles; his *I-hsüeh hsiang-shu lun* [Discussion of Numerology in the *Book of Changes*] and Hu Wei's *I-t'u ming-pien* [A Clarification of the Diagrams in the *Changes*] threw light on each other. His *Shou-shu sui-pi* [Desultory Notes on the *Book of History*] consisted of replies to Yen Jo-chü's questions. Thus the learning of Yen and Hu were all influenced by Huang, and his other accomplishments were of comparable merit.

Scholars of the early Ch'ing all emphasized the "useful application [of knowledge]," or the so-called "practical statesmanship."[3] Huang, from the vantage point of historical learning, argued for it with particular eloquence. His most influential work on modern thought was the *Ming-i tai-fang lu* [Plan for the Prince] which included this statement:

> The later sovereigns channeled all profits of the Empire to themselves and all national burdens to others . . . so that the people did not dare to think of their own interests. [The sovereigns] equated their own supreme private interests with the common good of the nation . . . and looked upon the nation as their enormous private property. . . . Thus the sovereigns must be held re-
> [*31] sponsible for the failure of the people to find security anywhere. . . . The people of the empire resented and hated their sovereigns, regarding them as enemies and calling them autocrats, which indeed they were. Yet petty scholars punctiliously stressed proper relations between sovereigns and subjects as universally indispensable and said that even the Chieh and Chou tyranny did not justify regicide. . . . They attempted to apply such abstract terms as "father" and "heaven" [to the sovereign] in order to inhibit men from action.[4*]

He went on to say:

> The later rulers, already possessed of the whole empire, feared that their heirs might not keep it; to prevent such an eventuality they made laws. However, what they called "law" was merely familial law, not law of the empire. . . . If an "unjust law" could be passed by earlier rulers who could not control their selfish desire for gain, it could also be broken by later ones who could not control their desire for gain. The lawbreaker was naturally a scourge to the empire, but the law-maker also was not free from being a scourge to the empire. . . . People say that when one has the rule of [good] men, one does not need law, but I say that until there is the rule of law, there is no rule of man."[5*]

This kind of argument, from today's standpoint, is, of course, fairly common and trite, but two hundred and sixty or seventy years ago it [*32] was really a very bold and original statement. It is small wonder that Ku Yen-wu sighed upon reading it, and said: "The government of the Three Dynasties [Hsia (2205?–1766? B.C.), Shang (1765?–1123? B.C.), and Chou (1122?–256 B.C.)] may yet be re-established." Later, when men like Liang Ch'i-ch'ao (1873–1928) and T'an Ssu-t'ung (1865–1898) advocated the doctrines of people's rights and republicanism, they printed several tens of thousands of copies of excerpts from this book for secret distribution. This contributed powerfully to the sudden alteration of thought in the late Ch'ing.

Ch'ing historical studies flourished abundantly in Chekiang province, the most outstanding exponent being Wan Ssu-t'ung of Ningpo who was a student of Huang's. The [standardl] histories since the T'ang had been collective works of official bureaus. Wan criticized this sharply, saying: "The officially prepared history was a hasty work of many hands; it was like inviting men in off the streets to discuss your household affairs." [6*] Wan completed the *Ming-shih kao* [*Draft History of the Ming*] single-handed, and knowledgeable men opined that he was the only one since Ssu-mu Ch'ien [7] and Pan Ku [8] [who had done such a thing]. Later, from Wan's county, came Ch'üan Tsu-wang (1705–1755) who also covertly modeled himself after Huang and won acclaim from students of "institutional history." Chang Hsüeh-ch'eng (1738–1801) of Kuaichi [part of the present Shao-hsing] who wrote *Wen-shih t'ung-i* [General Principle of History and Literature] had knowledge and judgment even superior to Liu Chih-chi (661–721) and Cheng Ch'iao (1108–1166).

Wang Fu-chih (1619–1692) of Hengyang was born and raised in the [literary] wilderness of the South and had no formal schooling under famous teachers. Also, after the dynastic change [from the Ming to the Ch'ing in 1643–1644] he disappeared into the distant mountains and lost contact with the scholars and officials of the time. Consequently, he was not known during his lifetime, yet because of this [isolation] he attained some unique achievements. He attacked the Wang [Yang-ming] school of learning emphatically, saying: "To misrepresent the words of the sages is the great evil of petty men. . . . Wang teachings [lit., "Yao-chiang," [*33] the native place of Wang] forcibly wrenched similar passages out of the sages and singled out a word or a sentence in order to smuggle in Ch'an [Zen] ideas by subtle means. How incredibly reckless!" [9*] He also stated:

> After several transmissions, it [Wang Yang-ming's teachings] became even more subject to this procedure and wholly different from the original truth. [Some men went so far as to] think that by examining isolated phrases and pairing them in different categories they displayed their ability to exhaust the

classics, [whereas in fact] these [techniques] were only useful in examination halls and literary games. The more extreme among them have gone astray through introspective speculation.[10*]

Such views are frequently found in [Wang Fu-chih's] posthumous works, and were certainly a reaction against the Ming learning which he felt had degenerated terribly. To salvage Ming [learning] by a return to the Sung, he especially recommended Chang Tsai's *Cheng-meng* [Correct Discipline for Beginners]. His method of learning initiated gradually the spirit of scientific research. He once said:

> The principles of things in the world are limitless; what is already excellent may become still more excellent. Changes take place with the passage of time, but nothing deviates from the correct path. But how can it be appropriate for a man to hold stubbornly to his own beliefs, leaving aside the possibility that what he regards as his own belief may be colored by inveterate habits or by adherence to a teacher's words, which he took to be from his own mind? [11*]

Wang's writing was voluminous; the 288 *chuan* printed in Nanking during the T'ung-chih period (1862–1874) did not even constitute half of it, and none of his works was guilty of "the inveterate habits" or of "adherence to the words of a teacher." His *Tu T'ung-chien lun* [Essays Written after Reading the *Comprehensive Mirror*] and *Sung lun* [Discussions on the Sung] frequently advanced new interpretations, and [*34] modern scholars like to study them. He was particularly profound in his cogitation and interpretations of logic and philosophy. His *Chang-tzu cheng-meng chu* [Commentary on Chang Tsai's *Correct Discipline for Beginners*], *Lao-tzu yen* [Commentary on the *Laotzu*], and *Chuang-tzu chieh* [Explanation of the *Chuang-tzu*] were all masterpieces, for he indeed attempted to form a school of philosophy of his own, though to no avail. His idea that "the Rational Principle of nature resides in human desires and that without human desires there can be no discovery of the Rational Principle of nature" [12*] may be considered an insight into what had not been thought of since the Sung (960–1279 A.D.) and Ming (1368–1643 A.D.). Later on, the doctrine of Tai Chen actually developed from this [idea] and for that reason, Liu Hsien-t'ing (1648–1695) admired and praised Wang Fu-chih highly in these words: "The vital spirit of heaven and earth, and the very heart of the teachings of sages [are contained] in this one line alone." [13*] Later on, Wang substantially affected the thinking of a scholar from his native town, T'an Ssu-t'ung, who once said: "Among the scholars of the past five hundred years, Wang alone was truly capable of comprehending natural and human causes." [14*] It is particularly interesting that in the catalogue of his *Posthumous Works* there were two [Buddhist] books, the *Hsiang-tsung lo-so* [Key to the Dharmalaksana Sect] and the *San-tsang fa-shih pa-shih kuei-chu-lun tsan* [A

Tribute to the Treatise on the Regulation of Eight Senses by the Master Hsüan-tsang].[15*] If a Confucian scholar in those days could study the Vijñānamātra sutra, should he not be called a spectacular man?

[*35] *Section 7. Yen Yüan (1635-1704)*

Ku, Huang, Wang, and Yen all reacted against the same Wang [Yang-ming] school of learning, but each reacted in a different way. From beginning to end, Huang never attacked the Wang school itself, but simply remedied the abstractness of its last phase. Both Ku and Wang [Fu-chih] de-emphasized Ming [learning] to preserve that of the Sung. Ku valued empirical research, Wang relished logical reasoning, but Yen was openly and bluntly opposed to the Ch'eng [brothers], Chu [Hsi], Lu [Chiu-yüan], and Wang [Yang-ming], also deprecating the pursuit of commentary, annotation, and empirical research. Therefore, the so-called "Sung learning" and "Han learning" were both rejected. Yen was particularly eminent and outstanding among scholars, yet in the long run his teachings did not achieve popularity during the Ch'ing period.

Yen Yüan (1635–1704) of Po-yeh was born in a remote area and grew up in someone else's family. Repeatedly experiencing sorrow and misfortune, he became eminently capable of facing difficulties with fortitude. His teachings were comparable to those of the "Stoic School" in Rome, and his independence of spirit vis-à-vis old ideas was most thorough. He once said:

> In making a statement one needs only to consider its rightness or wrongness and not its similarity or dissimilarity [to the ideas of others]. If it is right, then even if it is merely the view of one or two men, it cannot be altered. If it is wrong, then even if it is shared by tens of thousands of men, it should not be followed. Not only must we enlighten tens of thousands of men as seers do followers, but also [unravel] hundreds and thousands of years of confusion. There is absolutely no need to follow others and echo them.[1*]

[*36] His respect for his own conscience was such that it was thoroughly unwavering, and with respect to Sung learning, he made a positively unrestrained frontal attack in these words:

> Formerly I had reluctantly gone along with the Ch'eng [brothers] and Chu Hsi, and thought of them as a branch of the Confucian School, but during my trip to the South, I saw that every man was a Ch'an [Zen] Buddhist [in spirit] and that everybody indulged in empty verbiage in direct contradiction to the teachings of the Confucian school. [Realizing that] a man could study Confucius and Mencius only to the extent that he was able to break away from the Ch'eng brothers and Chu, I thereby concluded that Confucius and Mencius on the one hand and the Ch'eng brothers and Chu on the other, represented two

distinctly different ways, and that I would not be an obedient, careful villager [i.e., a mere follower] in the Sequence of Orthodoxy.[2*]

But how did Yen's learning differ from that of the Sung scholars? Yen's most important guiding principle was: "Stress more physical action and labor less with the mind."[3*] He elaborated this idea thus: "A man's time and energy are limited. A day spent in recitation and exposition is a day lost in actual practice. To work more with paper and ink is to have less practical experience of life!"[4*] Again he said: "A Sung scholar is like one who has got hold of an itinerary guide and pored over one item after another and become complacent in his mastery of all the routes of the world. He is popularly regarded as knowing the routes, whereas in fact he has not ventured a single step nor reached a single place."[5*] He said also: "Whether the discussions of the various scholars were con- [*37] cerned with the body or with the world at large, they were only paper work. Therefore, if what they said was contradictory to Confucius and Mencius, it was useless; and if what they said was not contradictory to Confucius and Mencius, it was also useless."[6*]

Moreover, he said:

> Take medicine for example. A reckless man, merely by poring over thousands of medical books and so familiarizing himself with their details, considers himself the leading authority of the empire. He regards taking pulses, making medicine, applying needles, and cauterizing as too vulgar to practice. His [reading] of books grows daily and his [theoretical] knowledge becomes more advanced daily. With one man fostering this [trend], the whole empire imitates him; and, while doctors fill the country, the people fill the sickbeds and die one after another.[7*]

Again he said: "To engage for a long time in a learning which emphasizes the love of inaction and empty talk will doubtless lead to a distaste for work, which will doubtless lead in turn to a neglect of it. In case of an emergency, [such a man] is completely lost. Thus, it was Sung learning which misled the talented people and ruined the affairs of the nation."[8*] He went on to say: "If a man looks at books and meditates with his mind, there is nothing to which [his imagination] cannot attain, but this is the easiest way to deceive himself and the world. Not only is he incapable but he is in fact ignorant."[9*] His discussions of the principle of learning were generally of this kind.

From the above standpoint, it is apparent that Yen not only considered Sung learning as no learning, but Han learning as well. His idea [*38] was that knowledge definitely could not be gained from books or lecture halls but from the daily events in society. He said: "If a man thinks of reading as learning, his is definitely not the learning of Confucius. If he can interpret books by reading books, his books cannot be those of Confucius."[10*]

Again: "Later scholars have turned extensive learning into extensive reading and writing." [11*]

What Yen advocated as learning was the "three kinds of rustic merit" of the *Ta-ssu-t'u* of the *Rites of Chou*: (1) the Six Virtues: knowledge, benevolence, saintliness, righteousness, loyalty, and harmony; (2) the Six Rules of Conduct: filial piety, brotherly love, good relations [with relatives to the ninth degree], good relations with maternal relatives, confidence [in upright friends], and charity; and (3) the Six Arts: ceremonies, music, archery, carriage-driving, calligraphy, and mathematics.[12] It was the Six Arts in particular that he himself practiced; thus [he emphasized] farming, medical practice, pugilism, training in military strategy and tactics, the practice of ritual and ceremony, and the study of music. In teaching students he insisted that each specialize in one art. He wholeheartedly embraced the idea of "the sanctity of work" as he said: "To nourish the body, there is nothing better than getting used to activity. Work during the day and rest at night; brighten your spirit and find work to do!" [13*] Again: "To live a day, one should serve the people a day." [14*] In fine, one seeks knowledge only because he intends to work; work is knowledge and without work there is no knowledge; this was Yen's basic creed. The substitution of practical learning for empty learning, of active knowledge for passive knowledge, of living knowledge for dead knowledge corresponded well with the new and latest [*39] educational trends, but were the things Yen considered practical, active, and living totally free from empty, passive, and dead elements? This was a matter of the times; we cannot measure past men by the social conditions of today.

The most outstanding students of Yen were Li Kung and Wang Yüan, both capable of carrying out his teachings. But Yen's way was too rigorous and ascetic, somewhat like that of Mo-tzu. It had only a few transmitters and not long afterward suffered an untimely death.

Section 8. Mei Wen-ting (1632-1721), Ku Tsu-yü (1631-1692), and Liu Hsien-t'ing (1648-1695)

The only really prominent sciences of our nation were astronomy and mathematics, which were particularly popular during the Ch'ing. All the scholars of classical learning were conversant with both [of these sciences], and the pioneering father [in these fields] was Mei Wen-t'ing (1632–1721) of Süancheng. Hang Shih-chün said:

Since Matteo Ricci entered China during the Wan-li period (1573–1620) of the Ming, quite excellent instruments and maps had been made – [Chinese]

scholars were too overwhelmed [by him] to be able to find time for a deep inquiry into the origin and development of Chinese mathematics. Frequently they took the superficial works that had been handed down for generations to be the complete picture of the ancient Nine Chapters [i.e., mathematics], and thus deprecated the ancient system as unworthy of attention. On the other hand, there were some who obstinately guarded the old learning and rashly spurned Western learning [lit., "men"] as heresy. Thus the two schools [East and West] kept apart from each other. Mei collected Western works and explained them in Chinese terms with slight modifications. For instance, [subjects like] trig-
[*40] onometry and ratio[?] were not originally included in the Chinese system, so he specially clarified them. The ancient [Chinese] methods of making equations were not known in the Western system, so he wrote monographs on them to clarify the essential ideas of the ancients.[1*]

Mei has more than eighty titles to his credit, all generally in such a spirit. He knew of no national boundaries to knowledge, and so he had no preconceived prejudices. His creative accomplishments are numerous and he himself explained: "In pursuing my work, I always went through great difficulties before I could make it simple and easy. My only wish is to make this science very well known so that forgotten knowledge may not be untransmitted. [If so], I will die with no regret!" [2*] Here we have a pure scholarly attitude.

The study of geography also flourished greatly during the Ch'ing, but after the Ch'ien-lung (1736–1795) and Chia-ch'ing (1796–1820) periods it generally over-emphasized investigations in historical geography, and its contributions were largely restricted ones. In terms of scope of study and quality of thinking, there has as yet been no work that can surpass the *Tu-shih-fang-yü chi-yao* [Essentials of Historical Geography] by Ku Tsu-yü (1631–1692) of Wusih. Wei Hsi (1624–1680) reviewed it as follows:

The various geographical works and maps that had inherited misinformation and errors from each other, confusing Name and Reality, were all collated and corrected [by Ku] on the basis of official histories. His book was hence utterly unique and unprecedented in [a period of] several hundreds and thousands of years. . . . He integrated the various histories and came out with his unique views. The profundity of his thinking and the keenness of his perception are beyond the expression of the spoken and written language.[3*]

In writing this book, Ku began the manuscript at the age of twenty-
[*41] nine and completed it at fifty, without a day's interruption. He himself said: "Whenever my boat and cart passed [a place], I had to see the inner and outer cities, study the mountains and rivers, examine the distance of the routes, and inquire about the water and land customs. I also engaged in uninhibited conversation with traders and travelers, as well as with veterans who have been on expeditions or guard duties, in order to examine and compare similarities and differences." [4*] This was certainly the modern scientific spirit.

There was a great scholar in the early Ch'ing whose work did not come down to posterity; he was Liu Hsien-t'ing (1648–1695) of Ta-hsing. Wang Yüan (1648–1710) wrote the following on his tombstone:

> He disengaged himself [from entanglement] in order to visit the entire Nine Provinces [China], studied the topography of mountains and rivers, visited famous retired men, made heroes his friends, observed local customs, assembled anecdotes widely – [all this] to broaden his experience even more, and to confirm his knowledge. . . . He discussed the changes in the ways of the universe and of the *yin* and *yang*, the grand strategies of the hegemons and kings, military arts, literature, institutions and regulations, and important points in various localities. . . . With respect to ceremony, music, astrology, medicine, calligraphy, mathematics, law, agriculture, mulberry [plantings] [i.e., sericulture], and the making of firearms for war, he had [studied them all] exhaustively, without limit, either [indirectly] via other fields or [directly] by extensive investigation.[5]*

But what is even more striking is Ch'üan Tsu-wang's description of his [Liu's] posthumous work, *Hsin-yün p'u* [New Scores of Rhymes].*

[*43] From the time that Shih Shou-wen of the T'ang (618–906 A.D.) first attempted to create new alphabets for China, until 1918, when the Ministry of Education promulgated the *Phonetic Symbols*, nearly a thousand years had elapsed before that task was completed. During this interval Liu was the man most capable of systematic and sustained thinking. If his book had been passed down to posterity, this problem might have been solved long before, and much scholarly energy [spent on] research over the past thirty years might also have been spared. Nevertheless, it was still fortunate that Ch'üan had passed on an outline [of Liu's work] as material for modern scholars to study. The present *Phonetic Symbols* has adopted a number of his proposed methods, and we have already benefited from him.

Ch'üan had also described Liu's views on geography, history, and "law of kinship," and came to this general conclusion: "What Liu wrote about [*44] was of such scope that it could not be accomplished by a single man at one time. Therefore, although he was earnest about his undertaking, it was difficult [for him] to complete the task." This is indeed true. But the fact of the matter is that learning has never been encompassed by one man at one time; it depends solely on whether posterity can make good use of the heritage and illuminate it. Was not [the system initiated in] Liu's New Scores of Rhymes brought to completion three hundred years later? Liu himself once said: "A man who cannot manipulate the natural course of events for the benefit of the world, but can only keep

* *Translator's Note*: Here follows a quotation from Ch'üan, describing Liu's unique accomplishments in phonology. Several of the terms and expressions used were too vague and abstruse to permit an accurate translation in terms used by modern phonologists. I take the liberty of omitting this quotation which is about a page long in the original text, pages 42–43.

his knowledge and ability for his own and his family's benefit, is not worthy of being called a man!"[6*] This is a general view of the main direction of his learning; it is regrettable only that his line [of thought] had not been transmitted at that time. Among his works only the *Kuang-yang tsa-chi* [Miscellaneous Records of Kuang-yang] is now extant. This is actually a random record of informal writings and quite inadequate to represent him.

Meanwhile, there was a certain Fu Shan of Taiyüan who was known for his quixotism during the dynastic change [i.e., from Ming to Ch'ing]. After this national change, Feng Ch'üan and Wei Hsiang-shu had tried hard to recommend him [to the Ch'ing court], [which he refused to serve] at the risk of near-martyrdom for himself. After that he changed into the attire of a Taoist priest. To someone who asked him about his views he said: "I study Chuang-tzu and Lieh-tzu; of all this business about benevolence and righteousness, I am truly ashamed to speak."[7*] Nevertheless, an historian said: "His knowledge was not equaled by anyone north of the Big River [Yellow River]."[8*]

[*45] *Section 9. Summary*

To sum up the above, we know that the intellectual milieu of the Formative Period was extremely complex and splendid by virtue of these four reasons:

(1) Having inherited the very abstract Ming thought, men [of the Ch'ing period] grew tired of it, and one after another turned to something with depth and solidity.

(2) After passing through a great upheaval, society was relatively peaceful; people therefore had leisure to improve themselves in learning.

(3) A foreign people [the Manchus] had entered to rule China and men of fortitude and integrity were ashamed to serve the court; therefore they avoided the limelight by concentrating their talents on sound learning [i.e., solid scholarship].

(4) The prestige and authority of the old school of learning had already disintegrated, but the system of the new school had not yet been established. There was as yet no limitation such as "conformity to one kind of orthodoxy," so the spirit of free learning was particularly vigorous.

This spirit of learning, under environmental stimuli, also developed in four directions:

(1) In order to correct the late Ming error of "no learning," people [*46] studied ancient books, but the more they studied, the more they realized the difficulty of understanding them rightly. Therefore they

studied as prerequisites philology, the semantics of technical terms, regulations and institutions, etc., and [out of this study] emerged the School of Empirical Research.

(2) The various great masters of that period were all elderly survivals of the previous dynasty who commonly harbored a concealed bitterness over the dynastic change and planned to restore [the Ming]; therefore they were interested in studying [the causes of] success and failure in ancient and modern historical records, geography, strategic forts and passes, and other matters of practical statesmanship.

(3) Since the last phase of the Ming (1368–1643), when Matteo Ricci and others introduced into China what was then known as Western learning, the method of scholarly research had changed [under pressure] from without. At first only astronomers and mathematicians credited [the new method] but later on it was gradually applied to other subjects.

(4) As the trend of learning was turning back from the abstract to the concrete, some men looked for the concrete in books and some in action. Southerners were generally quick and systematic, so they tended to develop in the field of writing; northerners were unpretentious, sincere, and persistent, so they tended to express themselves in action.

[*47] This is an overall view of the course of intellectual development in the Formative Period.

However, during the height of the second period, only the so-called Orthodox School [School of Empirical Research] developed to the fullest extent; all the other schools either languished or died premature deaths. Why was this so? I think there are four reasons here too:

(1) The Yen-Li school of action proclaimed fairly high ideals, but it could hardly escape the kind of criticism that Chuang-tzu leveled at Mo-tzu: "His way was too harsh; I am afraid the world cannot take it up." [1*] This kind of asceticism could be realized only by those with religious beliefs; it could not be expected of ordinary men. The teaching of Yen Yüan, which definitely lacked the ideas of "life after death" and "otherworldliness," insisted on maintaining a very bare, cold, and rigorous principle of moral obligation in everyday life and demanded of men the renunciation of all pleasures. This was, of course, not a broad way for the general public. His teaching was able to shine for a while because his disciples were directly inspired by his personality, but after several generations of transmission, its power of inspiration weakened as time passed. Its gradual decline and [final] extinction were only a matter of course. Moreover, because of social changes, not all of his so-called practical "arts" were actually practical. The one he emphasized most was *li* but this so-called *li* was only a kind of formality of two thousand years [*48] earlier that definitely could not be carried out in its entirety today. Since it could not [be practiced], the concrete had ironically be-

come abstract. This was incompatible also with the currently prevailing intellectual trend of seeking after the concrete, and it was only natural that it could not itself become established as a trend.

(2) I have said that the then-prevailing efflorescence of the "school of practical statesmanship" was caused by the determination of the various great masters to restore [the Ming]. The refusal of these great masters to serve the Ch'ing court had naturally rendered them highly suspect and later, when literary inquisitions took place all too frequently, scholars became increasingly concerned with self-preservation and dared not expound any doctrine that might arouse official suspicions. But the talents and intellect of brilliant and outstanding men could not remain unused forever; exegesis of ancient aphorisms and exhaustive searching into the semantics of technical terms could certainly be called [tasks which] "do not injure the world and do not conflict with men," and in these scholars found a refuge.

Moreover, what were called the "tasks of practical statesmanship" were supposed to meet the needs of the time and would serve no purpose after that time. If the men who engaged in this kind of learning could not put [their program] into practice immediately, [their only recourse] was to hide it away in [the recesses of] famous mountains [for posterity to read], and thus ultimately it could not help becoming a kind of empty declaration. As empty declaration, why couldn't shallow men plagiarize its ideas in order [to pose as] associates? When these "associates" grew numerous, they became indistinguishable from the original [exponents] and soon came to be regarded askance. Thus after the Ch'ien-lung and Chia-ch'ing periods (1736–1820), this school declined and [finally] became extinct; even the history and geography scholars all tended toward [*49] the field of empirical research, no longer able to carry on their work [mainly] by discussion and argument.

(3) To develop a body of learning, the first prerequisite is to have a superior methodology at the outset. With respect to the Ch'ing School of Empirical Research, the various masters such as Ku, Yen, Hu, Hui, and Tai had actually opened up a new road for all to travel; wise men followed it in a grand way, and unwise men in a petty way, but all alike could be spurred on. China had amassed several thousand years of civilization and her ancient books were really worthy of study, like a very rich vein in a gold mine. Unless we study and rearrange them we cannot enjoy their use, just as the gold [ore] in a mine must be dug out and processed in order to obtain it. Thus when the methodology was established, scholars not only became interested in it, but they realized the need for it too, and all of them came under its influence. The more they analyzed, the more tightly-knit [the methodology] became, and the more they dug, the deeper they got. As the school at that time allowed ample

scope for exploration, all those who joined it, regardless of their talent [lit., "big or small"], if only they worked faithfully, could in some way ultimately accomplish something. That is why [this school] stood head and shoulders above other schools in solitary eminence.

(4) Since the methodology of Ch'ing learning was almost "scientific," it seems appropriate that it [the learning] should develop in the scientific direction too. But why is it that it [the methodology] was applied only to antiquarian studies and that, apart from mathematics and astronomy, [*50] no other natural sciences developed? In general, the rise of a body of learning on the one hand considerably depends on its history, and on the other hand, on special opportunities. The learning of our nation over the past several thousand years concentrated on social studies as a rule, and was never really concerned with the natural world. This need not be denied. Also, at that time, there was no special motive force to turn scholars' attention in a new direction. Furthermore, during the youthful vigor of the new School of Empirical Research, there were simply too many fields [lit., "colonies"] open for exploration, towards which men of talent and intelligence were inclined; naturally they could not dissipate their energies in other directions. Since astronomy and mathematics were a traditional part of the classics and history, they could develop concomitantly in a subordinate capacity; all others, however, had no such [background]. Actually, European science did not prosper until modern times, and during the age of the "Renaissance," its intellectual trend also emphasized antiquarian studies. This indeed ought to be the inevitable procedure for the advancement of learning.

Now that I have concluded my discussion of the Formative Period, I shall consider the High Period.

PART II

The Middle Ch'ing Period:

The Dominance of the School of Empirical Research; The Beginnings of Reaction

Section 10. Hui Tung [1697-1758]

The School of Empirical Research did not embrace the whole academic world during the Formative Period, whereas it dominated it completely during the High Period. Therefore, anyone dealing with the in- [*51] tellectual history of the High Period need hardly look beyond the School of Empirical Research. Empirical research in the Formative Period made little more than a rough beginning, omitting and oversimplifying a good deal in its research methodology – for example, Yen Jo-chü's *Shang-shu ku-wen shu-cheng* was cluttered with different genres of writing such as diaries and letters, which resulted in a highly mixed and rambling presentation, and Hu Wei's *Yü-kung chui-chih* [Guide to the *Yü-kung Gazetteer*] for the most part discusses statesmanship and is a mixture of both the Han and Sung [approaches]. It is thus not strict in its methodology. Had it not been for the various masters of the High Period, it is doubtful that the School of Empirical Research could have developed by itself into an independent school, and without the School of Empirical Research there could have been no Ch'ing learning; hence a discussion of Ch'ing learning must focus on this [High] period.

In this period, the School had already become "popularized," with a good many powerful men in it who regarded each other as teachers and friends. Their pursuit of knowledge followed a fairly "uniform" [pattern] with no particular factions to speak of; I should like to discuss only one or two of them as representative of the rest. The great masters of that time were universally recognized to be Hui Tung and Tai Chen, and Tai's excellence and profundity of learning actually surpassed even that of Hui. I will now present in brief the writings and discourses of these two men and their lines of transmission for comparison.

Hui Tung of Yüan-ho [in Kiangsu] [came of a family which] for generations past had engaged in classical studies. His grandfather, Chou-t'i, and his father, Shih-ch'i, both had written [books] and were looked upon as masters among scholars. Heir to his family's scholarly tradition, Hui carried it even further and wrote the *Chiu-ching ku-i* [Ancient Interpretations of the *Nine Classics*], *I-Han-hsüeh* [Studies of the *Changes* According to Han Tradition], *Chou-i-shu* [Explanation of the *Book of Changes*], *Ming-t'ang ta-tao lu* [Principal Teachings Concerning the Luminous Hall], *Ku-wen Shang-shu k'ao* [A Study of the *Book of History* in Ancient Text], *Hou-Han-shu pu-chu* [Supplementary Commentary on the *History of the Later Han*], and others. His most outstanding pupils were Shen T'ung, Chiang Sheng, and Yü Hsiao-k'e. Yü's pupil, Chiang Fan (1761–1831), the author of the *Kuo-ch'ao Han-hsüeh shih-ch'eng chi* [Biographies of the Leaders of Han Learning under the Present Dynasty], considered Hui the orthodox [founder] of this [i.e., Han] School. But actually Hui was not qualified to represent all the learning of his generation, for he merely established the range and limits [of that school].

The Hui school was [characterized by] extensive reading and much memorization at the outset, with homage to antiquity and the adherence to its own methodology as the abiding and unchanging creed. Hui Shih-ch'i was so conversant with the texts of the *Nine Classics, Four Histories, Notes on the Various States of Tso-chuan* (*Kuo-yü*), *Strategies of the Warring States* (*Kuo-ts'e*), and the *Elegies of Ch'u*, that he once recited the entire Feng-shan chapter of the *Shih-chi* [*Historical Record*] before an assemblage of guests, without mistaking a word.[1*] Hui Tung studied under his father's tutelage and his [powers of] memory and recitation became even more amazing. His father said:

> Cheng Hsüan's [commentaries] on the three *Rites* [i.e., the *Rites of Chou, Ceremony and Rituals*, and the *Book of Rites*] and Ho Hsiu's [Commentary] on the *Kung-yang Commentary* often employed the Han method, because the Han was not far removed from antiquity. . . . But Chia Kung-yen . . . could not write a sub-commentary on such works as Cheng's commentary. . . . Since the Han was farther removed [from antiquity] than the Chou, and the T'ang was even further removed [from antiquity] than the Han, it was understandable that the [earlier] views were not thoroughly mastered; how much more so would this be the case [with men] after the Sung! [2*]

From this we see that the Hui family's criterion in their approach to learning was based on the antithesis "antiquity or modernity" and [*53] this is precisely the fundamental spirit of Hui Tung's approach. He said:

> Han scholars mastered the classics by means of their own method; thus, there were Masters of the Five classics, who gave oral instruction in philological glosses which were then recorded on bamboo slips and silk scrolls. In this way, the views of these Han classical masters were established, in the view of the officials in charge of learning, as equal in standing to the classics themselves. . . . Ancient characters and words cannot be understood without these classical masters. . . . Therefore, ancient philological glosses should not be altered and the classical masters should not be dispensed with. . . . My family has transmitted the classics for four generations, each time with a mastery of the ancient meanings. . . . I have therefore carried on the family tradition of learning in writing *The Ancient Interpretations of the Nine Classics*. . .[3*]

The Hui school's approach to learning can be summarized in eight characters: "That which is ancient must be authentic and that which is of the Han must be good." Hui Tung's statement that "the views of the Han classical masters were equal in standing to the classics" was made with the intention of elevating the views of these masters to the rank of the classics. Wang Yin-chih once said: "Although Hui Tung arduously studied antiquity, his judgment was not sound and his thinking not disciplined; when he saw something other than modern he usually accepted it without asking whether it was right or wrong." [4*] We may say this statement shows insight.

Hui was reputed to know well the *Book of Changes.* [As a result of] his study of this work, such terms as Cheng Hsüan's *hsiao-ch'en* (correlation of the twelve months with the twelve "lines" of the *ch'ien* and *k'un* hexagrams), Yü Fan's *na-chia* (correlation of the ten *kan-chih* with the hexagrams), Hsün Hsü's *sheng-chiang* (the rising of the *ch'ien* and the falling of the *k'un*), Ching Fang's *shih-ying* (the response of the "breaths" of the Earth to the "breaths" of the Heaven), *fei-fu* (the visible and [*54] invisible in divination), *liu-jih ch'i-fen* (six days and seven parts), and *shih-kuei* were all "clarified and illuminated" by him.[5] In Wang Chung's words, this is "the lost knowledge that was cut off from us for more than a thousand years," but as I see it, Hui was making a false claim; what [real] difference is there between his work and Ch'en T'uan's "River Chart and Lo Writing?" [6] And yet the latter was spurned because it had been studied by men of the Sung period, whereas the former was believed because it was advocated by men of the Han period. This seems highly confused and incomprehensible, but the men of that time were deluded and often regarded his work as a masterpiece. Chiang Fan (1761–1831), the legimate and direct heir of the Hui school, wrote the *Kuo-ch'ao Han-hsüeh shih-ch'eng-chi* [Biographies of the Leaders of Han Learning under the Present Dynasty] which contained a supplementary, concluding chapter listing the classical masters and classical tenets of the Ch'ing dynasty as follows:

> Although Huang Tsung-hsi's *I-hsüeh hsiang-shu lun* [Discussion of Numerology in the *Book of Changes*] condemns the works of Ch'en Tuan and K'ang Chi, it regards *na-chia* and *tung-hsiao* as false hexagrams, and considers the annotation by Wang Fu-ssu concise, precise, and devoid of superfluous interpretation. Although Huang Tsung-yen's (1616–1686) *T'u-shu pien-ho* [An Inquiry into Doubts Cast on the "River Chart and Lo Writing"] emphatically condemns Sung scholars, because it does not follow Han learning alone, he was not a man of profound conviction. . . . Although Hu Wei's *Hung-fan cheng-lun* [Correct Discussion of the *Hung-fan* Chapter of the *Book of History*] made a powerful attack on the errors of the "River Chart and Lo Writing," it also condemns the Han doctrines of Five Elements, and Visitations and Prodigies. This shows he did not know that Hsia-hou Shih-ch'ang's *Hung-fan wu-hsin chuan* [Commentary on the *Hung-fan* Chapter and the Five Elements] also derived [*55] from Fu Sheng. For this reason I cast it aside.

This kind of statement very clearly illustrates the central principle of the Hui school, which demanded that all doctrines be obeyed that stemmed from Han scholars, and held anyone an infirm believer who dared to criticize them. Later, when Juan Yüan (1764–1849) edited the *Explanation of the Classics in Hsüeh-hai-t'ang*, he used this [Hui-school principle] as a criterion, and therefore rejected most of the famous works by Ku, Huang, Yen, and Hu on grounds of impurity.

Speaking objectively, this school had both its merits and failings within the intellectual world of the Ch'ing period. Its strict observance of its own methodology consolidated the fortress of the so-called "Han learning" and distinguished it [from other schools of thought]; this is its merit. Its unyielding inertia, blind obedience, parochial outlook, and eagerness to reject opposition almost stifled the skeptical spirit and critical attitude of the Formative Period; this is its failing.

Ch'ing learning has often been labeled "Han learning" by various writers, but actually what the various masters before Hui – men like Ku, Huang, Wang, and Yen – dealt with was not "Han learning," and what was undertaken by the various later masters, such as Tai, Tuan, and the Two Wangs, was also not "Han learning." As for "pure Han learning," only the one school of Hui fully deserved the name; it did not ask whether "it was authentic or not" but whether "it was Han or not." Approaching the mastery of learning in this way, how could it achieve comprehensive understanding? Moreover, there were a great variety of schools of interpretation of the classics among the Han scholars, and it was not infrequent that two interpretations were diametrically opposed. Blind obedience to one would leave a man no choice but to reject the other. Hui [*56] was, of course, the man who raised the standard of "reverence to Han [learning]." On his interpretation of the statement "Philosopher Chi under a cloud," because he wanted to promote the view of Meng Hsi and suppress that of Shih Ch'ou and Liang-ch'iu Ho he remarked: "This is the transmission of an error which had its start in the Former Han Period (206 B.C.–24 A.D.)".[7*] This brought forth biting ridicule from Fang Tung-shu (1772–1851).[8*] Thus, the maxim that "that which is of the Han period must be good" could not be consistently adhered to. In the light of [the above], I really wonder whether Ch'ing learning could have established itself so eminently had it not been for Tai Chen.

Section 11. Tai Chen [1724-1777]

Tai Chen (1724–1777) of Siuning [on the southern border of Anhwei] studied under Chiang Yung, and his relationship with Hui Tung was something between that of teacher and of friend. At the age of ten Tai started his schooling, and when he came to the passages after the phrase "the preceding chapter of classical text" [1] in *The Great Learning*, he asked his school teacher, "How do we know that this is what Confucius said, as transmitted by Tseng-tzu, and how do we know that [the commentary] represents the views of Tseng-tzu as recorded by his disciples?" The teacher answered, "This is what the previous master Chu Hsi said in his commentary." He then asked, "When did Chu Hsi live?" and was answered, "Southern Sung (1127–1279 A.D.)." When he again asked, "When did Confucius and Tseng-tzu live?" the answer was "Eastern Chou (722–481 B.C.)." He pressed further: "How much time elapsed between the [*57] Chou and the Sung?" The answer was: "Almost two thousand years." Then he said, "How, then, could Chu Hsi know this for a fact?" The teacher could not answer.[2*] This anecdote is apt not only to illustrate the point of departure of Tai's learning, but it actually epitomizes the entire spirit of the Ch'ing school of learning of that age, for [Tai] was not in the habit of accepting anyone's statement readily without insisting on finding the evidence for it. He often found flaws in places others had neglected and, having found them, would press forward step by step until the point of exhaustion. If in the end he still could not find anything to warrant his confidence, then although they were the words of sages, philosophers, father, or teachers, he would not credit them. It is this kind of spirit of inquiry that really provided the basis for modern science; since Tai possessed this instinct even in childhood, it was quite logical that he should have been able to complete the task of establishing a school of learning in his own time.

Tai said:

> A scholar should be deluded neither by others nor by himself. He should not look for ephemeral fame just as he should not expect fame from posterity. The idea of fame has two disadvantages: [it drives] one either to attack past men in order to exhibit oneself, or to depend on ancient sages as props, in order to ride their coattails. . . . A man who tries to work through [problems] relying on his own wisdom may not attack others with the sole intention of self-display, [*58] but when he has accumulated enough errors he may unconsciously accept them as truths; what first enters his mind comes to dominate it and leads him astray for the rest of his life. Perhaps not all of his dependence on others is motivated solely by a desire of riding their coattails. Nevertheless, [in either case] although the mean motive may be absent, the evil consequence is just the same. . . .[3*]

"Not to be deluded by others and not to be deluded by oneself" are the two commandments from which Tai really derived most of his strength all his life. As the pursuit of knowledge is indeed a difficult task, a man who has barely set foot on the road can seldom avoid being deluded by others, and when he has gone deeper in his pursuit and tries hard to rid himself of the delusions of others, he may find that he is soon deluding himself. Unless a man can be imperturbably calm, open-minded, and level-headed, he will suffer from this mistake in one way or another. Tai attacked the "delusion by others" in this way:

To aspire to get at the truth, a man must purge himself completely of all of his dependence. Although the philologic [method] of the Han scholars was based on an orthodox line of transmission, at times it suffered from forced interpretations. The Chin men had even more farfetched interpretations and groundless speculations. Those of the Sung judged by introspection; thus they often accepted many errors, renouncing precisely what was not wrong. . . . Scholars since the Sung have wrenched their own ideas into identity with what the ancient sages and wise men intended to say, without really understanding their spoken and written language. With respect to worldly affairs, they [the scholars since the Sung] treated them dogmatically in accordance with what they called the "rational principle" without actually getting at the complete background and details of these affairs. Therefore, the great truth was lost and the affairs were badly conducted. . . . They themselves were not conscience-stricken, but the world suffered from their errors. Whose fault is it when the [*59] uninformed went so far as to consider them scholars who carried their ideas into practice? [4*]

Tai anathematized "self-delusion" as follows:

The reason I have investigated our inherited classics is that I am afraid that the suggestive sayings of the sages may become obscured in later generations, but some of my findings were based on thoroughly [lit., "ten parts"] conclusive evidence, some are not yet so based. By conclusive evidence I mean that they must be verified by ancient [works] as containing no discrepancy of any sort; it must be in so complete an accord with truth as to leave nothing debatable; it must exhaust both major and minor points and consider what is fundamental as well as what is of secondary importance.

But if I presume something to be correct merely on the basis of hearsay, or determine it as good merely by choosing the best of a variety of interpretations, or judge it on the basis of unfounded words, or call it valid on the basis of an isolated piece of evidence,[my evidence is inconclusive].

Although by following the stream one knows its source, still without an eyewitness to the source's outflow, [his evidence is inconclusive]. Although one can reach the tip of the smallest branch of a tree by following the root upwards, yet before he touches the network of branches with his own hands, his evidence is inconclusive. Studying classics in this way means losing the [true] meaning of "let your nay be nay" and simply creating one more error for learned men to expose. . . .

Only by getting close to the [truth] by profound thought and personal insight can one know what is conclusive finding and what is not yet conclusive. It is like measuring wood with a piece of string: what was formerly assumed to be straight is now shown to be crooked, or like measuring the earth by a surveyer's level: what was formerly assumed to be level ground is now revealed [*60] in its unevenness. Only in this way can one transmit what is authentic and not what is questionable; when in doubt, omit, so that a study of the classics may not exert harmful influence.[5*]

From a perusal of the first quotation we know that to regard Tai's learning as "Han learning" is quite improper; what Tai contemplated was "the elimination of the various kinds of dependence." The intellectual trends of the Chin and Sung naturally came under his attack, and even the men of the Han were merely regarded by him as having *chia-fa*, their "methodology," but he never asked people to follow them [i.e., Han scholars] blindly. Ch'ien Ta-hsin (1728–1804) spoke of him as "seeking the truth by investigating the facts" without patronizing any one school.[6*] Yü T'ing-ts'ai said:

> When there was a single character which was not based on the Six Scripts, or the interpretation of a single word which could not be uniformly applied to the various classics, he would not believe it without evidence. When he doubted, he had no peace with himself until he had repeatedly checked the references and evidence. Thus, what he perceived by his own mental effort usually transcended the formidable array of commentaries and sub-commentaries.[7*]

This quotation admirably conveys his spirit of freedom of thought.

An examination of the second quotation [reveals] that what he called conclusive evidence and inconclusive evidence are actually the counterparts of a scientist's law and hypothesis. The objective of science is to find a law, but a law must pass through an hypothesis-stage before it is established. When we first develop an idea, we do not dare consider it true; its degree of truth may be only ten or twenty per cent; but if we assume it to be close to the truth and use it as a [starting] point for study, then, the results of several trials may soon increase the degree of truth to fifty or sixty per cent, then to seventy or eighty per cent, and finally to a hundred per cent. Only then can we accept it as a law and proclaim it as such. That which cannot reach hundred-per-cent [certainty] may remain an hypothesis for later men [to work on], or it may be rejected outright by the man concerned; this indeed ought to be the attitude of all scientists. Tai's argument was certainly derived from hard [lit., "sweet and bitter"] experience. His statement, "What was formerly assumed to be straight is now shown to be crooked, and what was formerly assumed to be level [ground] is now revealed in its unevenness," shows quite truly the indispensable path in scientific research, and his determination to omit – to transmit only the authentic and not the questionable – is a most important ethical [principle] for the society of scholars.

Tai also said:

> There are three difficulties in learning: the difficulty of acquiring erudition, the difficulty of making decisive observations, and the difficulty of making critical judgments. I certainly do not measure up to these standards; but as a rule I merely act and write books keeping them in mind. Among previous men of extensive learning and powerful memory were men like Cheng Ch'iao (1108–1166) and Yang Shen (1488–1529), whose houses overflowed with their writings; erudition they certainly had, but hardly incisive judgment. . . .

The distinction between Tai's and Hui Tung's approach to learning was that the latter had only erudition whereas the former had both [the powers of] decisive observation and incisive judgment. Chang Ping-lin (1868–1936) has stated: "Tai in his study carried on close and rigorous [*62] analysis systematically, tracing back ancient meaning to their sources, evaluating them by his own standards." [8*] This is a most perceptive statement.

Ling T'ing-k'an (1757–1809) wrote *Shih-lüeh chuang* [A Brief Record of Activities] of Tai, with a statement attached as follows:

> Formerly, Prince Hsien of Ho-chien sought out the truth by investigating facts. With real facts in front of me, if what I say is right, it cannot be proved wrong by the forcible arguments of others, and if what I say is wrong, it cannot be proved right by their forcible arguments either. For instance, the subjects of the Six Scripts, the Nine Chapters of Ancient Mathematics, and the court regulations and institutions are of this kind. But with abstract arguments in front of me, not only may what I call right be considered wrong by others who have a different interpretation, but what I call wrong may also be considered right by others who have a different interpretation. For instance, the study of philosophical principle is a case in point.[9*]

These words sound very much like the language of the Positivist School of Philosophy and fittingly represent the spirit of Tai as well as the spirit of the Ch'ing school. It is a pity that this attitude was applied only to antiquarian studies and not to the natural sciences – a fact necessitated by the force of circumstance.

Tai frequently said: "Having an inaccurate understanding of ten [things] is worth less than having a true understanding of one [thing]." [10*] Therefore, although his learning was extensive it was not superficial, and [his areas of] specialization and particular excellence were traditional [*63] Chinese linquistics, the calendar and mathematics, and waterworks and geography. His works on linguistics included:

Sheng-yün k'ao [A Study of Phonetics], four *chüan*
Sheng-lei piao [Classified Tables of Sounds], ten *chüan*
Fang-yen shu-cheng [Commentary on the *Dialects*], thirteen *chüan*
Erh-ya wen-tze k'ao [A Study of the Language in the *Erh-ya*], ten *chüan*

His works on the calendar and mathematics included:

Yüan-hsiang [An Inquiry into the Origin of Astrology], one *chüan*
Li-wen [Questions on the Calendar], two *chüan*
Ku-li k'ao [A Study of the Ancient Calendar], two *chüan*
Kou-ku ke-huan chi [A Record of the Geometrical Measurement of the Circle], three *chüan*
Hsü t'ien-wen-lüeh [Supplement to the Brief Study of Astronomy], three *chüan*
Ts'e-suan [On the Use of Napier's Bones (Mathematics)], one *chüan*

His work on waterworks and geography included:

> *Shui-ti chi* [A Record of Waterworks and Geography], one *chüan*
> *Chiao Shui-ching chu* [Collation of the Commentary on the *Water Classics*], forty *chüan*
> *Chihli ho-chü shu* [A Book of Rivers and Streams in Chihli Province], sixty-four *chüan*

His other works will not be listed in full here. The Synopsis on the subject of astronomy-mathematics in the *Ssu-k'u ch'üan-shu* [*Complete Works of the Four Treasuries*] was entirely by his hand, and he also took part in the preparation of the other subjects. His masterpiece in later life was the *Meng-tzu tzu-i shu-cheng* [Elucidation of the Meaning of Words in *Mencius*].

This Elucidation of the Meaning of Words in *Mencius* went beyond the realm of empirical research and was intended to constitute "Tai's philosophy." Tai himself once said:

> The way of the sages was to see to it that there were no unexpressed feelings in the world; it sought to realize desires so that the world could be governed well. Later scholars did not understand that it is precisely when feelings reach their fullest and most unreserved expression that the "rational principle" is fulfilled. Their so-called "rational principle" was similar to what cruel officials call "law": cruel officials killed men with their "law," and later scholars killed men with their "rational principle." Gradually the appeal to "law" [of the legal-
> [*64] ists] was abandoned and "Rational Principle" took the center of discussion, yet [people] died. The situation became even more hopeless! [11*]

He said further:

> The Ch'eng [brothers] and Chu Hsi regarded "rational principle" as an entity of heavenly derivation yet immanent in human hearts, which opened the way for people of later generations the world over to rely on their own opinions and to insist on them as the "rational principle," to the detriment of the rest of men. They created further confusion with their doctrine of "Do away with desires," and became even farther removed from the [true] "rational principle," more insistent on maintaining their own opinion, and more disastrous to the people. Is it really "rational principle" that is detrimental to the people? It is rather that they were not conscious of the fact that it was their own opinion! [12*]

Also he said:

> Before the Sung (960–1279) Confucius and Mencius were distinctly Confucius and Mencius, and Lao-tzu and Buddha were distinctly Lao-tzu and Buddha. Those who discussed Lao-tzu and Buddha used exalted and abstruse language without leaning and depending on Confucius and Mencius, but since the Sung the works of Confucius and Mencius have completely lost their [correct] interpretation, for scholars have indiscriminately plagiarized the words of Lao-tzu and Buddha to interpret them. . . . It is like a grandson who has never seen his grandfather's face and mistakenly draws another man's face as his grandfather's, in order to make obeisance; indeed, the obeisance is made to his own grandfather, but the face is not his.[13*]

Tai wanted to eliminate the two delusions of "adulterating Confucianism with Buddhism" and "ignoring desires in favor of rational principles." Thus, late in life he wrote three chapters of *Yüan-shan* [On the Origins [*65] of Goodness] and also the Elucidation of the Meaning of Words in *Mencius* which [latter] consisted of the following essential points:

. . . The *Book of Rites* states: "In food and sex reside man's basic desires." When sages governed the world, they sympathized with the people's feelings and helped satisfy the people's desires, thereby establishing the kingly way. People in general know that Lao-tzu, Chuang-tzu, and Buddha differ from the sages, and when they hear the former's doctrine of doing away with desires, they will not believe in it. However, Sung scholars believed it and considered them as equals of the sages. The distinction between principle and desire, everybody can discuss. Therefore, today's rulers regard the ancient sages' sympathy with people's feelings and the satisfaction of their desires as frivolous and trivial [aims], and ignorance of these practices as no cause for alarm. When they [today's rulers] preach "rational principle," it is not difficult for them to find cases of extraordinarily high integrity in the world, as examples of righteousness to make people feel guilty [by comparison]. The high admonish the low with "rational principle"; the elder admonish the younger with "rational principle"; the noble admonish the ill-born with "rational principle" – even though they are in the wrong [their action] is considered proper. The low, the young man, and the ill-born may rebut with "rational principle," but even though they are in the right, [their action] is considered improper. Consequently, people of low status cannot manifest their feelings and desires to people of high status, and these [feelings and desires] are after all the same universally. The high binds the low with "rational principle," and the sins of every low person multiply to infinity. When a man dies at the hands of the law, there are people left who will pity him, but when a man dies at the hands of "rational princple," who will pity him?

[*66] He also said:

Mencius said: "To nourish the mind there is nothing better than diminishing desires." Knowing full well that desires could not be wholly eliminated, he wanted merely to diminish them. In the life of man there is nothing more distressing than an inability to live out his life; to live and let live is humane, but to live by injuring other people's lives without regard is inhumane. This inhumanity undoubtedly has its roots in [men's] desire to live out their life; thus, to rid them of such desire would certainly lead to the elimination of inhumanity. But when a man is void of all desire, he would take a wholly apathetical attitude toward the miserable and hardpressed life of the people throughout the world. To let others live, but not to live oneself, is against nature.[14]

He went on to say:

Chu Hsi often spoke of "delusion induced by human desires," but "desires" are related to nothing but the business of living and reproduction. The perversion of "desires" is "selfishness" and not "delusion"; when a man believes he has a "rational principle," whereas in fact what he maintains is false, this is "delusion." Man's great troubles are only "selfishness" and "delusion." "Selfishness" arises from a perversion of desire, and "delusion" arises from a perversion of "knowledge."

Again he said:

[*67] When the superior man governs the world, he makes it possible for everyone to express his feelings and satisfy his desires, not contradicting "truth" (*tao*) and righteousness. In governing himself, the superior man unifies feelings and desires in truth and righteousness. The evil of suppressing desires is even worse than that of stopping a flood; it kills feelings and eradicates intelligence as well as stifles benevolence and righteousness.

He went on:

Ancient sages did not seek benevolence, righteousness, propriety, and wisdom outside the realm of [human] desires, and did not consider these in isolation from blood, breath, mind, and spirit. However, later scholars seemed to believe in the existence of some other entities which are attached and combined to form [human] nature; they dabbled indiscriminately in Lao-tzu and Buddha because they did not well understand the words of Confucius and Mencius.

Again he said:

Question: With respect to the words of the Sung teachers . . . is it true that when they could not find a textual basis in the Six Classics they would borrow . . . [classical] language to embellish their own doctrines in order to win the confidence of scholars? Answer: to ignore the original intentions of the sages' utterances and regard one's own doctrines as the sages' statements is misrepresentation of the sages. To borrow their language to embellish one's doctrine, in order to win confidence, is to deceive scholars. Misrepresenting the sages and deceiving the scholars were things which the Ch'eng brothers and Chu Hsi were too wise to do, but since their works borrowed methods from [*68] Lao-tzu and Buddha, they have failings. When a man gets used to the word that has first entered [his head], he is likely to be deluded by it unconsciously.

Every word in this book *Shu-cheng* is distilled and essential. What has been recorded above is not even a tenth of it. Its contents may be summarized as an attempt to substitute "a philosophy of feeling" for the "philosophy of rational principle." From this point of view, it was extremely similar to the basic currents of the Age of Renaissance in Europe. At that time the human mind was bound by the Christian teaching of absolute asceticism and was extremely tortured. [Knowing] this was counter to human nature and yet not daring to break away from it, men followed one another in hypocrisy, thereby precipitating ironically a complete collapse of morality. The Renaissance movement remedied this by reviving the long-suppressed "Greek emotionalism" and civilization, once liberated, turned in a new progressive direction which prospered irresistibly.

Tai certainly had this situation in mind when he determined to give a new direction to Chinese civilization, and his philosophic position may truly be called a radical about-face from the previous two thousand years. His discussion of high and low as well as the proper and the improper in an above paragraph [reveals] unmistakably his egalitarian spirit, with which he launched a great revolution in ethics, and although his criticism of the Sung scholars' adulteration of Confucianism with Buddhism was couched in a language of restraint, his attitude was nevertheless very strict. He demonstrated everywhere the truth-seeking and fact-finding spirit of a scientist, and his book was thus the most valuable and unusual work of the last three hundred years. Tai himself was also very proud [*69] of this work, as he once said: "Among my life-works, in terms of greatness, the Elucidation of the Meaning of Words in *Mencius* ranks first." [15*]

Nevertheless, although the Tai school of learning held sway for a period, this book of his, strangely enough, exerted only a very minor influence. An account by Chiang Fan (1761–1831), reveals:

> In those days the readers of the *Shu-cheng* could not comprehend its meaning, and only Hung Pang (1745–1779) took an interest in it. Hung wrote a biographical sketch of Tai which included [Tai's] *Letter to P'eng Ch'ih-mu.*[16*] When Chu Kuei (1731–1807) saw this, he said, "This [item] need not be included. The work of Tai that is worthy to be handed down is not this piece." Hung wrote Chu a letter of strong protest but to no avail, and Tai's son, Chung-li, finally excluded this letter.[17*]

Thus it is evident that even the various members of the Tai school at that time held different opinions on this work. T'ang Chien (1778–1861) stated: "The master [i.e., Tai] was fundamentally a philologist; but wishing to conceal his ignorance of philosophical principles he specially wrote the Elucidation of the Meaning of Words in *Mencius* to criticize the Cheng brothers and Chu Hsi." [18*] T'ang was not a man who could understand Tai's work and his words were quite inconsequential, but they reflected the then-prevailing psychology of the majority of men.

Since Tai's followers in those days hardly studied and explicated this work at all, it was refuted only by one Fang Tung-shu (1772–1851),[19*] who, however, did not hit the mark. This book has not yet caused any [*70] repercussions even after a hundred-odd years; is it possible that they will come later on? Thus, in discussing the activities of the Ch'ing orthodox school of learning, we have no choice but to exclude this book. I have often said: "The movements of Ch'ing schools of learning were 'movements of research methodology' and not 'movements of ideology.'" Is this the reason that its achievements were not as great and stupendous as those of the European Renaissance Movement?" [20]

Section 12. Tuan Yü-ts'ai [1735-1815], Wang Nien-sun [1744-1832], and Wang Yin-chih [1766-1834]

Among the later scholars of the Tai school there were many prominent men, but none could reflect more credit on it than Tuan Yü-ts'ai (1735–1815) of Chin-t'an, and Wang Nien-sun (1744–1832) and his son Yin-chih (1766–1834) of Kaoyu [in Kiangsu]. They were collectively known to the world as Tai, Tuan, and the two Wangs. Among Tuan's writings, the most famous were his *Shuo-wen chieh-tzu chu* [A Commentary on the *Explanations of Script and Elucidation of Characters*] and *Liu-shu yin-yün piao* [Phonological Tables of the Six Scripts]. Among Wang Nien-sun's writings, the most famous were *Tu-shu tsa-chih* [Miscellaneous Notes on books] and *Kuang-ya shu-cheng* [Commentary on the *Kuang-ya*]. And among Wang Yin-chih's writings, the most famous were the *Ching-i shu-wen* [Interpretations of the Classics Heard from (My Father)] and *Ching-chuan shih-tz'u* [Explanation of the Particles in the Classics and Commentaries].

The learning of Tai, Tuan, and the two Wangs differed markedly from that of the Hui Tung school in that the latter studied classics in a way much like a man who reads European books without knowing European languages and therefore considers the translator unimpeachable. The Han scholars were the translators, who were to be believed and relied upon [*71] without the possibility of daring to deviate. The Tai school was not like this: it would not lightly credit translators and would not rest until it had sought out the correct original, authentic texts. The accomplishment of the Hui school lay in [the study of] discrete chapters and isolated sentences, simply citing ancient works in order to correct later works, but whenever the Tai school discovered a new interpretation it could be applied uniformly to all books alike with good sense. Hence the Hui school may be called the school of Han learning, but the Tai school is definitely the school of Ch'ing and not of Han learning.

Explaining the *Book of Changes* with *hsiao-ch'en* and *na-chia*,[1] interpreting the *Book of History* by means of the Five Elements and Visitations and Prodigies, and describing the *Book of Odes* by the Five Relations and Six Feelings,[2] as well as [interpreting] the meaning of the classics by means of injudicious citation from apocryphal and prognosticatory texts,[3] were the common practice among Han scholars. The Tai school of Ch'ing learning, however, did away with these [habits] and steered quite clear of them. It devoted its complete attention to philology, the study of terms referring to artifacts, and institutions, and although its discussion of philology and artifacts quoted the sayings of Han scholars frequently and extensively, it did not follow them without reservation.

For instance, the Miscellaneous Notes on Books and an Interpretation of the Classics Heard from (My Father) consisted entirely of corrections of errors in the old commentaries and sub-commentaries. These old commentaries were the works of Mao Kung (ca. 2nd century B.C.), Ch'eng Hsüan (127–200 A.D.), Ma Yung (76–166 A.D.), Chia K'uei (30–101 A.D.), Fu Ch'ien (2nd century A.D.), and Tu Yü (222–284 A.D.), and the old sub-commentaries were [those of] Lu Te-ming (d. 627 A.D.), K'ung Ying-ta (574–648 A.D.), and Chia Kung-yen (of the T'ang period). As to the works after the Sung (960–1279 A.D.), it was beneath their [the Tai scholars'] dignity to correct them. Thus, men like the Wangs, senior and junior, were actually the critics of Mao, Cheng, Chia, Ma, Fu, and T'u, and not their submissive followers. Not only would they not adhere to the ancients submissively, but they were uncompromising even [in the face of] their fathers and teachers. Tuan's respect for Tai truly [*72] knew no bounds, but a reading of his *Commentary* on the *Shuo-wen* will reveal expressions like "the Master's saying is wrong" and "the Master's saying is incorrect" everywhere. Even the junior Wang's Interpretation of the Classics contained quite a few deviations from the words of his father, Wang senior.

Not only were these people utterly uncompromising towards the errors in old commentaries and sub-commentaries, but they even dared to alter classical texts. This [practice] may seem to resemble the Sung and Ming scholars' fondness for altering ancient works, but it is, in fact, entirely different: the men of the Sung and Ming relied solely on subjective speculation whereas the scholars of the Tai school used objective research and comparative examination as a basis. Tuan Yü-ts'ai said:

> In collating texts it is extremely difficult to decide what is correct and what is incorrect. There are two kinds of truth and error: [the authenticity] of the original text and [the truth] of its thesis, and only after the correctness or incorrectness of the original text has been decided upon can one judge the correctness or incorrectness of its thesis. . . . What is an original text? It is the author's manuscript. What is a thesis? It is the author's exposition. . . . Without ascertaining what the original text is, one may distort the ancients, and without passing judgment on the correctness or incorrectness of the thesis one may mislead men of the present.[4*]

This statement clearly explains the position and value of the School of Empirical Research in the world of learning. [No problem arises] if we [*73] do not attempt to master an intellectual discipline, but if we attempt it, the first step must be a clear and precise understanding of the true aspects of this discipline; the second step is a criticism of its correctness or incorrectness and merits or demerits. For instance, nowadays if we want to criticize the doctrine of a certain European scholar and rely solely on an inferior and fallacious work of translation, upon which we will base our argument and discussion, then what we refute may still not be the original work. Isn't this a pitiable and ludicrous [state of affairs]! Although the study of ancient Chinese books will not show as many serious discrepancies, still, because of the difference between ancient and modern phraseology and the errors of copying, printing, and transmission, there are numerous passages that cannot be read and comprehended. If we criticize the correctness or incorrectness of the exposition of a book containing incomprehensible passages, it is inevitable that our criticism will in large measure go to waste. The Ch'ing scholars of empirical research made a tremendous effort in this first step of the work, and since their efforts were well spent, they were truly able to save us, their descendants, an enormous amount of energy which we may devote to the second step of the work. The value of Ch'ing learning lies entirely in this, as represented by the writings of Tai, Tuan, and the two Wangs.

Juan Yüan's preface to the *Ching-i shu-wen* states: "All the misinterpretations of ancient scholars were [re-examined on the basis of] extensive citation and abstruse parallels, in order to get at their original mean-
[*74] ing. If the ancient sages and wise men could see this they would smile and say: 'These are indeed my words; the misinterpretations of several thousand years have now been rectified.' . . ."

This statement is not unduly flattering, since even today when we read works by the Wangs, father and son, we cannot help feeling that every one of their points is clearly evident to our minds and that our old misunderstanding melts away on the spot, like ice. Even so vigorous an opponent of Han learning as Fang Tung-shu (1772–1851) had to concede: "The *Ching-i shu-wen* by Mr. Wang of Kaoyu can truly make Cheng Hsüan (127–200 A.D.) and Chu Hsi (1130–1200 A.D.) bow their heads. Since the Han (206 B.C.–220 A.D.) and T'ang, nothing compares with it."[5*] It is thus evident that an impartial judgment cannot be suppressed.

But how could these men have achieved such a record? In a word, [it is because they] used scientific methods. Read the writings of the Wangs, father and son, carefully, and [you will find that] they express this [scientific] spirit best. I have investigated their methods of learning [which may be summarized as follows]:

(1) *Alertness*: They were particularly adept at making scrupulous observations on points which ordinary people are apt to overlook, with a view to discovering the points worthy of special study; this is known as finding gaps in reading. For instance, since the creation of the world, apples have fallen to the ground innumerable times, but its [importance] was first recognized only by Newton. Water boils every day in every household, but its [importance] was recognized only by Watt. Since
[*75] childhood we have deftly recited the classical texts that the

Ching-i shu-wen corrected but only the Wangs had the capacity to see [mistakes] in them. All discoveries in knowledge must depend on this [kind of alertness] as a first-step task.

(2) *Open-mindedness*: If attention and observation give rise to doubts, people are prone to make snap judgments on the basis of subjective, momentary feelings; thus the newly discovered "gap" may soon be lost again. The advocates of empirical research were definitely not like this; they cleared their minds in advance so that not a shred of preconception could gain entry, and they collected only objective material for a highly impartial study.

(3) *Establishment of an hypothesis*: Research should not be random and undisciplined; instead, hypotheses would be set up in advance [to serve as working] formulae.

(4) *Collection of evidence*: Once an hypothesis was established, they would not accept it immediately as a definitive law, but would collect extensive evidence in order to find out whether this hypothesis would agree with all phenomena of the same category, as the biologist and botanist do with their daily collection of specimens and the physicist and chemist, with the daily laboratory experiments.

(5) *Conclusion of the case.*

(6) *Inference*: After repeated inductive investigation, a correct conclusion may be reached, and with this conclusion one may infer similar items without impediment.

[*76] Wang Yin-chih stated in his *Preface* to the *Ching-chuan shih-tz'u*:

> . . . I first took the twenty-eight chapters of the *Book of History* for investigation and found that the introductory and auxiliary particles of the text had been interpreted by men of the past as having real meaning, [which had] frequently [resulted] in the evils of misinterpretation. I attempted to explain them, but I lacked the courage to be positive about it, until I learned of my father's discussions of the various paragraphs in the Mao version of the *Book of Odes*, such as 'wild and windy was the day'.[6] . . . He elucidated their meaning and theme, and I felt [my difficulty] melt away like ice. . . . Then I extended his idea and exhausted this group of expressions. I extensively collected all the particles from the *Nine Classics* and *Three Commentaries* to the books of the Chou, Chin, and Former Han, and arranged them by word-entry in the ten *chüan* of the *Ching-chuan shih-tz'u.*

He stated also:

> [When an interpretation] is scrutinized and agrees with the original text and, upon examination, also applies to other books, even if it is not to be found among the old interpretations, at least we know its meaning. . . . All that one sees scattered throughout the classics and commentaries can be detected in this way, hence the collection of them grew. . .

This is a fairly detailed description of his own learning-procedure and method of application, and although it gives only the account of the writing of a single book, it may also be taken to apply to his other works and those of the other masters as well. It is in this that Ch'ing learning [*77] differed from that of the previous dynasty and because of this, it can serve as a model to us for all time.

Section 13. Summary

The intellectual tendency of the Orthodox School may be briefly characterized as follows:

(1) In order to be established, an interpretation must be based on evidence; that which is not based on evidence but on speculation is rejected without question.

(2) In selecting evidence, the more ancient is prefered; therefore, Han and T'ang evidence takes precedence over that of the Sung and Ming, and Sung and Ming evidence cannot supersede that of the Han and T'ang. With Han and Wei evidence as a basis, that of the T'ang may be rejected, and that of the Wei and Chin also, on the basis of Han evidence. Similarly, on the basis of evidence from the pre-Ch'in period and the Former Han, Later Han [evidence] may be rejected. Explicating one classical text by another could render all commentaries useless.

(3) An isolated bit of evidence cannot provide a definitive interpretation. Something that has no evidence to the contrary may be temporarily kept, and may gradually gain weight as more evidence is acquired, but if powerful negative evidence is found, it must be rejected.

(4) Concealing or distorting evidence is considered unethical.

(5) There is keen interest in categorizing similar items as a basis for comparative study in order to find a law.

[*78] (6) Citations of old interpretations must show their references clearly; plagiarism is considered highly unethical.

(7) In case of disagreement of viewpoints, people argue with one another [so freely] that even students do not hesitate to criticize or reject their teachers, and the recipient [of criticism] is never offended by it.

(8) An argument is limited to the problem at hand and the purport of its language must be solidly substantial and sincerely temperate. Even though men are not willing to sacrifice their own opinions, they nevertheless respect other people's opinions at the same time; it is considered unethical to show any sign of overriding intolerance, or to obscure an argument purposely by complicating it, or to imply any sarcasm.

(9) A preference is shown for specializing in one branch of learning for a "narrow but deep" study.

(10) In literary style, unadorned solidity and simple clarity are preferred; "superfluous phraseology" is profoundly detested.

The scholars of those days prided themselves on this kind of intellectual method and styled their [learning] "sound learning." The core of their study was the classics and auxiliary studies such as philology, followed in order by history, astronomy and mathematics, geography, phonology, music, bronze inscriptions, collation, cataloguing, etc., all of which were studied in this spirit of learning. In fine, all book-learning since the Han had been put through a refinng process and given a kind of organization, [*79] with these direct results:

(1) Ancient books which were always regarded by us as difficult to read and understand can now be read and understood.

(2) Awareness of the many forgeries and works that had been glossed over or spoiled makes us more selective in our choice, without any more dissipation of our energy.

(3) Long-lost philosophies or neglected subjects of learning have since emerged to the fore as subjects for specialized study, thus increasingly enriching the contents of our knowledge.

The indirect results are these:

(1) When we read the biographies and writings of the various great masters and recognize their [attitude of] "knowledge for the sake of knowledge" and their life-long pursuit of just one single subject of learning, in which they pieced together bits of information [into an integral whole], and [when we realize] the difficulties they underwent before achieving success, we are unconsciously inspired by their personalities, which impel us to learn.

(2) Applying their methodology to learning can make our minds more discriminating, and finding "gaps" in reading can make us honest without deceit; we are thus made independent without a tendency to imitate, humble and receptive without a stubborn insistence on one idea.

Whether the Orthodox School learning is useful or not is hard to say. Comparing it with the various fields of learning in the modern world, [*80] it is undeniable that most of it is useless, but nevertheless, usefulness and uselessness are only relative terms. Lao-tzu said: "We put thirty spokes together and call it a wheel; but it is on the space where there is nothing that the utility of the wheel depends." [1] This is to say that uselessness is [really] usefulness. In this view, the attitude of a true scholar must be that of knowledge for the sake of knowledge. Those who speak about utility regard it as an end, and knowledge as but a means to this end; but to those who acquire knowledge for its own sake, knowledge is an end in itself and there is no point in talking about its usefulness or uselessness. Chuang-tze said: "A medicine to cure chapped hands may in one case bring a man a title and in another, only the ability to wash silk." [2] That is to say, whether [a thing] is useful or not depends entirely on the person involved. Following this definition, the same learning which is useless when undertaken by a certain man at a certain time in a certain place may become extremely useful when it is undertaken by another man at another time in another place. For this reason it is hard to talk [about utility].

Actually, from the point of view of pure scholarship, one need only ask whether a body of learning is really learning, but not whether it is useful; unless this is so, knowledge cannot achieve independence and thus develop. Because the Ch'ing school of learning was truly capable of establishing itself as learning, it is valuable in our nation's cultural history.

[For Sections 14, 15, and 16, see Bibliography.]

[*100] *Section 17. Notation-Book and Literary Style*

Alas, by the time I was born the [ranks of the] scholars of the Ch'ien-lung and Chia-ch'ing periods (1736–1820) had been thinned to the point of virtual disappearance. But at thirteen I went to study at the *Hsüeh-hai-t'ang* [School of the Ocean of Knowledge] in Canton, established by the former Viceroy Juan Yüan (1764–1849) to teach "sound learning" in our province; its organization and regulations were exactly the same as they had been a hundred years earlier. At sixteen and seventeen, I visited the capital and made the acquaintance of several of the remaining old scholars who held unswervingly to the legacy of the masters of the past. During the interval of [these years], I had also leafed through the writings of the various great masters and had compared these with what I had heard and seen, so I can still see [in retrospect], if hazily, the general conditions of the "learned society" of that time.

In those days almost everyone interested in learning had his "notation book," in which he recorded his findings as he read. This was so because the father of Ch'ing learning, Ku Yen-wu (1613–1682), had transmitted this spirit to later generations in his *Jih-chih-lu*, as he himself said: "My work *Jih-chih-lu* contains more than thirty divisions. All my lifelong aspirations and efforts are concentrated in it." [1*] He also said (to a friend): "You have been solicitous to ask how many more of *Jih-chih-lu* have been completed, but since I left you a year ago, although I have studied day and night and carried on repeated investigations, I have accumulated only ten odd items." [2*] Such were his painstaking efforts and his seriousness about them!

I gather that the original purpose of a notation book was not the writing of a book, but the collection of material for writing one. Since Ch'ing scholars cautioned men sternly against writing books glibly and would [*101] not consent to pass on [their writings] as final unless the material was highly satisfactory, it is not strange that some of them actually spent all their lives preparing the material alone. Moreover, in writing books the first-class scholars of that time as a rule did not want to write a single word beyond what was gained from actual knowledge. A specialized monograph or treatise requires a relatively extensive scope, and it is unavoidable that such works will be rounded out with platitudes which go beyond the scope of one's actual knowledge. This the various masters were not willing to do, so they preferred to keep their writings simply in notation form.

I have reiterated earlier that the Ch'ing scholars' pursuit of knowledge was based solely on the inductive method and a scientific spirit, but what were the procedures whereby this method and this spirit were realized? The first step: it is necessary to observe things carefully first and detect the points requiring special attention. The second step: having noted a certain fact, it is necessary to list all other facts of the same or related categories for a comparative study. The third step: on the basis of the comparative study, one forms his own opinion. The fourth step: with this opinion as a basis, one further searches for extensive evidence from all angles: front, side, and opposite. When the evidence is complete, then [the opinion] may be adjudged final, or renounced in the face of strong negative evidence. The evolution of all the sciences of the modern world follows this course, and the evolution of every doctrine by Ch'ing empirical research scholars doubtless had to follow the same course. This being the case, try to imagine the amount of material and energy neces- [*102] sarily involved in each step forward! Without recourse to a highly systematized notation, how would this have been possible?

The famous models of philological investigation are commonly recognized to be Wang Nien-sun's *Ching-chuan shih-tz'u* [Explanation of the Particles in the Classics and Commentaries] and Yü Yüeh's *Ku-shu i-i chü-li* [Examples of Doubtful Meaning in Ancient Books]. An examination of their contents will readily reveal the presence of several thousand notations before these books were organized, and this is true not only of specialized books [on special topics] but even of the more outstanding notes themselves, which were always prefaced by first-draft notes. For instance, Ch'ien Ta-hsin (1728–1804) threw new light on the "unvoiced labials" as [recorded in] ancient books. Try to read the original itemized manuscript of his *Shih-chia-chai yang-hsin-lu* [Record of Cultivating New Knowledge in the Shih-chia Study], and you will find that it must first have required over a hundred first-draft items of notation before it could be written; therefore, Ku Yen-wu's statement that he could write only ten-odd notes a year is not a misrepresentation. From this point of view, note-taking is actually an absolute necessity in undertaking this kind of study, and if we want to know the Ch'ing scholars' procedure for learning and their source of strength, we should certainly look for it here.

There are numerous books in the notation-style. The most remarkable ones, apart from the *Jih-chih-lu,* include:

Yen Jo-chü, *Ch'ien-ch'iu cha-chi* [Notation Book of Yen Jo-chü]
Ch'ien Ta-hsin, *Shih-chia-chai yang-hsin-lu* [Record of Cultivating New Knowledge in the Shih-chia Study]
Tsang Lin, *Ching-i tsa-chi* [Miscellaneous Notes on the Meaning of the Classics]
Lu Wen-chao, *Chung-shan cha-chi* [Notes Made while Lecturing at Chung-shan]
——, *Lung-ch'eng cha-chi* [Notes Made while Lecturing at Lung-ch'eng Academy]
Sun Chih-tsu, *Tu-shu ts'o-lu* [Minor Reading-Notes]
Wang Ming-sh'eng, *O*[*or I*]*-shu-p'ien* [On the Gradual Development of Learning]
Wang Chung, *Chih-hsin-chi* [Record of Recent Knowledge]
[*103] Hung Liang-chi, *Hsiao-tu-shu-chai ssu-lu* [Four Accounts in the Hsiao-tu-shu Study]
Chao I, *Kai-yü ts'ung-k'ao* [Various Studies in Retirement]
Wang Nien-sun, *Tu-shu tsa-chih* [Miscellaneous Reading-Notes]
Wang Yin-chih, *Ching-i shu-wen* [Interpretation of the Classics Heard from (My Father)]
Ho Cho, *I-men tu-shu-chi* [Reading Notes of Ho Cho]
Tsang Yung, *Pai-ching jih-chi* [A Daily Record of My Reverence for the Classics]
Liang Yü-sheng, *Pieh-chi* [Notes on the Passing Scene]
Yü Cheng-hsieh, *Kuei-ssu lui kao* [A Variety of Manuscripts Written during the *Kuei-ssu* (1833) Year]
——, *Kuei-ssu ts'un-kao* [Supplementary Manuscripts of the *Kuei-ssu* (1833) Year]
Sung Hsiang-feng, *Kuo-t'ing-lu* [A Record of Learning in the Family Hall]
Ch'en Li, *Tung-shu tu-shu-chi* [Reading Notes of Ch'en Li]

The others cannot all be listed here.

The notation books of the various masters differ in degree of excellence or crudity, and even within the same book the value of the items differs: there are some that are made up of raw data; [3*] some that are more finished in a crude sort of way; [4*] and some that are finished products.[5*] However, both raw data and the crudely finished products serve as useful materials for the finished products of [later scholars], and are therefore also valuable. In sum, scholars of those days preferred to use notation books as a method of difficult and painstaking learning. That they were able to go both far and deep [in their pursuit] and out of it produce creative works was in large measure a result of this method, which has now been lost.

Since Ch'ing scholars were not interested in imitating the practice of the men of the Sung and Ming of gathering students and lecturing, and did not have meeting and lecturing places like those of the various learned societies and schools of modern Europe and America, their opportunities for exchanging information were inevitably few. They relied on corre-
[*104] spondence as a substitute; when a junior scholar wanted to visit a senior one, he usually wrote a courtesy-letter of introduction first to inquire about some learned problems and enclosed copies of his own writings if he had any. If his senior thought him educable, he would doubtless answer him, removing his doubts and problems and encouraging him to continue. This was true of people of equal rank also; when they found a [new] interpretation, they always sent letters to friends who had mutual interests for their comment, and these [friends] rarely neglected to respond to the best of their ability. When a book was written it had to go to several good friends of the author for a critical checking of its merits and demerits before it circulated at large, and the checking was all carried on by letter. Letters of this kind were all carefully prepared and were in fact works in themselves. Although this practice is occasionally also to be noted in other dynasties, it was particularly strong in the Ch'ing.

The style [of these men] was straightforward and expository, employing no language of circumlocution, and having the sole purpose of elegant directness. The dialogue style was frowned upon and archaic eccentricity was not cherished either. In discussing literary style, Ku Yen-wu stated: "Confucius says: 'Their scope reaches far, and the explanations attached to them are elegant,' [6] and again: 'Without elegant composition of the words, they [words] will not go far.' [7] Tseng-tze says: 'In his words and tone he keeps far from lowness and impropriety.' [8] Nowadays, teachers who begin their lectures with dialogue are usually not apt in their diction."

He also said:

> There are ancient and modern eras, but there are no ancient and modern styles; [9] the [histories] of the Two Hans could not be written today, just as the *Book*
> [*105] *of History* and the *Tso Commentary* could not be the [histories] of the Two Hans. Plagiarizing a method of writing from the *Historical Records* or *Histories of the Hans* in order to be considered ancient, or pilfering one or two words from them to use in your own writing is quite unbecoming. . . . Rejecting words in general use today and borrowing ancient words for use is [a device] of literati to conceal their shallowness.[10*]

Ch'ing learning patterned itself after Ku Yen-wu; so did its literary style. Its credos were: (1) not to be vulgar, (2) not to be archaic, and (3) not to be circumlocutory. This kind of literary style was most fitting for the exposition of learning, but for this reason it proved quite offensive to the so-called "ancient style writers" of that time. Belles lettres were not the forte of the Ch'ing scholars. Among the classical masters, there was hardly anyone who excelled in poetry. True, most of their collected works contain poems, but none is remarkable. Only one Chang Hui-yen (1761–1802) could compose the *tz'u*, and only K'ung Kuang-shen, Wang Chung, Lin T'in-k'an, Hung Liang-chi, Sun Hsing-yen (1753–1818), and Tung Yu-ch'eng could write in the double-harness style, and even then their prose revealed a conscious effort at eradicating surface beauty, in line with the general intellectual trend.

[*106] *Section 18. General Encouragement of Scholarship in the Society*

During the most flourishing period of this school of learning, most of the prominent figures were, relatively speaking, men of integrity and little ambition. The civil service examinations then prevailed over all the nation, and as might be expected, nine out of ten scholars followed this path of preferment. In general, dedicated young scholars who had not yet acquired governmental degrees, and new degree-holders, whose salary was meagre, were frequently invited by older scholars into their homes to tutor children. These older scholars treated them as protégés also, encouraging and prompting them to enrich their knowledge. There were also handsome book-collections in the homes of these older scholars for [the younger scholars] to study, and the social friends of [these older scholars] consisted largely of leading contemporary scholars; hence [younger scholars] could often secure a back seat [at social gatherings] to broaden their outlook, and gradually their learning began to bear fruit.

Official promotion was based on seniority; a man had small cause to quicken the pace of advancement, and even if he had [the ambition] he might not be lucky. The one who acquired degrees early and lived a long time could rise to be state minister or prime minister; otherwise he grew old in the Hanlin academy or in a government bureau. Inured to the customary pattern of frugality and thrift, they were easily able to provide for their parents and dependents, and poor scholars, used to a simple life, were able to shut out all conflicts with the world and to devote their whole lives to learning. As for officials in the capital, they too had very simple office work and very few deadlines to meet, facts that enabled them to take up studies day and night behind closed doors, and when time allowed, to meet with friends of similar interests to compare notes and ask each other questions. Their influence was contagious and gradually spread to booksellers on the Liu-li-ch'ang [street], to the delight of many [of the scholars]; passing through a store a man might spend as much as a whole day there. [These book stores] almost served as a public library for the scholars and officials of the capital. Lin T'ing-k'an completed his study while a bookstore employee. It was a most convenient arrangement for scholars.

Those who were sent out as educational commissioners or as high [*107] provincial officials often selected eminent men to fill their personal staffs, and upon reaching their destination, they collected retired men of talent from all over and absorbed rising young men into their staff. Those who joined their select group could not only earn a better living, but could also add to their own knowledge. Men whose work produced masterpieces but who were unwilling to take government posts were also welcomed almost everywhere else. The presidency of a private academy, the editorship of the local history of a province, prefecture, or county, composing genealogies for large clans, or collating manuscripts for influential men for publication were all possible professions for them. Since all these [lines of activity] yielded a handsome compensation, besides increasing one's knowledge, scholars usually were pleased to take on such work. I have frequently stated that if the culture of a nation is to advance, society must have considerable respect for the scholar, allowing him to make a living from his intellectual pursuit without fear of cold and hunger. Only then can he have the leisure to engage in more profound research and to refresh his knowledge daily. It was under these conditions that modern European learning was generally cultivated, and the Ch'ien-lung and Chia-ch'ing periods (1736–1820) of the former Ch'ing dynasty present an almost comparable [picture].

Although the European Renaissance arose out of the ferment of a given historical environment and was catalysed by two or three spectacular men, it was also assisted and patronized by background figures like Pope Nicholas V in Rome, the Medicis, father and son, in Florence, King Alfonso of Naples, and the various great mercantile clans of the free [*108] Italian cities. All of them were influenced by the current trend and vied in their patronage, directly or indirectly encouraging and promoting it to no small degree; thus their accomplishments became the more glorious. It was the same with Ch'ing learning in its High Period; Emperor Ch'ien-lung (1736–1795), who inherited the accomplishments of his grandfather and father [i.e., K'ang-hsi and Yung-cheng] and enjoyed peace and prosperity, considered himself the lord-patron of learning. Without a day's respite, he established the bureau [for the compilation of] the *Four Treasuries*, compiled the *I-t'ung-chih* [Gazetteer of the Ch'ing Empire], edited the *Hsü-san-t'ung* [Three Supplementary Encyclopedias to the *T'ung-tien*, *T'ung-chih*, and the *T'ung-k'ao*], and the *Huang-ch'ao san-t'ung* [The Three Encyclopedias of the Ch'ing Dynasty], and compiled the *Hui-tien* [Collected Statutes of the Ch'ing Dynasty] and the *T'ung-li* [General Ceremonies of the Ch'ing Dynasty]. All the work naturally had to be carried out by scholars. There were also quite a number of high officials both inside and outside [of the capital], who reinforced this trend by becoming enthusiastic patrons [of learning]. During the Chia-ch'ing period (1796–1820), men like Pi Yüan (1730–1797) and Juan Yüan, themselves originally masters of the classics, rose to prominence as high provincial officials, with means to support scholars and encourage learning wherever they went, as though they were its patron-saints.

The salt merchants south of the Huai River, already completely addicted to a life of luxury, were also eager to follow the trends of the times, hoping to associate themselves with cultural refinement. They rivaled each other in collecting [specimens of] calligraphy, paintings, books, and [art] objects, inviting renowned experts to judge for them, and rewarding them with clean living quarters and rich stipends. At that time the vogue of [private] book-printing was quite strong, and although men like Huang P'ei-lieh (1763–1825) and Pao T'ing-po (1728–1814) could select and collate [texts] themselves, most of the others [who printed books] were influential men who wanted to win acclaim by this means and so invited famous experts to handle the task. Even Wu Ch'ung-yao (1810–1863), who erected his family fortune on the opium trade, also published the *Yüeh-ya-t'ang ts'ung-shu* [The Collectanea of the Graceful Cantonese Hall], a work known, in fact, for its excellent judgment, and other [similar cases] can be inferred. Actually, what had these men to do with learning? Yet we certainly cannot say that they did not contribute to its growth; [*109] they played the same role as the great families and wealthy merchants of Italy [lit., "southern Europe"] during the Renaissance [lit., "like the two halves of the same tally"]. All this leads me to a realization of what a tide of thought in a given period really is. When a movement reaches the height of its meteoric course, it can envelop men from all quarters of society, and in China, the "philosophy of the Mind" in the late Ming period and the School of Empirical Research of the High Period of the Ch'ing are cases in point.

Section 19. The Ancient-Style Writers: The T'ung-ch'eng School and the Yang-hu School

The preceding sections have discussed the Orthodox School of the High Period, which originated as far back as the transitional period between the reign of Shun-chih (1644–1661) and K'ang-hsi (1662–1722), and which lasted until the time of Kuang-hsü (1875–1908) and Hsüan-t'ung (1909–1911). Its pervasive influence and after-echo declined but were never totally submerged. Its destiny was linked, as it were, to that of the Ch'ing dynasty itself. During the hundred-or-more-years period of Ch'ien-lung (1736–1795), Chia-ch'ing (1796–1820), and Tao-kuang (1821–1850), its influence engulfed the whole nation; in fact, no other schools were strong enough to compete with it. If we insist on finding a [competing school], the so-called "Ancient-Style writers" may be the only ones who continued to harbor antithetical views beneath the mantle of this all-pervading authority.

Only when the Neo-Confucianism of the Sung and Ming had seriously degenerated did Ch'ing learning rise [in its stead], and when Ch'ing [*110] learning began to prosper, Neo-Confucianists increasingly lost their positions. During the Formative Period, those who still held to the shattered bastions of the Ch'eng brothers, Chu Hsi, Lu Chiu-yüan, and Wang Yang-ming, were Sun Ch'i-feng (1586–1675), Li Chung-fu, Tiao Pao (1603–1669), Chang Li-hsiang (1611–1674), Chang Erh-ch'i (1612–1678), Lu Lung-ch'i (1630–1693), Lu Shih-i (1611–1672), etc. All of them cherished good reputation and integrity and stressed practical action. They were pure scholars, but since all of them were over-punctilious, their works could not achieve luster and greatness. Meanwhile, men like T'ang Pin (1627–1687), Li Kuang-ti (1642–1718), Wei Hsiang-shu (1617–1687), and Wei I-chieh (1616–1686) also studied Sung learning, but were indecisive and eagerly toadied to their current [Manchu] overlords in the hope of maneuvering themselves into prominence. At that time, the bastion of Ch'ing learning had not yet been firmly established; writings and discussions of the various great scholars frequently reflected both Han and Sung learning and did not distinguish between the philosophy (*tao*) and practice (*shu*) of [both schools].

At the beginning of the Ch'ien-lung period (1736–1795), Hui Tung and Tai Chen rose to prominence and the Han banner flew supreme. Men who had previously clamored for Sung learning paled considerably, but a certain Fang Pao (1668–1749), whose status and reputation were roughly comparable to those of T'ang Ping, Li Kuang-ti, and others, deeply revered Sung philosophy and actually practiced its teaching. He was also very interested in good composition. Fang was a native of T'ung-ch'eng and had studied literature together with Yao Fan (1702–1771) and Liu Ta-k'uei (1697–1779) of the same town, using Tseng Kung (1019–1083) and Kuei Yu-kuang (1506–1571) as their models, and formulating what was known as the "principle and method of writing in the ancient style," and [they] dubbed themselves the T'ung-ch'eng school. They were also interested in explicating Ou-yang Hsiu's (1007–1072) idea of "demonstrating the way through good writing." They considered themselves to be in the line of Orthodoxy extending back to Confucius,

Mencius, Han Yü, Ou-yang Hsiu, the Ch'eng brothers, and Chu Hsi, and [a spirit of] mutual contempt prevailed between them and the contemporary scholars of Han learning.

Yao Fan's nephew Yao Nai (1732–1815) wanted to study with Tai Chen, who, however, was not eager to teach and so politely declined [to
[*111] accept him]. Tai advised the Ancient-Style writers in this way: "You, sirs, speak of your object as truth and not [stylistic] technique; certainly there may be truth in it, but can we say that writings such as yours are not exercises in [stylistic] technique?" [1*] Ch'ien Ta-hsin (1728–1804) also commented: "Fang's so-called 'principle and method of writing ancient composition' is merely that of the selected ancient compositions in popular edition. . . . Not only was he ignorant of their principle, but he knew nothing about their method. . . . Fang is actually an extreme case of failure to read books, and yet you are partial to him simply because his literary style is close to that of the ancients. . ." [2*] Thereupon the various Fangs and Yaos were considerably perturbed, and Yao Nai repeatedly wrote articles condemning the fragmentation of Han learning, and Fang Tung-shu (1772–1851) wrote the *Han-hsüeh shang-tui* [Discussions of Han Learning], sparing no effort in his all-out attack on the learning of Yen Jo-chü, Hu Wei, Hui Tung, and Tai Chen. From that point on, the two schools [Han and T'ung-ch'eng] were on bad terms. Later, Yün Ching (1757–1817) and Lu Chi-lu of Yang-hu accepted the 'principle and method' of the T'ung-ch'eng school after slight modifications, and Chang Hui-yen (1716–1802) and Li Chao-lo (1769–1841), both of them trained in the School of Empirical Research and both fond of literary writing, made common cause with Yün and Lu, calling themselves the Yang-hu school.

Although the Tai Chen-Tuan Yü-ts'ai line of the School of Empirical Research held sway over the nation, its discipline was too rigorous and too unexciting to win popular interest. Therefore, those who studied in the two schools [i.e., T'ung-ch'eng and Yang-hu] of ancient style never receded from the scene, although they were weak in capacities and talents, and rarely developed any power. During the Hsien-feng (1851–1861) and T'ung-chih (1862–1874) periods, Tseng Kuo-fan (1811–1872) was a good writer and held the T'ung-ch'eng school in high esteem; at one point he made a *Sheng-che hua-hsiang tsan* [Tribute to the Pictures of the
[*112] Sages and Philosophers], in which he promoted Yao Nai to equal rank with the Duke of Chou and Confucius. Tseng's [political] accomplishments were so spectacular at that time that the T'ung-ch'eng school gained prestige by association; even today there are men who still use such connection to ingratiate themselves with high officials and snub the common people.

Speaking objectively, the founders of the T'ung-ch'eng school were prudent, men of integrity, and self-respecting; at the height of Han learning, they took a vigilant stand against it and as such, they certainly can be said to have had courage; we cannot blame the pioneers for the decadence of their epigones. Nevertheless, if we judge this school by its writings, it was imitative, overly punctilious, and devoid of substance; if we judge it by its teachings, it encouraged abstractness and stifled creativity and was therefore not beneficial to society. Moreover, it never occupied an important place in Ch'ing learned circles, and most certainly will not survive in the future. We may leave it without further discussion.

On the other hand, Fang Tung-shu's Discussions of Han Learning was a very valuable work of the Ch'ing period. It was written during the Chia-ch'ing period (1796–1820), when the fortunes of the Orthodox School were at their highest point, and its courage in opposing the latter made it a kind of revolutionary work in itself. Although its defense of Sung learning contained many archaic and pedantic points, its attack on Han learning deftly hit many of its weak spots. Among other [examples], his criticisms of the deceit and falsity among the proponents of the "Han [school] of the *Book of Changes*" and of the dissension among those who discussed government regulations and institutions were particularly perspicacious. Later, scholars of Han learning were quite inclined to harmonize the Han and Sung [schools]; for example, Juan Yüan (1764–1849) wrote *Hsing-ming ku-hsün* [Ancient Glosses on Nature and [*113] Destiny] and Ch'en Li (1810–1882) wrote *Han-ju t'ung-i* [A General Survey of Han Scholars], both proclaiming that Han scholars also spoke of the study of rational principle. Ch'en's *Tung-shu tu-shu chi* [Reading Notes of Ch'en Li] included a *chüan* on Chu Hsi, stating that Chu Hsi too spoke of empirical research. All this certainly reflected the influence of [Fang's] book.

During the interval betwen the High Period and the Period of Transformation there lived another important man, namely, Chang Hsüeh-ch'eng [3] (1738–1801), who differed from the Orthodox School in that he was not punctiliously concerned with empirical research, and differed from the Modern Text scholars also, as is evident from his statement that the "Six Classics are all histories" and from his great respect for Liu Hsin's *Ch'i-lüeh* [Seven Summaries]. His work *Wen-shih t'ung-i* [General Principles of Literature and History] was certainly a source for the liberation of thought after the Ch'ien-lung and Chia-ch'ing periods (1736–1820). [In it] he stated: "The wise and learned men learned from the sages, who in turn learned from the people. . . . It was the Duke of Chou and not Confucius who was the great synthesizer." [4*] Again: "The Six Classics are all histories, and [the works of] the various philosophers all found their origin in the Six Classics," [5*] and "There were no [private] writings before the Warring-States Period." [6*] Again: "The words of the ancients were public and were never held by anyone as his private property," [7*] and "the dregs of old can be the distilled essence of today." [8*] Furthermore, he said: "The preeminence of more recent learning over earlier learning is a natural outcome of cumulative wisdom and thinking," [9*] and "learning need not seek to be compatible with the current trend." [10*] "Writings are not interchangeable; one should not forgo his own pursuits [*114] in order to resemble the ancients," [11*] said he, "It is best to form one's own school of learning, but I need not feel ashamed of my inability to do what other men can do." [12*] Creative ideas of this kind abound in this book, which is not only the masterpiece of an historian but actually opened new intellectual vistas to late Ch'ing scholars.

PART III

The Late Ch'ing Period:

The Modern Text School and Other New Trends

[*114] *Section 20. Division in the Ch'ing School of Learning*

Why did the Ch'ing school of learning [i.e., empirical research] disintegrate after the Tao-kuang and Hsien-feng periods (1821–1861)? There were causes that originated with the school of learning itself, and others that were precipitated by environmental changes.

What were the internal causes arising out of the school of learning itself? For one thing, although the methodology of the School of Empirical Research was quite excellent, the scope of its studies was nevertheless restricted and rigid. Within this school, the highest distinctions were achieved only in the field of philology, which, however, had been exhaustively developed by the various great masters so that only the dregs were left. The study of the nomenclature of artifacts included investigations of the [Chou] sacrificial hall, royal sleeping chambers, hats and dress, and the system of conveyance, but since the originals [of these things] no longer existed now, disputes could not be finally settled. The topic of government regulations and institutions mainly covered funeral dress, imperial sacrifice, political feudalism, and the well-field system, but there had always been variations [in these things] in each period since ancient times; no general reconciliation of views could be achieved from [*115] the numerous books [on these subjects]. Ch'ing learning had replaced Ming learning and flourished in its stead for no other reason than that it was concrete while [Ming learning] was abstract. Now that [Ch'ing scholars] split over the indefinable technical terms and institutions, it too became abstract; how different were they from the [Ming] exponents of "Mind" and "Nature"? Even though those who studied the *Book of Changes* rejected the "River Chart and Lo Writing" in favor of "Breaths of the year and the correlation of the twelve months with the twelve lines of the *ch'ien* and *k'un* hexagrams," [1] their deceitful pretentions were similar. Cases like this were quite numerous and could not win over men. In short, Ch'ing learning flourished by advocating the one word "concreteness," and declined because of its inability to realize this word. Naturally, one reaps what one sows.

Secondly, when an organism grows to a certain point, it becomes static and does not continue to grow, and from this stagnation comes corruption and decadence; this is the unchanging principle of things. The transformation of political systems follows this law, as do schools of thought. The rise of Ch'ing learning was a revolution against the Ming "intellectual oligarchy"; but after the Ch'ien-lung and Chia-ch'ing periods (1736–

1820) it had itself become an imposing "intellectual oligarchy" par excellence. Take, for exmple, Fang Tung-shu's *Han-hsüeh shang-tui* [Discussions of Han Learning]: although it does frequently evince signs of temper and intolerance, it nevertheless aptly strikes at many of the then-prevailing shortcomings. This the various masters of the Orthodox School could not accept, and their opportunistic followers, riding their coat-tails, [*116] even took an arrogant and hostile attitude toward it. The intellectual world was thus turned into a "dictatorship of the Han school." When a school of learning is itself defective and furthermore acts "dictatorially," it portends its own extinction.

Thirdly, Ch'ing scholars on the one hand asked men to honor antiquity, and on the other taught them to be skeptical. If a man reveres antiquity, there is always something more ancient which he ought to revere more; if he is skeptical, why cannot he also doubt what is generally believed by his contemporaries? After its golden period in the Ch'ien-lung and Chia-ch'ing periods, Ch'ing learning [found itself in a position] much like that of the early period of Modern European history when nations enjoyed internal peace and order, and men, like Columbus, looking outward for new lands were bound to appear. Therefore, when there is a sudden offshoot from a certain school, the fate of that school is implicitly doomed; this is in the very nature of things.

In what way did the environment help to induce these changes? First, the early Ch'ing school of "practical statesmanship" suffered a premature death, in part because the prevailing intellectual trend toward the method of inductive research tended to shun abstract generalization, and in part because of the desire to avoid offending official sensibilities and [to secure] self-preservation. After the Chia-ch'ing and Tao-kuang periods (1796–1850), state power and control were increasingly relaxed, and the people's minds thus gradually became liberated. But, when the leisurely inertia of civil officials and the flighty irresponsibility of the military went to extremes, all men of some judgment knew that a great [*117] calamity was approaching. Looking for an explanation, they blamed the impracticality of learning, and the dignified "oligarchs of learning" could not but become the first targets of attack.

Secondly, the Ch'ing learning had its birthplace and base in Kiangsu and Chekiang provinces. During the [Taiping] rebellion in the Hsien-feng and T'ung-chih periods (1851–1874) these two provinces suffered the severest blows, and documents and materials were scattered and lost. Younger scholars fled from place to place, having no leisure to revitalize learning. The brilliant and outstanding men of that time were passionately absorbed in public affairs and could hardly pay much attention to learning. The continuity and development of learning require relatively peaceful times, and thus the sudden decline of all branches of learning during the Hsien-feng and T'ung-chih periods was quite understandable.

Thirdly, after the "Opium War" resolute men of purpose [lit., "clenching their fists and grinding their teeth"] considered it a profound humiliation and a singular catastrophe; they sought for ways to redeem themselves. The revival of the conception of practical studies for the service of the state burst forth like an unextinguishable, raging fire. With the lifting of the ban on oceanic communication, so-called "Western learning" gradually came in: first the study of industrial arts and then political institutions. Scholars hitherto had lived as if in a dark room, unaware of what was beyond it; now a window was suddenly opened, through which they peered out and discovered all sorts of radiant objects which they had never seen before. Looking back into their own room, [they saw] only depressing darkness and piled-up dust. Consequently, their yearning for foreign knowledge became stronger daily and their feelings of disgust with internal [developments] daily became more pronounced. To break through the wall and to get out of this darkness, it was necessary first to attempt to fight the existing political system. Therefore, with their very elementary knowledge of "Western learning" they coalesced with the so-called "school of practical statesmanship" of the Formative Period in early Ch'ing to form an independent school of their own, openly raising the rebel's flag against the Orthodox School. These were the main reasons for the disintegration of the Ch'ing school of learning.

[*118] *Section 21. Modern Texts versus Ancient Texts*

The spark that set off the distintegration of the Ch'ing school of learning was the dispute between the Modern and Ancient Text schools of classical learning. What are the Modern and Ancient Text [schools]? It [the distinction] had its origin in the book burning of Ch'in Shih-huang-ti when the Six Classics were destroyed. With the rise of Han the various scholars gradually began to teach on the basis of their [own] knowledge and different schools arose among them. With respect to the *Book of Changes*, there were three schools: Shih (Ts'ou), Meng (Hsi), and Liang-ch'iu (Ho), all of which evolved from T'ien Ho. As to the *Book of History*, there were the three schools of Ou-yang (Sheng), Ta Hsia-hou (Sheng), and Hsiao Hsia-hou (Chien), all evolving from Fu Sheng. With respect to the *Book of Odes*, there were the three schools of Ch'i, Lu, and Han: the *Lu Odes* coming from Shen Kung, the *Ch'i Odes* from Yüan Ku, and the *Han Odes* from Han Ing. In regard to the *Spring and Autumn Annals* there was only the *Kung-yang Commentary* [which was expounded by] the two schools of Yen (P'eng-tsu) and Yen (An-lo), both evolving from Hu-mu Sheng and Tung Chung-shu. Of

Li there was only the *Yi Li* [Ceremony and Ritual] [expounded by] three schools: Ta-tai (te), Hsiao-tai (sheng), and Ch'ing (P'u), all originating with Kao T'ang-sheng.

[*119] These fourteen schools were established with the officials of learning during the times of the Emperor Wu (140–86 B.C.) and Emperor Hsüan (73–48 B.C.) of the Han Dynasty, and Erudites were appointed to lecture [on them]. The texts they used were all written in the "seal writing," in use during the Ch'in and Han, and these were known as the Modern Texts. The transmission and teaching of the classical learning as stated in the "Biographies of Scholars" in the *Historical Records* ended here, and these were the so-called Fourteen Erudites.

Toward the end of the Former Han (206 B.C.–25 A.D.) there appeared the so-called Ancient Text classics and commentaries. There was a Fei [version] of the *Book of Changes* which was said to have been transmitted by Fei Chih of Tung-lai; there was also a K'ung [version] of the *Book of History*, which was said to have been proffered by a descendant of Confucius, Kung An-kuo, who discovered it stored within a wall. There was a Mao [version] of the *Book of Odes*, which was said to have been transmitted by the Erudite Mao Kung under Prince Hsien of Ho-chien. With respect to the *Spring and Autumn Annals*, there was the *Tso Commentary*, which was said to have been once taught by Chang Ts'ang. Of *Li* there were the thirty-nine sections of "Dispersed Rituals," which were said to have been obtained by Prince Kung of Lu from the dismantled house of Confucius. There was also the *Officials of Chou*, which was said to have been obtained by Prince Hsien of Ho-chien. As all these classics and commentaries were written in the tadpole characters [of ancient times], they were known as the Ancient Texts.

Most of the classical masters of the Two Han dynasties did not believe in the [authenticity of the] Ancient Texts, which Liu Hsin (ca. 46 B.C.–23 A.D.) repeatedly sought to establish with the officials of learning, but to no avail. He sent a letter to the Erudites of the Court of Sacrifices, accusing them of being "egocentric, hyper-conservative, cliquish, and jealous of the truth." When Wang Mang usurped the Han [throne in 9 A.D.], Liu utilized his [Wang's] power to establish [the Ancient Texts], but the Emperor Kuang-wu (25–58 A.D.) again abolished them. During the early periods of the Eastern Capital [i.e., Late Han], believers [in the Ancient Texts] were very few. Toward the end of Late Han, however, great masters like Fu Ch'ien, Ma Yung (79–166 A.D.), and Cheng Hsüan (127–200 A.D.), all honored and studied the ancient texts; as a result, the Ancient Text school of learning prospered greatly.

The focal point of the dispute then was the *Kung-yang Commentary* [*120] on the *Spring and Autumn Annals*. The great Modern Text scholar, Ho Hsiu (129–182 A.D.), wrote *Tso-shih kao-mang* [The Incurability of Mr. Tso], *Ku-liang fei-chi* [The Disabling Diseases of Ku-liang], and *Kung-yang mo-shou* [The Conservatism of Kung-yang]. On the other hand, the great Ancient Text scholar, Cheng Hsüan, refuted him with *Chen kao-huang* [Revitalize the Incurable], *Ch'i fei-chi* [Rehabilitate the Disabled], and *Fa mo-shou* [Enlighten the Conservative]. As Cheng Hsüan was very learned, he wrote commentaries extensively on the various classics. Later, Tu Yü (222–284) and Wang Su (195–256) of Chin, furthered his work. Hence the decline of the Modern Text School. This was the *cause célèbre* of the dispute between the Modern and Ancient Texts during the two Han dynasties.

[*121] From the period of Southern and Northern Dynasties (420–589 A.D.) on, schools of classical learning and interpretation argued only about Cheng Hsüan and Wang Su; and thus the dispute between the Modern and Ancient Texts came to an end. Lu Te-ming of the T'ang period wrote *Shih-wen* [Explanatory Notes] and Kung Ying-ta (574–648 A.D.) wrote *Cheng-i* [The Correct Meaning of the *Book of History*], both modeled after Cheng and Wang in a mixed manner. As to the *Shih-san ching chu-shu* [*Commentaries and Sub-Commentaries on the Thirteen Classics*] now in circulation, the Wang (Pi) Commentary is used for the *Book of Changes*; the fabricated commentary by K'ung An-kuo is used for the *Book of History*; Cheng's Sub-Commentary on *Mao's Commentary* is used for the *Book of Odes*; Chen's commentaries are used for the *Chou Rituals, Ceremony and Ritual,* and the *Book of Rites*; and Tu Yü's Commentary is used for the *Tso Commentary* on the *Spring and Autumn Annals.*

After the Sung (960–1127 A.D.), Ch'eng (Hao and Yi) and Chu (Hsi) and others also extensively annotated the various classics, thereby rendering the commentaries and sub-commentaries of the Han and T'ang obsolete. Coming into the Ch'ing Period, [one sees] the gradual revival of antiquity; men like Ku Yen-wu and Hui Shih-ch'i intensively promoted the subject of annotation and commentary, an occupation which revived [the studies of] the Six Dynasties and T'ang. After Yen Jo-chü attacked the fabricated *Book of History* in the Ancient Text and later proved its forger to be Wang Su, scholars once again opened the famous issue of Cheng (Hsüan) versus Wang (Su) of the Southern and Northern Dynasties, downgrading Wang and upgrading Cheng. This revived [the learning] of Late Han. After the Ch'ien-lung (1736–1795) and Chia-ch'ing (1796–1820) periods, every school [accepted] Hsü (Shen) and Cheng (Hsüan), and everyone [accepted] Chia (K'uei) (30–101 A.D.) and Ma (Yung). The learning of Late Han glowed as the mid-day sun. Like an avalanche which will not stop until it reaches the ground, the old issue of the Modern and Ancient Texts of the Former Han was inevitably reopened once more, as might be expected.[1]

Section 22. The Kung-yang Commentary

The core of the Modern Text School was the *Kung-yang Commentary*. The language of the *Kung-yang* scholars was aptly characterized as "abounding in unusually bizarre and eccentric ideas," [1*] and no one since the time of Wei (220–265 A.D.) and Chin (265–420) had dared to discuss it. Although the *Commentaries and Sub-Commentaries on the Thirteen Classics* now in circulation used Ho Hsiu's Commentary for the *Kung-yang Commentary*, there was a sub-commentary by Hsü Yen of the T'ang period (618–907), which however did not illuminate Ho's interpretation. The *Kung-yang Commentary* thus became a lost subject for almost two thousand years.

Since Ch'ing scholars were fully engaged in studying old classics, K'ung Kuang-shen, a student of Tai Chen, took the initiative in writing *Kung-yang t'ung-i* [A Comprehensive Interpretation of the *Kung-yang Commentary*], but because he did not understand methodology very thoroughly, it was not considered authoritative by Modern Text scholars.

The great pioneer of the Modern Text School was Chuang Ts'un-yü [*122] of Wu-chin, who wrote the *Ch'un-ch'iu cheng-tz'u* [Correct Commentary on the *Spring and Autumn Annals*]; he omitted trivial philological points and the nomenclature of artifacts, concentrating only on [elucidating] the so-called "great principles hidden in esoteric language"; thus he took an entirely different route from that of the school of Tai and Tuan. A later scholar of his native county, Liu Feng-lu (1776–1829), followed [his footsteps] and wrote *Ch'un-ch'iu Kung-yang ching-chuan Ho-shih shih-li* [Explanation of the Rules of Mr. Ho in His Study of the *Kung-yang Commentary* on the *Spring and Autumn Classical Annals*], which successively brought to light the meaning of such "unusually bizarre and eccentric ideas," to use an expression of Ho Hsiu's,[2] as the "Unfolding of the Three Epochs," "Going through the Three Periods of Unity," "Relegating the Chou Dynasty and Entrusting the Kingship to Lu," and "Receiving the Mandate to Reform Institutions."[3] His book employed a scientific, inductive, research method, consistent in reasoning and conclusive in judgment; among the writings of Ch'ing scholars, it is a most valuable creative work.

Tuan Yü-ts'ai's grandson, Kung Tze-chen, had studied philology with Tuan on the one hand and was interested in the Modern Text School on the other; he expounded the classics after the fashion of Chuang Ts'un-yü and Liu Feng-lu. By nature Kung was a lighthearted dilettante, unscrupulous about detailed rules of behavior; in this he was quite similar to Rousseau in France. He had a taste for oversubtle thinking, and employed unrestrained, picturesque, and ambiguous diction, a fact not appreciated by his contemporaries. But this delighted him all the more. He often quoted ideas from the *Kung-yang Commentary* to criticize and satirize current political events and inveigh against despotism. In later life he also studied Buddhism and liked to discuss logic.

All in all, Kung's studies had the defect of lacking depth; no sooner did his thinking reach the outer limits [of any field of learning] than it stopped, and it was also buried under luxuriant diction which made his ideas not easily accessible. Nevertheless, he did contribute to the liberation of thought in the late Ch'ing period. Most of the so-called "Scholars of New Learning" of the Kuang-hsü period (1875–1908) went through [*123] a period in which they worshipped him. A reading of his *Ting-an wen-chi* [Literary Collection of Kung Tze-chen] electrifies a man at first, but after a time one gets tired of his shallowness. Nevertheless, the development of the Modern Text School actually began with him. A poem by Hsia Tseng-yu to Liang Ch'i-ch'ao runs as follows:

Kung and Liu both evolved from Chuang,
This line, alone and dim,
Reached back to Tung Chung-shu.

This was a most lucid statement of the origins of the Modern Text School. To make a comparison with the men of the Orthodox School, Chuang is similar to Ku Yen-wu, and Kung and Liu, to Yen Jo-chü and Hu Wei.

In the early stage of the "Modern Text [Movement]," only the *Kung-yang Commentary* was discussed while other classics were left untouched; however, as a result [of this study] it became known that the approaches of the Ancient and Modern schools of classical masters were entirely different during the Han period. To know Chia K'uei, Ma Yung, Hsü Shen, and Cheng Hsüan was not to exhaust the entire Han learning. At the time, the work of assembling lost texts was highly popular, and no efforts were spared to collect even a single word or phrase of the ancient classics and other interpretations. Thus an increasing number of people studied the legacy of the Modern Text School:

Feng Teng-fu, *San-chia-shih i-wen shu-cheng* [Commentary on the Different Texts of the Three Schools of *Odes*]
Ch'en Shou-ch'i, *San-chia-shih i-shuo k'ao* [A Study of the Legacy of the Three Schools of *Odes*]
Ch'en Ch'iao-ts'ung, *Chin-wen Shang-shu ching-shuo k'ao* [An Examination of the Interpretations of the Classics according to the *Book of History* in the Modern Text]
——, *Shang-shu Ou-yang Hsia-hou i-shuo k'ao* [An Examination of the *Book of History* according to the Legacy of Ou-yang Hsia-hou]
——, *San-chia-shih i-shuo k'ao* [A Study of the Legacy of the Three Schools of *Odes*]
——, *Ch'i-shih I-shih-hsüeh shu-cheng* [Commentary on Mr. I's Work on the Ch'i *Odes*]
Cha Ho-shou, *Ch'i-shih I-shih hsüeh* [Mr. I's Work on the Ch'i *Odes*]

All of these concentrated solely on the similarities and differences between methodologies [of the Modern and Ancient Text Schools] without questioning their authenticity or spuriousness. By the end of the Tao-kuang [*124] period (1821–1850), Wei Yüan (1794–1856) wrote *Shih ku-wei* [The Ancient Hidden Meanings of the *Odes*], launching his first major attack on the *Mao Commentary* [on the *Odes*] and the *Big and Small Prefaces* [of the *Odes*], which he said were forgeries of a later origin. His arguments were erudite and convincing, like Yen Jo-chü's elucidation of the *Book of History*, and he sometimes advanced new interpretations also. He agued that poetry was not written to eulogize or criticize: "It is certainly true that eulogy and criticism are the order of the day with the Mao school of *Odes* . . . but the poet describes his emotions and stops when they are expressed. . . . How can there be genuine joy, sorrow, and happiness for subjects which require no emotion? [lit., "solely for the purpose of groaning for one who is not sick"]. . . ." [4*] This view has a deep affinity to the "art for art's sake" approach, and, in fact, breaks the fetters that had bound literature for the previous two thousand years. Again, on the identity of poetry and music, he said: "In ancient times music was based on poetry; Confucius rectified poetry by rectifying music." [5*] His ability to advance new interpretations gave new vitality to old books.

Wei Yüan also wrote *Shu ku-wei* [The Ancient Hidden Meanings in the *Book of History*] to state that not only was the *Book of History* in Ancient Text, which appeared late in Eastern Chin (317–420 A.D.) [i.e., the one attacked by Yen], a forgery, but the disquisitions on ancient texts by Ma Yung and Cheng Hsüan of the Later Han (25–221A.D.) was also not based on [the works of] K'ung An-kuo either. Meanwhile, Shao I-ch'en (1810–1861) also wrote *Li-ching t'ung-lun* [A General Treatise on the Classics on Rituals] to assert that the seventeen chapters of *Ceremony and Ritual* were complete in themselves, and that the thirty-nine chapters of the so-called *Dispersed Rituals* in Ancient Text were forged by Liu Hsin. Liu Feng-lu had also previously written *Tso-shih Ch'un-ch'iu k'ao-cheng* [The Textual Criticism on the *Tso Commentary* on the *Spring and Autumn Annals*], stating that the original title of that book was *Tso-shih Ch'un-ch'iu* [Mr. Tso's Spring and Autumn Annals] and not *Ch'un-ch'iu Tso-shih-chuan* [*Spring and Autumn Annals* according to Mr. Tso], and that it was in the same class as *Yen-tzu Ch'un-ch'iu* [Mr. Yen's Spring and Autumn Annals] and *Lü-shih Ch'un-ch'iu* [Mr. Lü's Spring and Autumn Annals], being a chronicle and not interpretation of the classics. [*125] Where the interpretations of classics did occur, they had been interpolated by Liu Hsin, who had even forged the title *Tso-shih-chuan.*

After Liu Feng-lu's book appeared, the question of the authenticity or spuriousness of the *Tso Commentary* arose. When Wei's book appeared, the authenticity of the *Mao Odes* was questioned; so was the *Dispersed Rituals* after the appearance of Shao's book. As to the question of the authenticity of the *Rites of Chou*, it had been an issue since the Sung dynasty (960–1127 A.D.). At first each of the various scholars merely selected a book for a limited study; but later, when they looked for the background of [these books], they found that all of them had appeared simultaneously at the end of the Former Han period (206 B.C.–25 A.D.), that their transmission-process could not be thoroughly investigated, and that Liu Hsin had been the man who sponsored and struggled for their establishment. In fine, the various classics in Ancient Texts were all related to each other; if one were authentic, then all were authentic, and if one were forged, then all were forged. So the whole question of the Ancient and Modern Texts of the Two Hans was reopened for examination, and the man who [undertook] this was K'ang Yu-wei.

The strong advocates of the Modern Text School were perforce Kung and Wei, during whose lives the Ch'ing government was already becoming weak and decadent. The whole nation was drugged by the enjoyment of peace at that time, but these men, as if they alone sensed national dangers and grievances, often came together to discuss [lit., "to point their fingers toward heaven and make designs on the earth"] grandiose plans for their country. Empirical research as a branch of learning had not [*126] originally been their specialty, but because everybody else was engaged in it, they too were able to do so, planning to open new frontiers of learning. Therefore, although they studied classics, they did so in a spirit quite different from that of the Orthodox School, which engaged in classical study for its own sake.

Both Kung Tzu-chen and Wei Yüan were fond of discussing governmental affairs and paid great attention to border events. Kung's *Hsi-yü chih hsing-sheng i* [Suggestion to Make the Western Territory a Province] was put into practice during the Kuang-hsü period (1875–1908), and it is today's Sinkiang Province. He also wrote *Meng-ku t'u-chih* [An Illustrated Record of Mongolia], dealing with Mongolian politics and customs, and including in it his own comments.[6*] Wei, who wrote *Yüan-shih* [A History of the Yüan Dynasty] and *Hai-kuo t'u-chih* [An Illustrated Gazetteer of Maritime Countries], was actually a pioneer among specialists in foreign geography. Therefore, it was their legacy that prompted later Modern Text scholars to discuss politics in classical terms.

Section 23. K'ang Yu-wei [1858-1927]

The Modern Text Movement centered around K'ang Yu-wei (1856–1927) of Nan-hai, who, however, was not its founder but its synthesizer. During his early life he had been very interested in the *Rites of Chou*, and after mastering it thoroughly, he wrote the *Cheng-hsüeh t'ung-i* [A General Discourse on Government and Learning]. Later, when he saw the writings of Liao P'ing (1852–1932), he gave up his old ideas entirely. Liao P'ing was a student of Wang K'ai-yün (1833–1916). Wang achieved fame in his time through his study of the *Kung-yang Commentary*, although his accomplishments in classical learning were quite superficial since he was fundamentally a belle-lettrist. Wang's work, the *Kung-yang* [*127] *ch'ien* [Explanation of the *Kung-yang Commentary*] was even less valuable than that of K'ung Kuang-sen (1752–1786). Liao studied with Wang and wrote the *Ssu-i-kuan ching-hsüeh ts'ung-shu* [Collection of Classical Studies of the Hall of Four Benefits], which contained more than ten pieces of writing, all of them quite firmly based on the methodology of the Modern Text School. Late in life he was pressured and bribed [1] by Chang Chih-tung into writing a book repudiating his former [beliefs]. As a man, he certainly had little to recommend him, but it is undeniable that he influenced the thinking of K'ang Yu-wei.

The first book K'ang wrote was the *Hsin-hsüeh wei-ching k'ao* [Study of the Classics Forged during the Hsin Period], the "forged classics" being the *Rites of Chou*, the *Dispersed Rituals*, the *Tso Commentary* (*Tso chüan*), and the *Mao Commentary* on the *Book of Odes*, works for which Liu Hsin (ca. 46 B.C.–23 A.D.) had tried hard to appoint Erudites [2] at the end of the Former Han (206 B.C.–46 A.D.). "Hsin learning" referred to the learning of Wang Mang of the Hsin Dynasty (9–23 A.D.). Contemporary Ch'ing scholars who modelled themselves on Hsü Shen (ca. 100 A.D.) and Cheng Hsüan (127–200 A.D.) styled their studies "Han learning," but K'ang considered it the learning of the Hsin Dynasty rather than that of the Han, and so changed its name.

The essential points of the *Hsin-hsüeh wei-ching k'ao* are these: (1) The classical learning of the Former Han had never had anything called the Ancient Texts and all the Ancient Texts had been forged by Liu Hsin. (2) The book-burning by the Ch'in [in 213 B.C.] had not impaired the Six Classics, and the ones transmitted by the Fourteen Erudites of the Han were all complete texts of the Confucian school, with nothing missing or omitted. (3) The written character used at the time of Confucius was the "seal character" of the Ch'in and Han, and moreover, as regards the "texts," there had never been the classifications of "Ancient" and "Modern." (4) Liu Hsin had tried to cover up the traces of his forgery by adding glosses and creating confusion among all the ancient works, while he was collating books in the imperial library. (5) The reason Liu Hsin had undertaken forgery of the classics was that he wished to help Wang Mang usurp the Han [throne] by conspiring in advance to distort and submerge Confucius' great principles hidden in esoteric language.

[*128] Whether these opinions are entirely correct need not be discussed here; what is important is that the appearance of this interpretation had two repercussions: (1) The foundation of the orthodox Ch'ing school of learning was basically shaken; (2) all ancient books had to be examined anew and reappraised. This was certainly a "hurricane" in the intellectual world.

K'ang Yu-wei had two students, Ch'en Ch'ien-ch'iu and Liang Ch'i-ch'ao (1873–1929), who had been following [the methods of] the School of Empirical Research for a long time, and Ch'en was particularly gifted and competent. When [the two of them] heard K'ang's doctrine, they gave up their own work completely and studied with him. [K'ang's] writing of the *Wei-ching k'ao* was accomplished with considerable participation by these two men, and although they were often troubled by their teacher's dogmatism, they could not influence him. Actually this book is quite excellent and competent on the whole, and the points that can be criticized are but minor ones. As to [K'ang's] arguments that Liu Hsin had secretly introduced several tens of items into the *Shih-chi* [Historical Records] and the *Ch'u-tz'u* [Elegies of Ch'u] and that he had secretly cast and buried the bells, tripods, and other ritual bronzes that had been excavated, in order to dupe posterity, these were certainly completely untenable even from a common sense viewpoint, and yet he maintained them stubbornly. Actually, the essential points of his thesis do not require these irrelevant remarks and forced arguments in order to be maintained, but because he was so anxious to be erudite and different, he often went so far as to suppress or distort evidence, thereby committing a serious crime for the scientist. This was his shortcoming.

As a man, K'ang was totally subjective in myriads of things. His self-confidence was extremely strong and he maintained it very stubbornly. [*129] As for objective facts, he either ignored them completely or insisted on remolding them to his own views. He was this way in his practical career as well as in scholarship. It is precisely because of this that he was able to found a school of thought and rise to fame with it for a time, and it was precisely for the same reason that he was unable to lay a strong and solid foundation for it. Reading his Study of the Classics Forged during the Hsin Period will readily reveal this. Barely a year after this work appeared, it incurred the displeasure of the Ch'ing court; its printing blocks were destroyed and its circulation was thus much restricted. Later, a certain Ts'ui Shih (1851–1924) wrote *Shih-chi t'an-yüan* [An Inquiry into the Origins of the *Historical Records*] and *Ch'un-ch'iu fu-shih* [The Restoration of the *Spring and Autumn Annals* in its Original Form]. These two books quoted and developed K'ang's ideas, making them more precise and terse. Ts'ui Shih was a late protagonist of the Modern Text School.

K'ang's second work was the *K'ung-tzu kai-chih k'ao* [A Study of Confucius on Institutional Reform] and his third, the *Ta-t'ung shu* [Book of the Universal Commonwealth]. If his Study of the Classics Forged during the Hsin Period is comparable to a cyclone, these two works were a mighty volcanic eruption and huge earthquake. He studied the *Kung-yang Commentary* without bothering with the minutiae of the rules of writing composition; he was only looking for the great principles hidden in esoteric language which Ho Hsiu (129–182 A.D.) labelled "the extraordinary and the marvelous." He decided that the *Spring and Autumn Annals* had been Confucius' creation for the purpose of institutional reforms, and that written words were nothing but symbols, like a secret telegraphic code and the notes of musical scores, which cannot be understood without oral instructions. Moreover, [he said that] not only the *Spring and Autumn Annals*, but all of the Six Classics had been written [*130] by Confucius; men in the past were wrong when they said that Confucius had merely edited them. [He believed that] Confucius wanted to establish an independent criterion by which to promote or demote the men of old and to select or discard the ancient texts. He always [tried to justify] his institutional reforms on the basis of antiquity, relying on Yao (2357?–2256? B.C.) and Shun (2255?–2206? B.C.), although we do not know whether there actually were such men, and even if there were, they must [in all probability] have been very ordinary men; their salient virtues and great accomplishments, depicted in the classical canon, were all figments of Confucius' imagination. Not only was this the case with Confucius, but all the philosophers of the Chou (1122?–256 B.C.) and Ch'in (255–207 B.C.) too advocated institutional reforms on the basis of antiquity. For instance, Lao-tzu relied on the Yellow Emperor; Mo-tzu, on the Great Yü; and Hsü Hsing, on the Divine Husbandman.

More recently, men who have looked to Ho Hsiu (129–182 A.D.) for guidance in the study of the *Kung-yang Commentary* like Liu Feng-lu (1776–1829), Kung Tzu-chen (1792–1841), and Ch'en Li (1809–1869) have all talked of changing institutions, but K'ang's doctrine was quite different from theirs. What he called institutional change involved a kind of political revolution and reform of society; for this reason he liked to talk about "going through the three periods of unity." "Three periods" implied that the three dynasties of Hsia (2205?–1766? B.C.), Shang (1766?–1123? B.C.), and Chou (1122?–256 B.C.) were different from each other; hence, reforms should be made as time went on. He was also fond of speaking of "the unfolding of the three epochs," the "three epochs" being "the epoch of disorder," "the epoch of rising peace," and "the epoch of universal peace." The more one made changes, the more one would progress. K'ang's advocacy of political "reform and restoration"[3] was indeed based on these ideas. He said that Confucius' institutional reforms had covered a hundred generations before him and a hundred generations after him, and therefore K'ang honored him as the founder of a religion. But since K'ang mistakenly considered Christian worship in [*131] Europe as the basis of good government and state power, he frequently attempted to equate Confucius with Christ by quoting a variety of apocryphal prognostications to support [his thesis], and consequently, Confucius, as K'ang saw him, was imbued with a "quality of mystery." These, in brief, are the contents of his Study of Confucius on Institutional Reform. The influence of this work on the intellectual world may be said to have been the following:

(1) It taught men not to study the ancient works with the intention of seeking out the trivialities of commentary on isolated phrases, or philology, or the terms for artifacts, or [minute details] concerning institutions, but [to study them] for their general meaning. On the other hand, their general meaning was not to be found in the discussion of Mind and Human Nature,[4] but rather in the basic ideas with which ancient men initiated laws and established institutions. As a result, both Han and Sung learning were rejected, and this opened up new frontiers to the academic world.

(2) In asserting that Confucius' greatness lay in his establishing a new school of learning [i.e., initiating a religion], it encouraged men's creative spirit.

(3) Since the *Wei ching k'ao* had already condemned the majority of the classics as Liu Hsin's forgeries, and the *Kai-chih k'ao* had gone further to say that the entire corpus of the true classics had been created by Confucius under the pretense of their antiquity, the classical canon, which had commonly been considered sacrosanct and inviolable for the past several thousand years, was now laid open to question to its very foundations. This prompted scholars to a [more] critical and skeptical attitude.

[*132] (4) Although [K'ang] praised Confucius highly, he nevertheless said that Confucius had established a school of learning with the same motives, the same means, and the same objectives as had the other philosophers in establishing theirs. In this way he relegated Confucius to the rank of other philosophers, dissolving the so-called notion of "a black-white demarcation and a fixed orthodoxy" and so leading men into comparative studies.

Section 24. K'ang's Ta-t'ung shu

The two works mentioned above represent K'ang Yu-wei's reinterpretation of the older learning; his own creative work was the *Ta-t'ung shu* [Book of the Universal Commonwealth]. Formerly, when K'ang had completed his studies with Chu Tz'u-ch'i, he had withdrawn into solitude on the Hsi-ch'iao Mountain for two years in order to engage in deep meditation alone, by which he hoped to probe exhaustively the way of Heaven and Man and then create his own school of learning by applying [what he had learned] to practical affairs of the world. He interpreted the *Li Yün* [The Evolution of Li] [1] in terms of the "three epochs" of the *Ch'un-ch'iu* and asserted that the "epoch of rising peace" was "partial security" and the "epoch of universal peace" was a "universal commonwealth." As The Evolution of Li has it:

> When the Grand Course was pursued, a public and common spirit ruled [*133] all under the sky; they chose men of talents, virtue, and ability; their words were sincere, and what they cultivated was harmony. Thus men did not love their parents only, nor treat as children only their own sons. A competent provision was secured for the aged till their death, employment for the able-bodied, and the means of growing up to the young. They showed kindness and compassion to widows, orphans, childless men, and those who were disabled by disease, so that they were all sufficiently maintained. Males had their proper work, and females had their homes. [They accumulated] articles [of value], disliking that they should be thrown away upon the ground, but not wishing to keep them for their own gratification. [They labored] with their strength, disliking that it should not be exerted, but not exciting it [only] with a view to their own advantage. . . . This was [the period of] what we call the Grand Union [Universal Commonwealth].[2]

If this paragraph is translated into modern terms, it contains the ideas of *democracy* ["a public and common spirit ruled all under the sky; they chose men of talents, virtue, and ability"], a *League of Nations* ["their words were sincere and what they cultivated was harmony"], *public upbringing of children* ["men did not treat as children only their own sons"], *sickness and old-age insurance* ["a competent provision was secured for the aged . . ."], *communism* ["they accumulated articles of value . . . but not wishing to keep them for their own gratification"], and the *sanctity of labor* ["they labored . . . but not with a view to their own advantage"].

K'ang held that this was the ideal social system of Confucius and was actually the "epoch of universal peace" mentioned in the *Ch'un-ch'iu*. He developed these ideas into a book, which may be summarized as follows:

(1) No nations; the whole world should set up a single government and be divided into several regions.

(2) Both the central and regional governments should be popularly elected.

[*134] (3) No family and clans; a man and a woman should cohabit not more than a year together; upon expiration of this term, there should be a change of mates.

(4) Pregnant women should go to an institution for pre-natal education, and babies after birth should go to nurseries.

(5) Children should enter kindergarten and respective schools according to age.
(6) Upon coming of age they should be assigned by the government to various duties in agricultural, industrial, and other types of productive enterprise.
(7) The sick shall go to hospitals, and the aged to Homes for the Aged.
(8) The establishments for pre-natal education, the nurseries, the kindergartens, the hospitals, and the homes for the aged should be the highest institutions within the regional [government]; those who enter them should obtain the highest satisfaction.
(9) Adult men and women should as a rule serve in these establishments for a certain number of years, as they do at present in the military.
(10) Establish different classes of public dormitories and dining halls so that each may freely enjoy and use them according to his working income.
(11) Reproach for idleness should be the severest form of punishment.
[*135] (12) Those who make new discoveries in learning and those who serve with special distinction in the five establishments of pre-natal education, etc., should receive specific rewards.
(13) There should be cremation of the dead, and fertilizer factories in the neighborhood of the crematoria.

This, briefly, is the outline of the Book of the Universal Commonwealth. The whole work runs to several hundred thousand words, discussing heatedly and minutely the roots of human suffering and happiness and the standards of good and evil, and going on to state the reasons for his [proposed] legislation, the crucial point of which was the destruction of family and clan. K'ang states that since a Buddhist renounces his family in order to find escape from suffering, it would be better to arrange it that he has no family to renounce; that since private property is the source of quarrel and embroilment, who without a family would enjoy having private property? As for nations, they too will follow the family and die out.

K'ang set up these objectives as the ultimate aim of human evolution, but he did not state by what method these could be attained. He does not satisfactorily explain either whether his first objective — a time limit on the cohabitation of a man and a woman — accords with human nature. Nevertheless, when he wrote this book thirty years ago, he relied on nothing and he plagiarized nothing [from others]; yet his ideas correspond in many ways to the internationalism and socialism of today, and in statement
[*136] of high principle he even surpasses them. Yes, he may certainly be called a spectacular man!

Although K'ang had written this work, he kept it secret from other men and never taught its ideas to his students, averring that the present was but the "disordered" epoch, in which one could speak only of "partial security" and not of the "universal commonwealth." To speak of the latter would be like committing mankind to floods and ravening beasts.[3] Among his students only Ch'en Ch'ien-ch'iu and Liang Ch'i-ch'ao were permitted to read this book at first. They enjoyed reading it tremendously and were bent on making parts of it public. K'ang did not encourage this, but he could not prevent them from doing so either, and from that time forth, students at the *Wan-mu ts'ao-t'ang* ["the grass hut amidst a myriad of trees"] all talked about the universal commonwealth. Nevertheless, K'ang from beginning to end advocated salvation of the present world by the principles of "partial security" alone; in regard to the problems of politics as well as social ethics, he considered it his duty to maintain the status quo. He had formulated a new ideal which he considered most worthy and most perfect, yet he did not desire its realization and even fought with all his might to suppress it. I suppose the strangeness and unpredictability of human nature can hardly exceed this.

Immediately after the Sino-Japanese War (1894–1895), K'ang gathered several thousand young scholars [4] to present a memorial on current affairs, known as the "*Kung-ch'e shang-shu*" ["Memorial Presented by Provincial Candidates"]. This is actually the beginning of the "mass political movement" in China.

Since K'ang wanted to practice his doctrine of "partial security" in [*137] the government, he had to look for [patronage] from others, but they steadfastly refused to use him and frequently drove him away. Moreover, the younger generation for the most part disliked his conduct and exchanged criticisms with him, while K'ang, for his part, being over-confident, was contemptuous of these younger men, taking an even more recalcitrant attitude toward them. He is now old and much retired from the world; thus a great thinker of our country does not lend his lustre to his countrymen, which is indeed a pity.

Liang asked him repeatedly to print and distribute his Book of the Universal Commonwealth, but for a long time he would not consent. Finally, it was printed in the *Pu-jen tsa-chih* [Pu-jen Magazine]; but when barely one-third of it was published, the magazine stopped publication and never resumed again.

Section 25. Liang Ch'i-ch'ao [1873-1929]

One vigorous propagandist of the Modern Text School was Liang Ch'i-ch'ao of Hsin-hui. At thirteen he had studied with his friend Ch'en Ch'ien-ch'iu at the *Hsüeh-hai-t'ang* [School of the Ocean of Knowledge], concentrating on the study of Tai Chen, Tuan Yü-ts'ai, Wang Nien-sun, and Wang Yin-chih; because of this association [Liang] received considerable help and benefit from Ch'en Ch'ien-ch'iu. Three years later, when K'ang Yu-wei was sent home as a result of his presentation of a memorial while a mere commoner [1895], and at a time when the whole nation regarded him as an eccentric, Ch'en and Liang were curious about this and went to see him. At first sight, they were thoroughly taken with him and formally became his students, urging him to open a school and give lectures. The [school] was [later] known as the *Wan-mu ts'ao-t'ang* ["the grass hut amidst a myriad of trees"]. After studying there for several [*138] months, the two ardently proclaimed what they had learned [to people] at the *Hsüeh-hai-t'ang*, and severely attacked the old learning; not a day went by that they did not argue with their elders and contemporaries.

K'ang did not lightly impart his knowledge to others. The regular curriculum at the school included, apart from the *Kung-yang Commentary*, punctuation and reading of the *Tzu-chih t'ung-chien* [Comprehensive Mirror for Aid in Government], the *Sung-Yüan hsüeh-an* [Writings of Sung and Yüan Philosophers], the *Chu-tzu yü-lei* [Classified Conversations of Chu Hsi], and others. Frequently old ceremonies were performed too, and since Ch'en and Liang had little taste for this, they changed to the study of the Chou and Ch'in philosophers and the Buddhist scriptures; they also browsed through various political works by Ch'ing scholars as well as translations of Western works, turning to K'ang for solutions to their problems. It was not until a year later that they learned about the idea of the universal commonwealth and, ecstatically delighted as they were, wished very much to publicize it. K'ang felt that the time was not ripe, but he could not stop them. Two years later, Ch'en died [at the age of 22] and Liang felt the more impelled [to continue] single-handed.

Liang studied the *Wei-ching k'ao* [Examination of the Forged Classics], but since he was often unable to bear his teacher's dogmatism, he left it completely, without further ado. His teacher was in the habit of quoting apocryphal works to explain Confucius in mystic terms, and he did not approve of this either. Liang maintained that the Confucian school of learning had evolved in time into the two factions of Mencius and Hsün-tzu, the latter expounding [the idea] of partial security [relative order], and the former, that of a universal commonwealth [Great Harmony]. The classical masters of the Han Dynasty, whether of the Modern or Ancient Text Schools, had all evolved from Hsün-tzu [according to Wang Chung]; therefore, over the past two thousand years, even if the schools had often changed, all of them had changed uniformly within the framework of the Hsün-tzu school. The school of Mencius was thus discontinued and hence that of Confucius also declined. [Liang] there-

[*139] fore took upon himself the task of raising the banner: "disregard Hsün-tzu and emphasize Mencius." He drew a number of ideas from *Mencius* – among them, killing and punishing "enemies of the people"; "autocrats"; "having those skilled in making war suffer the highest punishment"; and "distributing land in order to regulate property holdings" – which he felt embodied the fundamental essence of the universal commonwealth idea. He promulgated these daily, and as he was also partial to *Mo-tzu*, he read and proclaimed its ideas of "universal love" and "non-aggression."

Liang often visited the capital and gradually came into contact with leading scholars and officials of the time, among whom his most intimate academic friends were Hsia Tseng-yu (1865–1924) and T'an Ssu-t'ung (1865–1898). Hsia was at that time beginning to study the Modern Text learning of Kung Tzu-chen and Liu Feng-lu, and whenever he developed a [new] idea he shared it with his bosom friends. Later when Liang went into exile in Japan, Hsia presented him with a poem which read in part:

A nether gloom shrouds the gate of Lan-ling [home of Hsün-tzu],
    Myriads of ghostly heads [swarm about] like ants;
A demon [Hsün-tzu] lifts his hand, and
    The sunlight is blotted out;
We tuck up our sleeves to attack him,
    With one blow we fell him like a pig,
Flushed with drink we throw away our glasses and rise,
    Laughing and looking about, carefree, and gay:
Within the universe, only this can give us joy.

From this we can discern with what a spirit of high exuberance the "anti-Hsün" movement of that generation was actually carried on. T'an was then beginning his study of Wang Fu-chih and liked to discuss logic and statesmanship, but upon meeting Liang he became greatly obsessed with the idea of the universal commonwealth [Great Harmony] also and promulgated it with even greater vigor [see next section for details]; on the other hand, Liang's views were in turn greatly influenced by Hsia and T'an.

Thereafter, the movement of Liang and his associates took on even stronger political overtones. Liang started a magazine at Shanghai pub-
[*140] lished every ten days, known as the *Shih-wu pao* [often called "The Chinese Progress"], and wrote *Pien-fa t'ung-i* [A General Discussion of Reform], which criticized the worthless government and proposed to abolish the old examination system and establish modern schools as ways of remedying the crisis. From time to time he also wrote on "popular sovereignty" but he touched on this only very generally, not daring to espouse it too overtly.

Shortly afterwards, T'an Ssu-t'ung, Huang Tsun-hsien, and Hsiung Hsi-ling, among others, established the *Shih-wu hsüeh-t'ang* [School of Current Affairs] at Changsha, inviting Liang to be head lecturer, with T'ang Ts'ai-ch'ang and others as assistant instructors. Liang went there and lectured on the *Kung-yang Commentary* and the *Mencius*, also teaching his students the methods of note-taking. There were only forty students altogether, the most outstanding being Li Ping-huan, Lin Kuei, and Ts'ai Ao. Liang remained in the lecture hall for four hours a day, and at night wrote comments on the students' notes, a single comment sometimes running to several thousand words; it was not unusual for him to spend whole nights at this without sleep. His discussions were concerned, in the main, with the current version of the theory of popular sovereignty, and he also talked of historical events of the Ch'ing dynasty, listing [episodes of] misgovernment and strongly advocating revolution. As for his views on learning, he excoriated pitilessly all the scholars from Hsün-tzu down to those of the Han, T'ang, Sung, Ming, and Ch'ing.

At that time, all the students lived in dormitories and had no contact with the outside world; the atmosphere within the school became more radical day by day, but the outside world had no way of knowing this. Then, when the new year vacation arrived and the students went home, they showed their notes to relatives and friends, causing a great stir throughout the entire Hunan province.

Prior to this, T'an Ssu-t'ung, T'ang Ts'ai-ch'ang, and others had established a Reform Association of China for group discussions; they also published *Hsiang-pao* [*The Hunan Daily*] and *Hsiang hsüeh-pao* [*The Hunan Journal*] [published every ten days]. Although their writings were not so radical as those of [Liang's] school, these men were in fact secretly acting in concert with it. They also reprinted clandestinely the *Ming-i tai-fang lu* [Plan for the Prince], *Yang-chou shih-jih chi* [Record of Ten [*141] Days in Yang-chou], and other books, with editorial comments, for secret distribution as a means of disseminating revolutionary ideas. Their followers increased day by day and a bitter quarrel between the new and old parties of Hunan arose. Yeh Te-hui wrote *I-chiao ts'ung-pien* [Collected Works in Defence of Confucianism] which ran to several hundred thousand words of bitter, item-by-item refutation of K'ang Yu-wei's books, Liang's comments on [his students'] notes, and the various articles in the *Chinese Progress*, the *Hunan Daily*, and the *Hunan Journal*. Chang Chih-tung too wrote the *Ch'üan-hsüeh p'ien* [Exhortation to Learning] with more or less the same intent. Before the *coup d'état* of 1898, a certain censor memorialized the throne to impeach [Liang] by listing several tens of his comments on the [students'] notes, comments criticizing the Ch'ing ruling house and advocating popular sovereignty. This ultimately led to a large-scale inquisition which resulted in the death of T'an, the exile of Liang, the expulsion of T'ang and others, and the dissolution of the school. The academic conflict thus was enlarged to become a political one.

As Liang was living in exile in Japan, eleven of his students, including Li, Lin, and Ts'ai, left their homes to follow him. T'ang also traveled back and forth many times to plan a revolution with them, and after more than a year's [preparation], he started an uprising at Hankow; these eleven men returned [to China] one after another, and six of them died with him [in the attempt]. Liang too hurried back from America, but the rising had already failed when he reached Shanghai, and from that time on he once again devoted himself solely to the task of propaganda, publishing *Hsin-min ts'ung-pao* [New People's Periodical], *Hsin-hsiao-shuo* [New Works of Fiction], and other magazines to expound his [revolutionary] ideas and objectives. His countrymen vied eagerly [for an opportunity] to read them, and although the Ch'ing government strictly prohibited this, it could not be stopped. For each issue that ap-
[*142] peared [in Japan], there were usually more than ten reprinted editions in China. The thinking of students for the past twenty years has been much influenced by them.

Liang never liked the ancient-style writing of the T'ung-ch'eng school. His own early writing had been modeled after that of Han, Wei, and Chin, and was quite cogent and skillful, but at this point he liberated himself from it, and made it a rule to be plain, easy, expressive, and fluent of communication. He interlarded his writings with colloquialisms, verses, and foreign expressions fairly frequently, letting his pen flow freely and without restraint. Scholars hastened to imitate his style and it became known as the New-Style Writing; however, the older generation were bitterly resentful of it and condemned it as heretical [lit., "a wild fox"]. Nevertheless, his style had a clear structure and the flow of his pen was often passionate, with a rare magical kind of power for the reader.

Section 26. Contrast between K'ang and Liang

While Liang Ch'i-ch'ao daily espoused the revolutionary and republican cause against the Manchus, his teacher K'ang Yu-wei strongly disapproved of it, frequently reprimanding Liang and following this with tactful persuasion. In a period of two years his letters [to Liang] ran to several tens of thousands of words. Liang, on his part, had also become somewhat displeased with the work of the revolutionaries, and in a mood of precaution [lit., "once burned by hot soup, thereafter blowing upon even cold salad"] he slightlely altered his stand. Nevertheless, his conservative instincts and his progressive instincts frequently fought against each other within himself whenever his emotions were aroused, and his views of one day often contradicted those of an earlier day. He once [*143] spoke thus of himself: "I do not mind criticizing myself of yesterday with myself of today." Since men generally considered this a shortcoming, the effectiveness of his words was often compromised. This [mercurial quality] was probably the result of an inherent weakness of character.

After thirty, Liang never again spoke of the "forged classics," nor did he refer very often to "institutional reforms." On the other hand, his teacher K'ang Yu-wei vigorously advocated the creation of a Confucian Association, the establishment of Confucianism as a state religion, and the worship of Confucius together with Heaven. He did not lack adherents in the nation, but Liang could not agree with him and several times rose to repudiate him as in the following words:

> The intellectual world of our nation was never more illustrious, and its personages never greater, than at the time of the Warring States, and this was clearly a result of freedom of thought. When the First Emperor of Ch'in burned the works of the Hundred Schools [of philosophy], thought was stifled for the first time, and when the Han Emperor Wu apotheosized the Six Arts, suppressing the Hundred Schools, thought was stifled once more. Since the Han dynasty, it has been said that Confucianism has prevailed for over two thousand years, and yet the so-called "spirit of apotheosizing this man and deprecating that one" was persistently maintained. Consequently, there were disputes between the orthodox school of learning and the unorthodox and between the Modern Texts and the Ancient Texts. Those who were engaged in empirical research wrangled over the authenticity of interpretation, and those who discussed Human Nature and Rational Principle argued over the Proper Line of Orthodoxy. Each group considered itself the Confucian school, and rejected others as not Confucian. . . . Confucius was gradually metamorphosed into [*144] Tung Chung-shu (179?–104? B.C.) and Ho Hsiu (129–182); then into Ma Yung (79–166 A.D.) and Cheng Hsüan (127–200); then he became Han Yü (768–824) and Ou-yang Hsiu (1017–1072); again he became Ch'eng I (1033–1108) and Chu Hsi (1130–1200); then again he became Lu Hsiang-shan (1139–1193) and Wang Yang-ming (1472–1529); and still again he became Ku Yen-wu (1613–1682) and Tai Chen (1723–1777). This all happened because thinking was tied to one fixed point and could not break out into new directions. It was exactly like a band of monkeys, leaping and clutching at some fruit, or a group of old women struggling over a penny and cursing each other. What a pitiful situation it was! This was the result achieved by the party for the preservation of the [Confucian] cult during the past two thousand years. . .[1*]

Again Liang stated:

> The advocates of the preservation of the [Confucian] cult today have identified themselves with the new learning and the new principles of modern times and say: 'This Confucius already knew and that Confucius already said.' . . .

But they follow the new learning and the new principles not precisely because these latter are palatable to their minds but because these things secretly coincided with 'their' Confucius. Thus, what they love is still Confucius and not truth. If they search the *Four Books* and the *Six Classics* and still cannot find anything to identify themselves with, then they do not dare maintain [their own ideas], even if they clearly know it is the truth, and if others criti- [*145] cize their ideas as unConfucian, they do not dare not to relinquish them. Because of this, the truth can never be revealed to our countrymen. Therefore I despise the shoddy scholars who toy with words and are ever anxious to engraft Western learning upon Chinese learning under the pretext of introducing new things but who, in fact, want to preserve [the old ones]. They nurture a slavish spirit in the intellectual world.[2*]

Liang went on to say:

Snatching single phrases and isolated passages from ancient works and identifying them with modern ideas will very easily produce two kinds of error: (1) It is fine as long as the ideas to be proved analogous correspond with each other in all respects, but if the analogy is forced even slightly, it will most probably lead our people into misconceptions, and explanation of new learning in terms of old sayings will only nurture the growth of errors. For example, not long ago when the advocates of a constitution and a republic happened to see a certain word or phrase in classical canon which was close to the ideas of "constitution" or "republic," they were always ready to fix on it with a self-congratulatory air, claiming these institutions as indigenous to us; whereas in fact the modern republican and constitutional institutions developed a mere one hundred years ago even in the West. It is impossible to find them in ancient Greece and Rome, let alone in our country! Also, when the analogous words have a wide currency, many people will be limited in their thinking to the [*146] words and phrases used in the analogy. They will come to regard the so-called 'constitution' and 'republic' as mere commonplaces and will no longer look for the true meaning [of such institutions themselves]. . . . This kind of habit, once formed, will very readily prove to be a devilish stumbling block to our people's pursuit of practical studies. (2) Persuading people to implement a certain institutional reform by telling them that our ancient philosophers did it in the past, and urging them to study a certain subject by telling them that our early philosophers studied it, is of course a relatively easy way of introducing [Western things]. Yet repeated pronouncements of this kind will lead people to suspect that any institutions not initiated by our early philosophers are impracticable and that the pursuit of any studies not engaged in by our ancient philosophers is inadvisable. Unwittingly, this [practice] often strengthens the tendencies toward prejudice and complacency, and blurs one's [power of] discernment necessary in selecting the right thing to follow. . . . I will never pick the tempting and luscious peach and plum blossoms of my next-door neighbor to set off the old trunks of fir and pine around my own house, thereby becoming elated and self-satisfied. If indeed I love peaches and plums, I should think of transplanting them. Why cause them to be confused with fir and pine in Name and Reality?[3*]

Although these discussions were aimed at specific problems, they reveal briefly Liang's general appraisal of our country's traditional thought and his opinions on the proper way in which new thought should develop in the future.

[*147] The chronic trouble with Chinese thinking was its "tendency towards reliance on [ancient authority]" and its "confusion of [Name with Reality]." For instance, the introduction of Buddhist elements into Confucianism or the proneness to forge texts all originated in this kind of spirit, or take the case of Ch'ing scholars: Yen Yüan's (1635–1704) thinking was close to Mo-tzu's, and yet he felt impelled to claim Confucius as his source; Tai Chen's (1723–1777) thinking was entirely Western,[4] yet he felt obliged to state that he derived it from Confucius; K'ang Yu-wei's Universal Commonwealth was a creative masterpiece without precedent, yet he had to claim a Confucian origin for it. As to why Confucius had to use antiquity to justify his institutional reforms and why the various philosophers all relied upon antiquity, we scarcely need look beyond these [phrases] "reliance on [ancient authority]" and "confusion of [Name with Reality]." If the root of this disease is not eradicated, there can be no hope for the liberation and independence of thought. Liang tried to re-emphasize this point repeatedly. His opinions ofter disagreed with those of his teacher, hence the K'ang-Liang school split.

In intellectual circles, Liang's destructive force was far from negligible, while his constructive [contributions] are not evident. He was partly to blame for the superficiality and vulgarity of the late Ch'ing intellectual world. Nevertheless, he frequently quoted the Buddhist saying: "Before being able to save myself, I try to save others. This is the Bodhisattva's motivation." Thus he produced a great many works in the course of his life, for whatever he had to say he published it! He once spoke of himself: "By the time I had read as far as 'Human nature was originally good,' I was already teaching others about 'In the beginning of man.'"[5] He did not think of the fact that he had not mastered the passages after the phrase "By nature they are similar to one another," and possibly he [*148] did not even [completely] understand [the phrase] "In the beginning of man." Teaching in this way, how was it possible not to mislead men?[6]

Liang always maintained that all the doctrines of the world should have free entry [into China], and this was quite right. However, unless what were introduced bore authentic resemblance to the respective [schools] of thought and [unless they] contained their complete systems and features, they could not provide our countrymen with material for a well-founded study. This type of work cannot be carried on without a division of labor among a number of specialists.

Liang tended to be extensive and thus superficial, scarcely reaching the outer limits of [a field of] learning when he began to discuss and expound it. For this reason, there are many dubious generalizations in his writings, and in extreme cases there were outright errors. When he discovered this and attempted corrections, he had already lapsed into inconsistency. Nevertheless, speaking objectively and taking into account the isolation and moribundity of the intellectual world of twenty years ago, without this type of crude and wide-ranging approach the pioneer work of opening up new fields would not have been possible. From this point of view, Liang Ch'i-ch'ao may be considered the Ch'en She [7] of the new intellectual world. However, what his countrymen require and expect of him does not end here; with his innate forcefulness and the qualifications accumulated over a thirty-year period, he ought to try his utmost to lay groundwork for our new intellectual world. If this man lives out his life in the present manner,[8] we cannot but say that it is a great loss insofar as Chinese cultural history is concerned.

[*149] The point of greatest contrast between Liang and K'ang is that the latter had too many fixed ideas and the former too few, and this was reflected in the ways they managed their affairs as well as in their methods of study. K'ang often said, "My knowledge was complete by the time I was thirty; from that point on I made no more progress, as indeed there was no need to advance." Liang was different, feeling always that his knowledge was still incomplete and worrying that it might never be complete. For several decades he wandered about seeking [knowledge] daily. Consequently K'ang's knowledge now can be discussed definitely, whereas Liang's cannot. Because Liang had too few convictions, he would often be carried away by events and abandon positions he had held. We can say quite definitely that he had less creative power than K'ang.

Liang had a burning "desire for knowledge" and a great variety of interests. Whenever he took up a task, he immersed himself in it and concentrated his energies on it at the expense of everything else; after some time he would move on to another task and discard the previous one. Thus, because he concentrated his energies [on one point], he often produced results, but because he drifted along and forsook his old [work], he could not go deeply [into any subject]. He once wrote this poem for his daughter Ling-hsien's *Diary in I-heng-kuan*: "The flaw in my learning is my love of extensiveness; therefore it is superficial and discursive. A still greater trouble is my lack of persistence; whatever I won I quickly lost. You may imitate me in a hundred things, but not in these two!" He may be said to have had the wit to know himself.

[*150] Although Liang realized his shortcomings, he did not try hard to correct them. Moreover, he was interrupted intermittently by frequent foolish political activities which sapped his energy and caused him to neglect his study. Knowledgeable men say that if Liang can leave politics forever and limit his thirst for knowledge by concentrating on

one or two subjects, he will make even greater contributions to the intellectual world of the future. Otherwise he may just be the last representative of the intellectual history of the Ch'ing period.

Section 27. T'an Ssu-t'ung [1866-1898]

T'an Ssu-t'ung (1865–1898) of Liuyang (Hunan) was a meteor in the intellectual world of the late Ch'ing period. As a child he was fond of writing in the "double-harness style," from which he plunged into the Modern Text learning. A poem of his states that "only Wang Chung, Wei Yüan, Kung Tzu-chen, and Wang K'ai-yün are men of talent," which reveals the major influences on him. He was also interested in Wang Fu-chih's writings and liked to discuss logic, but after he met Liang Ch'i-ch'ao, his scholarly interests underwent a change, and after studying Buddhism with Yang Wen-hui (1837–1911) his interests underwent yet another change. He once assembled his early poems and writings for publication under the title "Early Studies of Ch'ien-ming of Tunghai written before Thirty," indicating that thereafter he would no longer occupy himself with that [type of writing]. His work of the "New Studies" was the *Jen-hsüeh* [The Book on Benevolence], also known as "The Writing [*151] of a Formosan," containing many sharp satires on the Ch'ing court, in which he assumed the guise of a Formosan giving vent to his anger. Having completed the manuscript, he kept it to himself and sent a duplicate to his friend Liang Ch'i-ch'ao, who published it for distribution in Japan, and the book thus came into general circulation. The author's preface to the *Jen-hsüeh* states:

> I shall shed tears of agony and make strong outcries in order to hasten the breaking out of the entangling nets [in which we are enmeshed]; to break out of the entangling net [created by] the pursuit of selfish interests and of official emoluments; to break out of the net of such vulgar teachings as those of the school of textual criticism and of stylistic formalism; to break out of the net of all [confining] theories and teachings throughout the globe; to break through the trammels imposed by rulers; to break out of the net of the "basic human relationships"; and to break out of the net of "heaven." . . . Since these nets can be broken through, they really do not exist, and it is only when there are no nets in reality that it is possible to speak of breaking through. . .

This, in brief, is the spirit of *Jen-hsüeh.* The Englishman Newton inaugurated modern science when he advocated "iconoclasm"; T'an's "breaking out of the nets" was in this same vein.

The *Jen-hsüeh* was written with the intent of fusing science, philosophy, and religion in a single furnace to make them more useful to human [*152] life. This can indeed be called an extremely bold and far-reaching project. However, while I dare not say that such a project may not be carried out someday, yet when viewed in the light of the general state of the intellectual progress of the modern world, it still seems somewhat premature. How much more so in the China of T'an's day!

As a boy, T'an had studied mathematics with considerable success, and had also read exhaustively various translations in the field of what was called "physics" and made full use of all the scientific knowledge then available to him. He had also studied the "Vijñānamātra" and "Avatamsaka" schools of Buddhism,[1] using them as the basis of his thinking and correlating them with science. Furthermore, he adopted the ideas of "The Universal Peace" and "The Universal Commonwealth" of the Modern Text scholars as the ultimate goal for a "World Order," also correlating these ideas with Buddhism. His book derived its material from these three fields [i.e., science, philosophy, and religion], which he organized as a basis for his own ideas, and while it is undeniable that it contains many inconsistent, disorderly, and childish arguments, still it broke so entirely free and independent of the fetters of the traditional thinking that it had no equal throughout the Ch'ing period.

At bottom, T'an opposed the idea of revering antiquity. He once asked, "If antiquity is so admirable, what is the point of being a modern man?"[2*] His general criticism of Chinese history runs as follows:

> The governments of the past two thousand years have all been modeled on that of the Ch'in, hence all of them have been great predators. The [dominant] doctrine of the past two thousand years has been Hsün-tzu's, which [*153] has produced good prudent villagers [i.e., sycophants]. It is the great predators who have utilized the good prudent villagers, and it is the good prudent villagers who have known how to flatter the great predators.[3*]

At that time, the pronouncements of T'an Ssu-t'ung, Liang Ch'i-ch'ao, Hsia Tseng-yu, and their circle were mostly based on this thesis, and T'an was the bravest of them all. The [idea of] "breaking out of the entangling nets," as advocated in his *Jen-hsüeh*, permeated the whole book and cannot be described here in full, but a few passages may serve as examples. He made an overt and bold attack on *ming-chiao*, the [objective] norms of social conduct [in Confucian ethics],[4] in the following words:

> Vulgar scholars and shallow dabblers are wont to talk about norms of social conduct [in Confucian ethics]. To equate these norms of social conduct with true [Confucian] teachings is to convert the Confucian teachings into a counterfeit image of reality, certainly not the reality itself. What is more, the norms of social conduct are man-made; they are used by those above to control those below, and the latter have no choice but to accept them. This is the origin of the terrible sufferings and heartless cruelties which have arisen out of the "three bonds" and "five constant relationships."[5]. . . If we take the word *jen*, or humanity, [we find that] it implies [an equal], reciprocal relation-

ship; rulers and fathers use it to lay obligations on subjects and sons while subjects and sons may in turn use it to lay obligations on rulers and fathers, and thus it is not a convenient device by which to exercise coercive control. Therefore, it became necessary to invent norms like "loyalty, filial piety, incorruptibility, and integrity" in order to create all kinds of distinctions in rank. . . . Since loyalty and filial piety are norms of social conduct which apply solely to subjects and sons, they do not in the least imply the necessity of reciprocity. Even if they [i.e., subjects and sons] could find other grounds for their arguments and wanted to reject [these norms], they could not in the end take a stand against the norms of loyalty and filial piety, sanctified by the Confucian ethics. . . . Where norms of social conduct are concerned, not only are men's lips shut so that they do not dare speak out, but their minds are locked too, so that they do not dare begin to think. . .

[*154] T'an had peculiar opinions about good and evil. He said: "There is no such thing as evil in the whole universe; evil is only a notion,[6] not a reality," and also, "vulgar scholars consider Divine Law good and the human desires evil, without realizing that without human desires there can be no Divine Law."

In order to substantiate his theory that "evil originates in [ascriptions to] norms of conduct," he advanced a very curious and sophistic argument as follows:

There are no greater evils than lust and murder. . . . The intercourse of men and women stems from lust, which is a conventional notion. Since time immemorial people have accepted this notion of lust without changing it and a habit has thus been formed to regard it as evil. Suppose from the origins of mankind, people had been accustomed to considering lustful practice an honorable ritual in state visits and festivities, in courts and temples, in cities and towns, and in crowded places before the public, as if it were the deep bow and kotow of China and the hugging and kissing of Western nations, who then would call it evil?

Destroying life is called murder, which is again only a conventional notion. If killing is evil, then all kinds of killing are evil. Men should not be killed, but why should tigers, wolves, oxen, horses, chickens, and pigs be killed? Why is [this kind of killing] not considered evil? Some may say: "All men belong to the same species, whereas tigers and wolves are not of the same species as man." When tigers and wolves kill men, they are consequently called evil, yet men kill tigers and wolves too, why are men not called evil? . . .

[*155] This type of argument borders on the sophistic, yet it is exactly here that his skeptical spirit and his courage to liberate [the minds of men] may be seen.

The second half of the *Jen-hsüeh* concerned itself mostly with politics. It begins with a discussion of the origin of states and of democracy.[7*] This was actually the basic creed of the contemporary T'an-Liang circle, who endeavored to propagate it in the spirit of martyrs. Looking at it from the present [standpoint], their views seem most commonplace and general; yet at that time these people had never so much as dreamed of the title of Rousseau's *Social Contract*, with which many of their ideas unwittingly coincided. Such a result could not have been achieved unless their minds had been liberated.

T'an advocated revolution against the Manchus in irresistibly sharp tones:

> [The claim] that the world is the private property of the ruler did not begin today. . . Yet who realizes that the sins of the Liao, Chin, Yüan, and Ch'ing [barbarian dynasties] are greater than those of their predecessors? Their land was of dirty soil; their people, nomadic; their hearts, those of beasts; and their customs, crude foreign customs. By violence, cruelty, rapine, and wanton killing, they snatched women, children, and wealth away from the heartland [of China] . . . and were still unsatisfied. They blocked our ears and eyes, bound us hand and foot, suppressed our thinking, frustrated our integrity . . . and then said: "This is quite proper for any subject who eats our food and lives in our land." But who, in fact, is eating whose food and who is living in whose land? . . .

Again he said:

> We Chinese would do well not to speak about Washington and Napoleon. Men of determination and good will should seek to imitate Ch'en She and Yang Hsüan-kan as vanguards of the sages,[8] for [in so doing] they will die without regrets. If such an opportunity does not arise, then it would be preferable to be a knight [an assassin], for this can at least uplift the popular morale and promote the spirit of bravery.

This kind of statement was made [lit., "written on bamboo tablets and silk"] some fifteen or sixteen years before the formations of the T'ung-meng Hui and of the Kuang-fu Hui.[9]

Political discussion in the *Jen-hsüeh* finally takes a turn in the direction of "one-worldism." T'an said: "[According to] the idea of the Great Unification in the *Ch'un-ch'iu*, there should be no nations in the world." And again: "I wish to save not only my own country, but also all the highly affluent Western nations and even all living species. . . . One should not call oneself the national of a certain country, but should look equally upon all nations as one's own and all peoples as one's compatriots." Ideas like this permeated the whole book and were espoused daily by the Modern Text School of that time. Later, when Liang Ch'i-ch'ao lived in the East [i.e., Japan] and was gradually subjected to the vulgar influence of Europe and Japan, he ardently promoted a narrow nationalism – what an affront to his late friend!

T'an met his end at the age of only thirty-three. Had he been given [*157] more years, his accomplishment would have soared to unpredictable heights. Though he left behind only one book, he shed infinite light, and although he passed away in the twinkling of an eye, he had no equal as a sweeping and cleansing force. It is for this reason that I compare him with a meteor.

Section 28. Chang Ping-lin [1868-1936]

During this period of transformation and decadence in Ch'ing learning, one man, Chang Ping-lin (1868–1936) of Yühang, was able to stand forth as a protagonist of the Orthodox School. In youth he had studied with Yü Yüeh (1821–1907), concentrating rigorously on traditional linguistics, and, as a native of the eastern part of Chekiang, he was quite profoundly influenced by Ch'üan Tsu-wang (1705–1755) and Chang Hsüeh-ch'eng (1738–1801). He made a very careful study of historical events of the transitional period from the Ming to the Ch'ing, and was strengthened daily in his anti-Manchu conviction.

Chang was by nature a very systematic and careful man. However, his early political tracts were intentionally limited to the single "doctrine of racial revolution," in order to make it easily understandable to the masses. As a result, his propagandist influence was very great. Beginning in middle age he immersed himself in the study of Buddhism, concentrating on the Vijñānavāda as interpreted in the *Abhidharmakośa* Treatise, and made some progress. After having gone into exile in Japan, he leafed through [numerous] Western works also, and with this new knowledge added to the old learning, he became more erudite and far-ranging every day. His study of linguistics had phonetics as its backbone, as he believed [*158] that words had spoken sounds before they had written forms and that the creation and growth of characters were all based on sounds. His works *Wen-shih* [The Origin of Writing] and *Kuo-ku lün-heng* [Essays on Traditional Learning] contained several chapters on linguistics and phonetics, [elucidating] a number of essential ideas that the old masters of the Ch'ien-lung and Chia-ch'ing periods (1736–1820) had not come upon. While he used the methodology of the Orthodox School, he also widened its content and opened up new paths. This was indeed a great accomplishment of Chang Ping-lin.

Chang interpreted Lao-tzu and Chuang-tzu in terms of Buddhism in a very cogent manner. Although his work *Ch'i-wu-lun shih* [Explanation of the "Discussion on Equalization of Things"] occasionally contained some unconvincing points, it still opened up new vistas to those who study the "philosophy of Chuang-tzu." His *Tao-Han wei-yen* [Candid Opinions on the Great Han Learning] contained many profoundly searching ideas. In his other works, such as the *Kuo-ku lün-heng, Chien-lun* [Selected Essays], and *Wen-lu* [Collected Essays], consistencies often entwined with contradictions. He once described the evolutionary processes of his learning in the following words:

> In youth, I studied the classics, adhering strictly to "sound learning." But what I elucidated and confirmed was limited to linguistics and [the study of]

ritual objects and numbers. Although I also widely read the various philosophers and understood in general the larger ideas contained in their subtle language, I was merely following the old interpretations. . . . Then I studied the Buddhist canons, browsing through the various sutras such as the Avatamsaka, the Saddharmapundarīka [Lotus], and the Nirvāna, and gradually came to understand their meaning more deeply, although I never really mastered them thoroughly. When I was imprisoned in Shanghai, I devoted myself single-mindedly to the work of Maitreya and Vasubandhu,[1] whose approach is to start to analyze "psychic phenomena" and who end by disproving [the existence] of these phenomena. This approach resembled my life-long [pursuit] of sound learning and was therefore easy to accept. . .

. . . In expounding Hsü's work [Hsü Shen's (ca. 100 A.D.) *Shuo-wen chieh-tzu* (Explanation of Script and Elucidation of Characters)], I suddenly came to an understanding and perceived clearly the origins of the language and script. Then I started to write *Wen-shih* [The Origin of Writing]. . . The [*159] insight I gained from this is quite different from the [ordinary] atomistic commentaries and subcommentaries. . .

In explaining Chuang-tzu to the students, I deliberated day and night before I came to some insight. Sitting upright in deep cogitation, I explained *Ch'i-wu* and integrated it with the Yoga [2] and Avatamsaka. . .

In my opinion, my lifelong pursuit of knowledge began with transforming the ordinary [level of Truth] into the transcendent [level of Truth] and ended with returning the transcendent to the ordinary [level of Truth]. The Ch'in and Han [scholars] had gone astray because they never perceived the difference between the two, cramped as they were within a circle. . .[3*]

His description of himself was not over-boastful, since his accomplishments beginning in middle age quite exceeded the limits of Ch'ing learning; his influence on the academic world in recent years has also been very great. Nevertheless, he had the deeply ingrained habit of narrowly adhering to the methodology of [his own school] and at times he could not avoid bias against other schools. For instance, in linguistics, he rejected bronze and oracle bone inscriptions, and in the classics he rejected the Modern Text School. His words often exceeded the bounds of propriety. He was probably less bold and determined in thought-liberation than the Modern Text scholars.

[*160] *Section 29. Translation of Western Works and the "Scholars of New Learning"*

After Hsü Kuang-ch'i, Li Chih-tsao, and others of the Ming period (1368–1644) had translated a number of [Western] books on mathematics, astronomy, and hydraulics, European works began to flow into China, influencing early Ch'ing learning to some extent, although their scope was limited to the fields of astronomy and mathematics. After the

"Opium War" (1839–1842) people began to sense the danger of foreign aggression, and during the Taiping Rebellion, when they enlisted foreign aid to quell domestic troubles, they marvelled even more at the Westerners' "strong ships and effective guns." The upshot was the establishment in Shanghai of the [Kiangnan] arsenal with a language school attached, the opening of the *T'ung-wen kuan* [i.e., Interpreters' College] in the capital, and the sending of students to the United States. The purpose [of these measures], however, was only to train able interpreters, and the aspirations and capacity of the students themselves probably never went beyond this [goal]. Consequently, during the ensuing several decades, they wrought no change in the intellectual world.

However, at the arsenal there had been translated twenty to thirty scientific works, with Li Shan-lan, Hua Heng-fang, and Chao Chung-han responsible for the [Chinese] versions. Since all of those men had a good foundation in [Chinese] studies and an extremely keen interest and a strong sense of responsibility in their work of translation, their accomplishments can be compared, in a way, to those of Hsü and Li of the Ming. [Foreign] churches in China produced a number of translations also, and the so-called "Scholars of New Learning" of the Kuang-hsü period (1875–1908), who were looking for knowledge from abroad, all regarded these works as invaluable [lit., "the secret treasure in the pillow case"], for their "hunger for knowledge" was then at a high point.

The defeat in the Sino-Japanese War (1894–1895) produced nationwide consternation, and assertive young men bitterly and determinedly [*161] talked of "Renovation and Reform"; high provincial officials like Li Hung-chang (1823–1901) and Chang Chih-tung (1837–1909) gave them moderate encouragement. Among the prevailing slogans was the phrase "Chinese learning for the fundamentals and Western learning for practical use," which Chang Chih-tung delighted in promulgating, and which the whole nation regarded as a keynote, since the men of that time positively would not admit that the Europeans and Americans, apart from their ability to make [guns], explore [terrain], sail [ships], and drill [troops], had any other kinds of knowledge. A search of the Western works translated would also not reveal any other kinds of knowledge.

Men like K'ang Yu-wei, Liang Ch'i-ch'ao, and T'an Ssu-t'ung were born and brought up in this environment of a "hunger for knowledge," absorbing themselves in introspective meditation and exhausting searching, in the hope of founding a new school of learning which would be "neither Chinese nor Western but in fact both Chinese and Western." This [possibility] was already precluded by that time, since not only was the indigenous traditional thinking too inveterate and deep-rooted, but the new foreign thought had too shallow and meager a source, which dried up easily once tapped and, quite expectedly, died of exhaustion.

The *coup d'état* of 1898 and the subsequent Boxer Rebellion exposed the weakness of the Ch'ing dynasty even more; young students went abroad for education one after another, and because of her proximity Japan drew the largest number. During the period 1902–1904 the translating profession flourished particularly, and there were more than several dozen periodicals with fixed dates of publication; for each new book [*162] that appeared in Japan, there were often several translations [of it into Chinese]. New ideas swept in like a raging fire, but they were all introduced [into Chinese literature] in the so-called "Liang Ch'i-ch'ao style"—disorganized, unselected, incomplete, ignorant of the various schools [of thought], and with an over-emphasis on quantity. Still, [Chinese] society welcomed these ideas, just as people in an area ridden by disaster will gulp down grass roots, tree bark, frozen birds, and putrescent rats, ravenously and indiscriminately, without asking whether these things are digestible or not, let alone whether they may cause sickness. In point of fact, nothing good and sanitary existed that could serve as adequate substitutes [for these things] either.

Nevertheless, there was at that time the unique Yen Fu (1853–1921) of Hou-kuan, who translated a number of books in succession, such as Huxley's *Evolution and Ethics*, Adam Smith's *The Wealth of Nations*, John S. Mill's *A System of Logic*, and *On Liberty*, Montesquieu's *De l'esprit des lois*, and Herbert Spencer's *The Principles of Sociology*, all of them famous works, although half were old and rather out-of-date [lit., "removed from the trends of the time"]. Nonetheless, among the students who had returned from the West, Yen Fu was the first to make connections with the intellectual world of China.

There was also a certain Lin Shu (d. 1924) who translated well over a hundred and several dozen works of fiction, which were quite popular at that time although most of his translations were made from [works by] second or third-rate European writers. Lin was accustomed to the old-style writing of the T'ung-ch'eng school, and whenever he translated a book he "demonstrated the Way through good writing," and therefore [established] no relationship with the new thinking.

A most unfortunate aspect of the late Ch'ing movement [for study of] [*162] Western thought was the almost total absence from it of the entire body of students returned from the West; the core and motivating force of the movement still rested with men who did not understand Western languages. Due to the limitations of their abilities, it was plainly unavoidable that they should have had such shortcomings as lack of selectivity in their introduction [of ideas], fragmentariness, generality, superficiality, and errors. As a result, the movement went on for almost twenty years without ever establishing a solid foundation; no sooner had it arisen than it collapsed, to be condemned by society. Speaking from this point of view, the Western-trained students in those days were deeply remiss toward the nation.

There was a fundamental general reason for the failure of the so-called "Scholars of New Learning"; namely, that they regarded knowledge not as an end but as a means. At that time, the [Manchu] overlords were enticing the nation along with promises of profit and position; schools became no more than the old examination system under a different name, and the new learning, merely a modified form of the eight-legged essay [training]. Eight or nine out of every ten students had impure motives in seeking knowledge, using it as a "pass key," to be discarded after use; these were the worst among them and need not be discussed. The better ones took "practicability" as their creed, saying that only by practicing what one learned in study could he fulfill his obligation; little did they realize that knowledge must be divorced from "practical" considerations [*164] and must exist for itself, as the maxim goes: "One should do what is proper with no thought of gain, and one should elicit truth with no consideration of reward." In other words, without "bookworms" there would no no knowledge. Among the "Scholars of New Learning" of the late Ch'ing, hardly any shared the spirit of "studying the classics for the sake of the classics" which their predecessors had had during the zenith of the Ch'ing. Is it at all surprising that they could achieve nothing? Therefore, the transition from Kuang-hsü (1875–1908) to Hsüan-t'ung (1909–1911) can only be called the Period of Decadence in Ch'ing learning; even [so modest] a name as the "Formative Period of the New Thought" may not be conferred upon it lightly.

Section 30. Buddhism in the Late Ch'ing

In the intellectual world of the late Ch'ing there was a side current; namely, Buddhism. During the early dynasty of Ch'ing, Buddhism had been extremely weak; there were few eminent monks, and indeed, if there were any at all, they had no relation to the intellectual world. Among the lay converts, Wang Fu-chih of the early Ch'ing was fairly well acquainted with the Dharmalaksana [*Fa-hsiang*] Sect,[1] though it was not his field of special interest. During the Ch'ien-lung period, P'eng Shao-sheng (1740–1796) and Lo Yu-kao (1734–1779) devoutly embraced this faith and the former even argued repeatedly [about Buddhism] with Tai Chen.[2*] Later, Kung Tzu-chen received instruction in Buddhism from P'eng[3*] and accepted the Bodhisattva vows late in life.[4] Wei Yüan, also, [*165] did so late in life, and changed his name to Ch'eng-kuan; among his writings was the *Wu-liang-shou-ching hui-i* [A Collection of Translations of the *Sukhāvatīvyuhasūtra*]. Both Kung and Wei received acclaim from Modern Text scholars, many of whom consequently studied Buddhism also.

Yang Wen-hui (1837–1911) of Shih-tai, who had served on the staff of Tseng Kuo-fan as a young man, and who later went to England in the retinue of [Minister] Tseng Chi-tse [i.e., the Marquis Tseng], had set his heart on Buddhist scriptures many years; his learning was immense, and his conduct and morality lofty. He retired to Nanking late in life, [directing himself] solely to the task of printing [Buddhist] scriptures and disseminating its doctrine, dying only a day before the Wu-han revolution in 1911. He knew the two sects Dharmalaksana and Avatamsaka thoroughly, and explained the Sukhāvatī Doctrine [i.e., the Pure Land Sect] to his students, whose respect and confidence he gradually won.[5] T'an Ssu-t'ung joined his circle for a year and drew upon what he learned there to write the *Jen-hsüeh* [The Book on Benevolence]. T'an quite frequently urged his friend Liang Ch'i-ch'ao [to study Buddhism] also. The latter, though unable to learn very much about it, was nevertheless inclined towards it, and his writings often held Buddhism in esteem. K'ang Yu-wei had always been fond of discussing religion, and it was not unusual for him to twist Buddhist sayings to fit his own meaning; Chang Ping-lin also was interested in the Dharmalaksana Sect, and wrote about it. Thus, among the late Ch'ing "Scholars of New Learning," there were almost none who did not have some connection with Buddhism, and true believers in general clustered about Yang Wen-hui.

Because the scriptures were more widely circulated, it became easier to learn about [Buddhism] and an increasing number of people studied it. These generally fell into two groups: those studying it as a philosophy [*166] and those believing in it as a faith.

With the introduction of Western philosophy, there naturally arose a kindred interest in Indian philosophy, with which our country had an extremely close historical relationship, so that studying it was not only easier but was a natural responsibility for us to shoulder, in the interests of the civilization of the world. Ambitious men were quite willing to take this task upon themselves, but they were so few that their work is not yet worthy of discussion at this point.

Because society had long been subject to a series of misfortunes and disorders, it was only natural that the anti-worldly type of thinking should emerge. In this unclean and evil world, men developed all sorts of vexation, frustration, grief, and sorrow; seeking a refuge that could offer security of life and peace of mind, men with some spiritual proclivity naturally fled to Buddhism. Buddhism, by nature, was neither renunciatory nor negativistic, but men who studied it faithfully and could truly maintain it with a positive spirit [were so few] that it would have been difficult to find even one or two, apart from T'an Ssu-t'ung.

With the study of Buddhism becoming a vogue of the time, certain men appeared who associated with [this religion] in order to acquire a high reputation. Frequently, malefactors of the past or bustling self-seekers of the present commended themselves to the study of Buddhism; one day they would listen to the scripture and squat cross-legged, and on the following day, slyly adulterate their products to victimize men. The Sukhāvatī [i.e., Pure Land] Sect, preaching salvation to Amitabha's paradise by faith,[6] originally included the precept of "salvation even for sinners," but malicious men took this precept out of context and fear- [*167] lessly indulged in evil doings every day, relying on a single invocation of "Amida Buddha" to effect a total redemption. This was almost equivalent to the [situation at] the lowest ebb of the Roman Catholic Church when indulgence in sins and repentence of sins could exist side by side without contradiction.

Moreover, the Chinese had always been quite badly tainted with the poison of superstition; as Buddhism became prevalent, all sorts of belief in evil spirits and unorthodox doctrines as well as methods for public deception and popular delusion were revived in its wake. Altars of divination [horoscope] filled the city, and prognosticatory diagrams were spread all over the writing tablets. Students of Buddhism little realized that Buddhistic teachings frowned upon this; indeed, they acted in such a way as to further the trend [lit., "push the wave and help the tide"], and even men who had been pillars of the New Learning twenty years ago talked about it avidly. If this [trend] continues unchanged, then Buddhism will become a great obstacle in our intellectual world, and even those of us who have always treated Buddhistic teachings with respect will henceforth be tongue-tied and afraid to discuss it any more.

Chiang Fang-chen has said: "The dawn of modern European history came from two great waves of [light]: one, the revival of Greek thought, which was the "Renaissance," and the other, the resurgence of primitive Christianity, which was the "Reformation." Our country's new turning point hereafter should also develop from two directions: one, the emotional, which [involves] a new literature and a new art, and the other, the rational, which [involves] a new Buddhism." [7*] I very much agree with his words. There is no doubt that Buddhism in China, which could [*168] not be suppressed or eradicated even by those who hated it intensely, will always be an important factor in our social thinking; whether this is beneficial or baneful to our society depends solely on whether the new Buddhists appear.

Another point which should be mentioned in passing is Christianity, which, because it is by nature alien to our national character, had a fairly negligible influence. Its earliest missionary [endeavor] came via the "Jesuit" order of the Old Religion [i.e., Catholicism], but although scholars and high Ming officials such as Hsü Kuang-ch'i believed in it for a time, it declined at the beginning of the Ch'ing period. Moreover, repeated missionary incidents nourished popular antagonism more and more, so that when the New Religion [i.e., Protestantism] first appeared, it suffered from [this ill-will] also. Later, our countrymen gradually made their peace [with Christianity] but the power of this religion in Europe had weakened considerably by this time. Churches of the various denominations within our country had carried on quite a number of works, with special emphasis on education, but all of them were obsolete and lacking in vitality. [Not only did the churches] not take part in the several movements of the New Thought, but they may even have indirectly exercised an obstructive influence on them. Christianity during the Ch'ing period may be said to have been neither reprehensible nor praiseworthy, and if this state of affairs is not changed hereafter, it will ultimately go into oblivion entirely.

[*169] *Section 31. Ch'ing Arts and Literature*

The intellectual atmosphere of the late Ch'ing dynasty is comparable in many ways to that of the European Renaissance, but what distinguishes the two sharply is the lack of progress of [Ch'ing] art and literature. Although Ch'ing art, especially painting, cannot be called greatly inferior to that of the previous dynasty, it certainly never developed in any new direction; this we need not dwell upon in detail here. Ch'ing literature, its poetry for example, certainly was in a state of extreme deterioration. Despite Wu Wei-yeh's vapidity and Wang Shih-chen's fragility and thinness, these men were hailed as the leading poets during the period of the founding of the Ch'ing dynasty, and during the high period of Ch'ien-lung (1736–1795), the so-called "three great masters," Yüan Mei, Chiang Shih-ch'üan, and Chao I, smelled of corruption. The collected works of the various classical masters and Ancient-Style writers usually contained poems which, however, were only very bad and clumsy agglomerations of rhymes. During the Chia-ch'ing (1796–1820) and Tao-kuang (1821–1850) periods, Kung Tze-chen, Wang T'an, and Shu Wei were hailed as [originators] of a new style, which was in fact crude and superficial. After the Hsien-feng (1851–1861) and T'ung-chih (1862–1874) periods, men tried hard to imitate Sung poetry, [producing works] that were even more raw and fumbling, and of even less lasting attraction. Writers who were somewhat readable were, quite unexpectedly, men from remote areas, like Li Chien and Cheng Chen, while no one from central China was ever heard of. Not until the last years [of the Ch'ing] were there such men as Chin Ho, Huang Tsun-hsien, and K'ang Yu-wei, who, in view of the richness and vitality [of their writings], could be called eminent great masters.

With respect to the *tz'u* [a kind of song-poem], the Ch'ing period had writers truly superior to those of the Yüan and Ming periods; [writers] like Na-lan Hsing-te, Kuo Lin, Chang Hui-yen, Hsiang Hung-cha, T'an [*170] Hsien, Cheng Wen-cho, Wang P'eng-yün, and Chu Tsu-mou were all famous men, but the *tz'u* was commonly regarded as a trivial form of art.

As for the *ch'ü* [drama], apart from K'ung Shang-jen's *Tao-hua-shan* [The Peach Blossom Fan] and Hung Sheng's *Ch'ang-sheng-tien* [The Palace of Long Life] no other works were worthy of mention; men like Li Yü and Chiang Shih-ch'üan were insipid and superficial.

With respect to novels, the *Hung-lou-meng* [*Dream of the Red Chamber*] stood unique for all times; the rest were unworthy of attention.

With respect to prose, masters of the classics set forth their principles starkly, with no literary flavor at all, and the T'ung-ch'eng school went so far as to approach writing [with rules as rigid as those of] "legal document." [1] During its early period, Wei Hsi and Wang Yüan were comparatively readable, and in its last period, there were Wei Yüan, Tseng Kuo-fan, and K'ang Yu-wei.

Ch'ing scholars were quite proud of their "double-harness" [2] writings, while in fact there was only one writer, Wang Chung (1714–1794), who was highly polished; Kung Tzu-chen and T'an Ssu-t'ung were next, in that order. But the best-known writers like Hu T'ien-yu, Shao Ch'i-t'ao, and Hung Liang-chi [on the other hand] wrote mellifluously without vigor; the others were even less worthy of mention. To sum up, I can assert quite assuredly that Ch'ing learning was very valuable in Chinese intellectual history, but Ch'ing literature and arts were of very little importance in Chinese literary and art-history.

Why did Ch'ing [learning] follow another path than that of the European "Renaissance"? The so-called "Renaissance" was, in a word, [*171] a return to Greece; Greek civilization had had art as its original basis and without it there was no Greece, as art was the special product of a volatile people [living] in a scenic and beautiful island-nation of the south; Italy's position is exactly the same. The primary art of Greece was sculpture, most of the products of which had come down to posterity; hence the excavation of the statue of the Goddess Venus — the sculptured nude Goddess — was the earliest motivation in the Renaissance, and the study of ancient canons as an intellectual pursuit came later. Therefore, it is quite appropriate that special emphasis was placed on art. Our country's civilization began in the great Northern plain, which was grandly majestic and spacious in its reaches, although somewhat unchanging and unfit for artistic development. The so-called "revival of antiquity" here meant the revival of the spirit of the ancient plains-civilization, and it is also quite understandable that [this spirit] should be deficient in the essential elements of the arts.

Still, why was [Ch'ing] literature not developed? Since European scripts are phonetic, the [linguistic] differences and changes between ancient and modern times are drastic, whereas the Chinese script is ideographic and therefore differences and changes [that have occurred] between ancient and modern times are trivial. Although Europeans at the time of the Renaissance tried hard to study Greece and even composed poems, songs, and other works directly in Greek, still, if they wanted to popularize Greek learning, they were forced to translate Greek into Latin or into the vernacular languages of the different nations; otherwise people could not read it. Consequently, the so-called "new writing style" [i.e., new vernacular literature] came into existence spontaneously, just as the translation of the Buddhist scriptures during the Six Dynasties, the Sui [*172] (590–617 A.D.), and the T'ang (618–906 A.D.) periods produced a kind of new writing style, and just as present translation of Western works has produced a new writing style. We have here a case of cause and effect.

It was different with our country, where changes in the form of words have not been radical; in studying ancient works, there was no need for transcriptions or translations. The *Analects* and *Mencius* could be read by all who were even slightly literate; those who could not read them could not read *Shui-hu* [All Men Are Brothers] and the *Dream of the Red Chamber* either. Therefore, scholars of ancient learning found no reason to change the written or spoken language, and since the written and spoken language did not change, even if the substance of knowledge was altered the written and spoken styles which narrated and transmitted this knowledge were not altered. This is the main reason why Ch'ing literature lacks its own characteristic [style]. Moreover, the various great masters of the age advocated [special] emphasis on solid [learning] and de-emphasized beauty [of style]; Ku Yen-wu said: "He who once styles himself as a literary man is no longer worthy of attention." [3*] The so-called "pure literary" writings were very much despised, and men of high calibre all concentrated in the one field of "scientific, empirical research," while all those who made a living by literary activities were second-rate men or worse. This is why [literature] could not develop.

[*173] *Section 32. An Evaluation of Ch'ing Scholarship*

A question: You have repeatedly mentioned that Ch'ing intellectual pursuits were rich in scientific spirit; why, then, did natural sciences not develop during that period? The answer: there is a reason for this. The progress of civilization frequently depends on the inheritance by later generations of bequests of knowledge from their predecessors and on their continuous enrichment. Generally speaking, a people who come into such an inheritance must order it first before attempting to develop it further; this is an inevitable step and the merit of the European Renaissance lay exactly here. Thus, in the days [of the Renaissance] science did not develop either; it had barely emerged and was obliged to await the future. [Similarly], Ch'ing scholars were determined to put the inheritance of the previous three thousand years thoroughly in order by the use of scientific methods, and they did succeed in part.

In general, within a certain period, a people can gather only enough strength to complete one task, and only by so acting can they really reach that goal. Ch'ing scholars concentrated their energies on this point [i.e., exegesis of old classics] and made a fair contribution to our civilization, and we certainly should not ask more of them. Moreover, they certainly tended to approach [their problems] in a solid and realistic manner. For instance, those who studied ancient phonology started by studying only the rhymes in the *Book of Odes* and the *Book of Changes*; then they proceeded to examine [phonetic] changes in the various dynasties, then advanced to an examination of the ancient and modern sounds in the dif-
[*174] ferent localities, and finally reached the study of the structure and functions of the human vocal system. This is clear evidence that empirical research in extensive antiquarian studies lead to empirical research in the natural sciences. Therefore, the path taken by the Ch'ing scholars was actually a preliminary series of steps toward the development of science; that they could not reach the goal [i.e., full scientific development] all at once was because of the [limitation] of time.

Furthermore, the development of knowledge must be based on publicity and interest, and there must be a comparative abundance of research material. The archaic notion of our people that "virtue makes for superiority and technology makes for inferiority" has a long tradition, and it has not been easy [for us] to free ourselves from it all at once. It need not be denied that we have always lacked interest in the study of natural objects and phenomena. Although there has not been a generation which has not made some scientific discoveries, all of them were shrouded in an atmosphere of mystery and thus could not be widely heralded. Some, in fact, were lost immediately after their discovery [lit., "after one turns the heels"]; for instance, in the medical field, many [methods of] diagnosis and prescription were lost because of the secrecy [surrounding them].

In general, the act of invention is often fortuitous. The inventor may not even be able to explain the "why" of it or may explain it without hit-ting on the truth. Not until he makes public the result of his invention to the world at large, and not until it is studied by many people by various methods and from various aspects, does the fortuitous fact become a definite law. Unless this kind of enterprise is supported by various public [*175] institutions of learning such as schools, learned societies, and newspapers, it cannot, by itself, profit from the benefits of mutual aid and the undertaking cannot be fully developed. How was this possible during the Ch'ing period? This is another reason why sciences could not develop.

Nevertheless, in discussing the rise and fall of the learning of an age, we need not be concerned with the kinds of study but only with the spirit in which study [is undertaken]; when this spirit is unerring, then it may be applied to one kind [of study] or another, with equally beneficial results. The spirit of the Ch'ing Orthodox School tended to de-emphasize subjectivity and emphasize objectivity, and to disregard the deductive [method] in favor of the inductive. Although it sometimes went too far in correcting errors, in it, nevertheless, resided the right procedure for learning. Its later offshoot [the Modern Text School] evinced a capacity for bold skepticism and liberation [of thought] which are, as a rule, the precursors of creative endeavor. Is this not the reason why Ch'ing learning is of value?

Section 33. General Conclusion

If the reader of my book finds that the material I have assembled is reasonably accurate and my comments not too erroneous, he will doubtless be prompted to a few reflections such as the following:

[*176] (1) It is evident that our people are richly endowed with the "instinct for knowledge" and that our cultural history is really worthy of study. These qualities may be seen, in a general way, in the history of even a single dynasty. Therefore, although we of the present generation should, on the one hand, absorb as much new culture from outside as possible, we should never, on the other hand, rashly indulge in self-depreciation and so sacrifice our heritage.

(2) On the "scholarly personality" of previous generations we need to develop a certain kind of outlook. The so-called "scholarly personality" seeks knowledge for knowledge's sake, and positively not as a means for anything outside itself. Therefore the character of the [true] scholar is straightforward and his purpose single. Although the world may not concede his usefulness at once, the progress of civilization in each age depends on this kind of man.

(3) We learn that the value of knowledge lies in the inclination to doubt, the pursuit of truth, and creativity; the spirit of learning may be

summed up by this point. No matter the object of the scholar's doubt, pursuit, and creativity, nor the degree of his attainment, once learning is undertaken, a contribution to knowledge will emerge. Only in this sense can we speak of an increase in our heritage. This is so with our national [*177] heritage and should also be so with the heritage of all humanity the world over.

(4) A comparison of present and past intellectual trends will lead us to discover our various shortcomings and to realize that the various bad features of modern learning, such as its vague generalities, confusion, and shallowness, have actually been produced by ourselves. Not until these faults are thoroughly corrected will there be any hope of independence for our learning. Moreover, those who are intent upon meddling in politics make their influence felt even beyond the world of learning. Is our generation to be a benefactor to the future world of learning, or a sinner against it? We have no choice but to bear in mind the successes and failures of previous generations as a means of self-instruction and encouragement.

This, briefly, is my purpose in writing this book and I am extremely optimistic about the future of intellectual life in our country because, after examining history and assessing the force of circumstance as well as judging our national character, I am convinced that in the near future several kinds of trends will develop, each one fulfilling itself to the maximum. Here I attempt to make this prediction and pray that my observations are not inaccurate and my hope not unfounded.

[*178] (1) After having gone through the training of the School of Empirical Research during the Ch'ing period of the last two-hundred-odd years — which has created a kind of tradition — the minds of the scholars in our nation have gradually become cool and systematic. These qualities are essential to the establishment of science. In our country the science of "form" [mathematics] has a long history [lit., "source"] and a solid foundation, but the science of "substance" [physics], because the time is inopportune, has not developed for the time being. Hereafter, the sciences of Europe and America will flow in steadily and our countrymen, applying the excellent scientific minds which they have inherited to these rich materials and using them as a basis for exhaustive study, will undoubtedly become one of the first-class "scientific peoples" of the world.

(2) Buddhist philosophy has always been a precious legacy of our forefathers, but because of its overdevelopment errors arose in the long run and scholars of the Ch'ing period reacted violently against it. However, as Ch'ing learning itself became overdeveloped, it too declined in the end, bringing into being a reverse reaction. It so happens that the intellectual atmosphere of the world has undergone a similar tendency: overdevelopment of material civilization has made "spiritual hunger" all

the more acute. Buddhist philosophy is a good answer [lit., "remedy"] to [*179] the need of the age. Our national character is especially fit for this kind of knowledge. That is why it could develop in the past; in the future this special character will undoubtedly reassert itself. Nevertheless, just as Buddhism of the Sui and T'ang was not Indian Buddhism, the revived Buddhism of the future will not be the Buddhism of the Sui and T'ang kind. In other words, it will be a "Buddhistic Reformation."

(3) The basic concepts of the so-called school of "practical statesmanship" were transmitted from Confucius and Mencius and promoted and expounded under various dynasties, and the schools in the formative and later stages of the Ch'ing period further enlarged its scope. The banner upheld by these schools proclaimed: the chief concern of knowledge is the improvement of society and the increase of happiness. In slogan form this is known as "economic welfare and people's livelihood." Therefore, its focus of discussion was quite naturally the problem of livelihood.

Our people's attitude toward the problems of livelihood, ever since the great philosophers of the pre-Ch'ing period, has always been characterized by ideals close to the "socialism" of modern times. During the past two thousand years the organization of our social economy has benefited considerably from this ideal, and was egalitarian and sound. Now this problem is common to mankind the world over, and the minds of [*180] scholars of all nations are vexed by it. I dare say that our country's social economy will prove to be the best testing-ground for the new doctrines of the future and that scholars of our country will have first priority of opinion on this problem. They should realize even more fully that they should assume the chief responsibility [for the solution to] this problem.

(4) The literature and arts of our country have very deep foundations and impressive bearing. But because they are products of a plains-civilization there have been relatively few changes, although traces of their gradual evolution are nevertheless discernible. Moreover, whenever they came in contact with foreign sects and schools, they were frequently capable of absorbing [these elements] for their own enrichment. Since first-rate men in the Ch'ing period did not devote their energies to these areas [i.e., literature and arts], there seems to have been a deterioration in this area. However, the signs of reaction could be seen even then. Hereafter Western literature and arts will be introduced [into China] to the full, and undoubtedly, in the near future many talented men will appear among our countrymen who will assimilate them, to the enrichment of our inheritance. A new school will come into being, in responsive relationship with other [fields of] learning, for the purpose of carrying out an extremely arresting popular cultural movement.

(5) As society daily becomes more complex and the subjects of learn-

ing to be undertaken more numerous, scholars certainly cannot limit themselves to the study of old canons, as the Ch'ing scholars did. On the other [*181] hand, the indigenous heritage cannot be relinquished either. Therefore, a new school of scholars must appear in the future who will use the latest scientific methods to recategorize the old learning according to subjects, extracting its essence and preserving its value, continuing the work left unfinished by the Ch'ing scholars but with even greater vigor and quality. This [procedure] will not only save the energies of later scholars, but will also keep past accomplishments from deterioration. And men all over the world who engage in "Sinological studies" may also have recourse to it [i.e., the reinterpreted old learning].

It is my hope based on my observations that the new age which is to replace the Ch'ing period will carry on at least the five currents listed above, each bringing its force to bear on our intellectual world and each occupying an important position in it. Now is the time to commence the new age. I shall now go on to state some further views to encourage myself as well as my countrymen.

(1) In studying we may find ourselves distracted by many interests; we must give up some before we can specialize. Of each branch of learning we should make a thorough and honest study and never allow ourselves to be "taught only to become a semi-scholar" of the type Liu Hsien-t'ing satirized.[1*] We must vigorously expunge the late-Ch'ing faults of generality, shallowness, and confusion.

[*182] (2) The men who are fond of political discussion find themselves speaking of "regional and professional self-government." So is it with knowledge, which should be developed in accord with locality and profession [division of labor]. The idea of development by division of labor according to profession is easily comprehensible and needs no elaboration. By "division of labor according to locality" I mean that, since the territory of our country is comparable in size to the whole of Europe, since the climate comprises three zones [torrid, temperate, and frigid], and since the various provinces are located either in the plains or along the seacoast or in the mountain valleys, each of these three areas comprising people with distinct characteristics, it behooves us to develop more than three types of culture. After our country eventually establishes the political foundations of provincial self-government, [each of these provinces] should, according to its characteristics, select one or two fields of learning as a major undertaking. For instance, the people of a certain province may be most fit for science and those of another, for literature and arts. Special emphasis must be placed [on these facts] in order to insure maximum development. Only in this way can we make maximum contributions to the civilization of our country and to that of the world.

(3) Knowledge cannot be exhausted by one school alone. Anything

that pertains to knowledge is by its very nature beneficial and good. We should never pursue conformity of thought, exemplified in the two-thousand-year-old practice of "extolling So-and-so and deprecating So-and-so." Knowledge is not afraid of argument and criticism, but when a man is expounding his learning he should also respect that of others. Only by this [*183] means can he avoid considering one school master, because he is affiliated with it, or the slave, because he is not, and avoid repeating the faults of the intellectual trends of previous dynasties.

I have now completed this book and am deeply grateful to our forefathers for their enormous bequest. I feel that there is a very splendid and dignified future lying before us.

NOTES

INDEX

Notes

Introduction by the Translator

1. I differ somewhat from Professor Schwartz on the subject of Manchu "repressiveness." Mr. Schwartz seems to suggest that the alien dynasty of the Ch'ing was, on the whole, no more oppressive than its predecessor, the absolutist Ming. I would go along with him so far as non-political, non-racial, purely intellectual pursuits were concerned, but in the fields of politics and administration I do think that alien rulers were more sensitive, suspicious, vigilant, and prone to take Draconian measures. The fear aroused by literary inquisitions was not limited to the literati alone, but extended to society in general. People inferred that if an inadvertent slip of the pen could send a man and his family to death, it would be infinitely more dangerous to engage in politics! The very fact that the powerful and high-handed rulers, like Yung-cheng and Ch'ien-lung, were foreigners was an added cause for concern. It was therefore not unnatural that Chinese talents should turn to such safe yet prestige-laden professions as scholarship and teaching.

On the "scientific" nature of the "school of empirical research," I am inclined to think that "science" here is used in a general, liberal sense, as in the term "social science." Whether social science is really science is still a matter of debate among Western scholars. When we speak of *historical science* today, we certainly do not mean it in the same sense as *natural science*. The "school of empirical research" per se was of course not a scientific school, but its objective, inductive methodology in historical and textual research may be considered scientific by eighteenth-century standards. In that sense, the Ch'ing methodology is scientific, or to be safer, proto-scientific. There is some truth in the assertion that this proto-scientific approach was partly influenced by the introduction of Western science in the late Ming and early Ch'ing, and that such famous empirical research scholars as Tai Chen and Hui Tung were well conversant with Western astronomy and mathematics. See Chang Yin-lin, "Ming-Ch'ing chih-chi Hsi-hsüeh shu-ju Chung-kuo k'ao-lüeh" (A Brief Study of the Introduction of Western Learning into China during Late Ming and Early Ch'ing), in Li Ting-i, ed., *Chung-kuo chin-tai-shih lun-ts'ung* (Collection of Essays on Modern Chinese History) (1st Ser.; Taipei, 1956), II, 21–22.

2. For details, see Joseph R. Levenson, *Liang Ch'i-ch'ao and the Mind of Modern China* (Cambridge, 1953).

3. Kuo Chan-po, *Chin wu-shih-nien Chung-kuo ssu-hsiang shih* (History of Chinese Thought in the Last Fifty Years) (2nd ed.; Shanghai, 1936), 35–36, 54.

4. James Legge mentions his difficulties in the various prefaces, prolegomena, and footnotes of his monumental work, *The Chinese Classics* (7 vols.; Oxford, 1893–1895), reprinted in Shanghai, 1939. See also Derk Bodde, "On Translating Chinese Philosophic Terms," *The Far Eastern Quarterly*, 14:231–244 (Feb. 1955); Edward H. Schafer, "Nontranslation and Functional Trans-

lation," *FEQ*, 8:251–260 (May 1954); Arthur F. Wright, "The Chinese Language and Foreign Ideas," and Achilles Fang, "Some Reflections on the Difficulty of Translation," both in Arthur F. Wright, ed., *Studies in Chinese Thought* (Chicago, 1953), pp. 286–303, 263–285, respectively.

5. Liang Ch'i-ch'ao, *Chung-kuo chin-san-pai-nien hsüeh-shu shih* (Chinese Intellectual History of the Last Three Hundred Years) (4th ed.; Shanghai, 1929), 3.

Generally speaking, the Northern Sung Confucianists stressed both political affairs and classical studies, but the Southern Sung Confucianists stressed metaphysical discourse on Mind and Nature at the expense of practical affairs. Cf. Ch'ien Mu, *Chung-kuo chin-san-pai-nien hsüeh-shu shih* (Chinese Intellectual History of the Last Three Hundred Years) (Shanghai, 1937), 5.

6. For discussions on Neo-Confucianism, see Feng Yu-lan, *A History of Chinese Philosophy*, trans. Derk Bodde (Princeton, 1953), vol. II, Chap. X, "The Rise of Neo-Confucianism and its Borrowings from Buddhism and Taoism," pp. 407–433.

7. W. Theodore de Bary, "A Reappraisal of Neo-Confucianism," in Wright, *Studies in Chinese Thought*, pp. 81–111.

8. Liang, 4.

9. David S. Nivison, "The Problem of 'Knowledge' and 'Action' in Chinese Thought since Wang Yang-ming," in Wright, *Studies*, pp. 112–145.

10. Ch'ien Mu. 8–17.

11. Liang, 11–16.

12. Arthur W. Hummel, ed., *Eminent Chinese of the Ch'ing Period* (2 vols.; Washington, 1944), I, 532–533.

13. *Ibid.*, I, 314–316.

14. *Ibid.*, II, 690–691.

15. Liang, 22; Ch'ien Mu, 177.

16. Quoted in Ch'ien Mu, Preface, 2.

17. Liang, 27.

18. *Ibid.*, 34–35.

19. *Ibid.*, 41.

20. Hummel, I, 288–290.

21. *Ibid.*, I, 373–375; Liang, 40.

22. Feng Yu-lan, *Chung-kuo che-hsüeh shih* (History of Chinese Philosophy) (Shanghai, 1934), 1011.

The Translation

[Starred (*) numbers indicate parenthetical references by Liang within his text; plain numbers indicate comments by the translator, Hsü.]

Foreword by Chiang Fang-chen

1. The propriety of comparing Ch'ing learning to the European Renaissance is doubtful. I do not subscribe to this comparison and, needless to say, assume no responsibility for it.

2. At the end of the Ming, Catholic Fathers Michael Boym and Andreas Xavier Koffler succeeded in winning the trust of the Emperor Yung-li (better known as the King Kuei) of the Southern Ming Court in Kwangsi and in con-

verting two Empress-Dowagers, christened Helena and Maria, an Empress, christened Anne, and a Crown Prince, christened Constantinus. Dowager Helena even sent a letter of admiration to the Pope Innocenzo, through Father Andreas Xavier Koffler. See Hsiao I-shan, *Ch'ing-tai t'ung-shih* (General History of the Ch'ing Period) (Shanghai, 1927), I, 604–606. For more information on late Ming Catholic activities, cf. Ch'en Shou-yi, "The Religious Influence of the Early Jesuits on Emperor Ch'ung-cheng of the Ming Dynasty," *T'ien Hsia Monthly*, 8: 397–419 (May 1939); 9: 35–47 (August 1939).

As regards the Jesuit influence on early Ch'ing emperors, we know that Emperor Shun-chih was extremely respectful to Adam Schall von Bell, whom he looked up to as the "ma-fa," meaning "father" in the Manchu language. Shun-chih visited him twenty-four times in a two-year period, 1656–1657. Emperor K'ang-hsi, needless to say, was well known for his fondness for Western astronomy and for some of the Jesuits. Cf. Fang Hao, *Chung-Hsi chiao-t'ung shih* (History of Sino-Western Intercourse) (Taipei, 1954), V, 111.

3. Emperor K'ang-hsi's eighth son, Yin-ssu, was assisted by a Portuguese Jesuit father, Ioannes Mourao, in his struggle for the throne. The fourth son, Yin-chen, who succeeded in getting the throne and became Emperor Yung-cheng, was naturally unfavorably disposed toward the Jesuits. See Hsiao I-shan, I, 656, 668–669, 706–713; Fang Hao, V, 169–172.

Author's First Preface

1. See Section 1, note 1.
2. *La Rekonstruo*, III, No. 3 (Nov. 1920), No. 4 (Dec. 1920), No. 5 (Jan. 1921), Shanghai.

Author's Second Preface

1. His name was Ting I, a famous literatus in the Han period and a friend of Ts'ao Chih. He made the statement when he asked Ts'ao to polish his writing. Cf. Chang Hsüeh-ch'eng, *Wen-shih t'ung-i* (General Principles of Literature and History) (2nd ed.; Shanghai, 1934), *chüan* 4, p. 1.

1. Introduction

1. The term *k'ao-cheng hsüeh* has usually been translated as "textual criticism," but this seems too narrow to cover the full implications of the term, since *k'ao-cheng* includes the investigation of ancient texts as well as artifacts. I have translated it more broadly as "School of Empirical Research," in spite of the modern connotation of this phrase.
2. This is a quotation from the Confucian *Analects*, Book 19, Chap. 23, verse 3. James Legge's translation in *The Chinese Classics*: Vol. I, *Confucian Analects, The Great Learning, and The Doctrine of the Mean* (Oxford, 1893), p. 347, is somewhat different: "The ancestral temple with its beauties, . . . all the officers in their rich array."

2. General Setting

1. This term "River Chart and Lo Writing" has been explained by Derk Bodde in his translation of Feng Yu-lan's *A History of Chinese Philosophy* (Princeton, 1953) as follows:

The "River Chart" (*Ho-t'u*) was a diagram supposed to have been borne out of the Yellow River on the back of a "dragon horse" during the reign of the legendary Fu Hsi. Some accounts say it contained the delineation of the "eight trigrams" of the *Book of Changes*, whereas according to others it merely contained the data from which Fu Hsi was able to construct them. (II, 8, n. 3.)

The "Lo Writing" (*Lo-shu*) was a similarly mystic diagram, supposed to have been borne out of the Lo River on the back of a tortoise at the time when the legendary Yü was draining off the waters of the great flood. (II, 89, n. 2.)

2. *Hsiao-hsüeh* is "the study of language," but to distinguish it from modern linguistics I have added the word "traditional" to qualify it. It may be rendered as philology, but I think it is closer to linguistics in its broader sense than to philology in its narrower sense. Also, I have rendered *hsün-ku* as "philology."

3. For details of the Modern Text of classical learning, see Section 21.

3. *Reaction to the Sung-Ming Neo-Confucianism*

1. The meaning of the original Chinese sentence is not clear.

2. *K'uang* means "wild"; *ch'an*, or *zen* in Japanese, means "meditation" (*dhyāna*), and is the name of an esoteric Buddhist sect. The expression *k'uang-ch'an* therefore denotes a type of men who acted in an eccentric, unrestrained, and unworldly manner, in order to be considered by others as deep and learned.

4. *Ku Yen-wu (1613–1682)*

1*. *T'ing-lin wen-chi*, "Ta yu-jen lun-hsüeh shu" [Collected Writings of Ku Yen-wu, "Letter of Reply to a Friend on Learning"].

2*. *Jih-chih-lu* [Record of Daily Knowledge], 18.

3. *Ch'ing-t'an* is translated by Bodde as "the art of conversing about philosophy and abstract topics only, and avoiding all mundane matters." See Bodde, II, 206, n. 1.

4. " 'Liang-chih' literally (means) 'good knowledge,' a term derived from the *Mencius*, VIIa, 15: The knowledge possessed without the exercise of thought is the 'good knowledge.' " Taken from Bodde, II, 601, n. 4.

5. Taken from James Legge, *The Chinese Classics*: Vol. II, *The Works of Mencius* (Oxford, 1895), Book 3, Part 2, Chap. 9, verse 2, p. 279.

6*. *Jih-chih-lu*, 18.

7*. Ch'üan Tsu-wang, *T'ing-lin hsien-sheng shen-tao-piao yin* [Foreword in the Epitaph on Ku Yen-wu's Grave].

8*. *Jih-chih-lu*, 18.

9*. *Ibid.*, 19.

10*. *Ibid.*

11*. *T'ing-lin wen-chi*, "Yü yu-jen shu, shih-ch'i" [Collected Writings of Ku Yen-wu, "Letters to Friends, No. 17."]

12*. *Chi-ch'i-t'ing chi*, "T'ing-lin hsien-sheng shen-tao-piao" [Collection of Chi-ch'i-t'ing, "Epitaph on Ku's Grave"].

13*. *Yin-lun* [On Sound].

14*. *T'ing-lin wen-chi*, "Yü yu-jen shu, erh" [Collected Writings of Ku Yen-wu, "Letters to Friends, No. 2."]

5. *Yen Jo-chü (1636–1704) and Hu Wei (1633–1714)*

1. The "River Chart and Lo Writing" is a kind of mystic art of divination. For details, see Section 2, n. 1, above.

2. For details of the controversy between the Modern and Ancient Text schools of classical learning, see Joseph R. Levenson, *Liang Ch'i-ch'ao and the Mind of Modern China* (Cambridge, Mass., 1953), Appendix, "The Controversy over the authenticity of the Confucian classics." See also Sections 21–23 of the present translation.

3*. Ling T'ing-k'an (1757–1809), *Chiao-li-t'ang chi*, "Wang Jung-fu mu-chih-ming" [Chiao-li-t'ang Collection, "Tombstone Inscription on Wang Chung's Grave"].

4. Bodde, II, 440.

5. *Ibid.*, 435.

6*. This expression is taken from Hu's own preface.

7. Renan's *Life of Jesus* was published in 1863 and Darwin's *Origin of the Species*, in 1859. Liang was wrong in saying they were published within two years of each other.

6. *Huang Tsung-hsi (1610–1695) and Wang Fu-chih (1619–1692)*

1*. *Ch'ing-shih*, "Huang Tsung-hsi chuan" [Ch'ing History, "Biography of Huang Tsung-hsi"].

2*. Ch'üan Tsu-wang, *Chi-ch'i-t'ing chi*, "Huang Li-chou hsien-sheng shen-tao-pei" [Collection of Chi-ch'i-t'ing, "Epitaph to Mr. Huang Tsung-hsi"].

3. Literally, "task of governing the world."

4*. *Yüan-chün* [*Origin of the Sovereign*].

5*. *Yüan-fa* [Origin of Law].

6*. Ch'ien Ta-hsin, *Ch'ien-yen-t'ang chi*, "Wan Chi-yeh hsien-sheng chuan" [Collection of Ch'ien-yen-t'ang, "Biography of Wan Ssu-t'ung"].

7. Ssu-ma Ch'ien (145–ca.86 B.C.) completed the first dynastic history, the *Shih-chi* or *Historical Records*, extending from the beginnings to ca. 100 B.C.

8. Pan Ku (32–92 A.D.) compiled the *Ch'ien-Han Shu*, or *History of the Former Han Dynasty*.

9*. *Ssu-chieh*.

10*. *Chung-yung pu-chuan yen*.

11*. *Ssu-chieh*.

12*. *Cheng-meng chu* [Notes on Cheng-meng].

13*. *Kuang-yang tsa-chi* [Miscellaneous Records of Kuang-yang], *chüan* 2.

14*. *Jen-hsüeh* [The Book on Benevolence], *chüan* 1.

15*. Unpublished.

7. *Yen Yüan (1635–1704)*

1*. Chun Ling, *Yen Hsi-chai yen-hsing-lu*, "Hsüeh-wen p'ien" [Record of Words and Conduct of Yen Yüan, "Chapter on Knowledge"].

2*. Li Kung, *Yen Hsi-chai hsien-sheng nien-p'u* [Nien-p'u of Yen Yüan], last *chüan*.

3*. *Ibid.*

4*. *Ts'un-hsüeh pien*, "Lun chiang-hsüeh" [Knowledge-Preservation Collection, "On the Exposition of Learning"].

5*. Li Kung, *Nien-p'u*, last *chüan*.

6*. *Hsi-chai chi-yü Wei-chui chi hsü* [Preface to Yen's Supplement to the Wei-chui Collection].

7*. *Ts'un-hsüeh pien*, "Hsüeh-pien" [Knowledge-Preservation Collection, "Argument on Learning"], I.

8*. Li Kung, *Nien-p'u*, last *chüan.*

9*. Chung Ling, *Yen Hsi-chai yen-hsing-lu*, last *chüan.*

10*. *Ibid.*

11*. Li Kung, *Nien-p'u*, last *chüan.*

12. There is a French translation of the *Rites of Chou*: E. Biot, *Le Tcheou-Li*, or *Rites des Tcheou* (2 vols.; Paris, 1851). Biot's translation of the "three kinds of rustic merit" is as follows (I, 213–214):

1. Premier genre de mérite: les six vertus: le savoir, l'humanité, la sagesse, la justice, la fidélité envers le prince, l'union.
2. Second genre de mérite: les six actions louables: la piété filiale, l'affection entre frères, l'amitié envers les parents des neuf degrés, les bonnes relations avec les allies du côté de la mère et de la femme, la fidélité envers les amis, la charité.
3. Troisème genre de mérite: les six sortes de sciences: les rites des céremonies, la musique, l'art de firer des flèches, l'art de conduire un char, l'écriture, le calcul.

13*. Chung Ling, *Yen Hsi-chai yen-hsing-lu, chüan* 1.

14*. Li Kung, *Nien-p'u*, last *chüan.*

8 *Mei Wen-ting (1632–1721), Ku Tsu-yü (1631–1692), and Liu Hsien-t'ing (1648–1695)*

1*. Hang Shih-chün, *Tao-ku-t'ang chi*, "Mei-ting-chiu-cheng-chün chuan" [Collection of the Hall of Antiquarian Description, "Biography of Mr. Mei Wen-ting"].

2*. *Ibid.*

3*. Wei Hsi, *Shu-tzu chi*, "Tu-shih fang-yü chi-yao hsü" [Collection of Shu-tzu, Preface to "Tu-shih fang-yü chi-yao"].

4*. Author's Preface to "Tu-shih fang-yü chi-yao."

5*. Wang Yüan, *Chü-yeh-t'ang chi*, "Liu-ch'u-shih mu-piao" [Collection of Chü-yeh-t'ang, "Tombstone Essay of Laybrother Liu"].

6*. Wang Yüan, *Mu-piao yin* [Introduction to Liu's Tombstone].

7*. Ch'üan Tsu-wang, *Chi-ch'i-t'ing chi*, "Fu Ch'ing-chu shih-lüeh" [Collection of Chi-ch'i-t'ing, "A Brief Record of Fu Shan"].

8*. Wu Hsiang-feng, *Jen–shih* [History of Man].

9. *Summary*

1*. *T'ien-hsia p'ien* [Chapter on T'ien-hsia].

10. *Hui Tung (1697–1758)*

1*. Ch'ien Ta-hsin, *Ch'ien-yen-t'ang chi*, "Hui T'ien-mu chuan" [Collection of Ch'ien-yen-t'ang, "Biography of Hui Shih-ch'i"].

2*. *Li-shuo* [On Propriety].

3*. *Chiu-ching ku-i shou-su* [Opening Passages of *Chiu-ching ku-i*].

4*. *Chiao-shih ts'ung-shu* [Correspondence of Wang Yin-chih, in Chiao's Collection], *chüan* 1.

5. These terms are "explained" in Hui's *I-Han-hsüeh*, but readers will soon find out that the author of the present work (Liang) does not think Hui really understood these terms. My translation of these terms was made after consulting Hui Tung's *I-Han-hsüeh*, I, 1–3; IV, 7, 106; V, 5; and Bodde, II, 107 ff., 118.

6. For an explanation of this term, see Section 2, note 1 of this translation.

7*. *Chou-i-shu* [Explanation of the *Book of Changes*], *chüan* 5.

8*. *Han-hsüeh shang-tui* [Discussions of Han Learning], last *chüan*.

11. Tai Chen (1723–1777)

1. This quotation, the first sentence of a commentary on *The Great Learning*, by the Sung philosopher Chu Hsi, usually appears at the end of *The Great Learning*. James Legge, in his *The Chinese Classics*, Vol. I (Oxford, 1893), p. 360, translates the first few sentences of this commentary as follows: "The preceding chapter of classical text is in the words of Confucius, handed down by the philosopher Tsang [Tseng-tzu]. The ten chapters of explanation which follow contain the views of Tsang, and were recorded by his disciples."

2*. Wang Ch'ang, *Shu-an wen-ch'ao*, "Tai Tung-yüan mu-chih-ming" [Literary Collection of Shu-an, "Tai Chen's Epitaphs"].

3*. *Tung-yüan wen-chi*, *"Ta Cheng Yung-mu shu"* [Literary Collection of Tai Chen, "A Reply to Cheng Yung-mu's Letter"]. [In the original text of the letter, first three words of this quotation ("A scholar should . . .") do not appear. – Tr.]

4*. *Tung-yüan chi*, "Yü-mou shu" [Collected Works of Tai Chen, "Letter to X"].

5*. *Tung-yüan chi*, "Yü Yao Chi-chuan shu" [Collected Works of Tai Chen, "Letter to Yao Chi-chuan"].

6*. *Ch'ien-yen-t'ang chi*, "Tai Chen chuan" [Ch'ien-yen-t'ang Collection, "Biography of Tai Chen"].

7*. Yu T'ing-ts'ai, ed., *Kuo-ch'ao ch'i-hsien lei-cheng*, "Tai Tung-yüan hsien-sheng shih-lüeh" [Selected Biographies in Our Imperial Dynasty, "A Sketch of Mr. Tai Chen"], *chuan* 131.

8*. *Chien-lun*, "Ch'ing-ju pien" [Selected Essays, Chapter on "Ch'ing Scholars"].

9*. *Chiao-li-t'ang chi* [Collection of Chiao-li-t'ang].

10*. Tuan Yü-ts'ai, *Ching-yün-lou chi*, "Yü-ch'in ya-yen hsü yin" [Collection of Ching-yün-lou, "Introduction to the Preface to Yü-ch'in ya-yen"].

11. *Tung-yüan wen-chi*, "Yü Mou-shu" [Literary Collection of Tai Chen, "Letter to X"], *chüan* 8. [In Chu Hsi's philosophy, *li* is the immanent nature of things, without which nothing can exist. Derk Bodde translates it as "principle," and I translate it as "rational principle." Chu Hsi himself remarks: "When a certain thing is made, there is in it a particular Principle (*li*). For all things created in the universe, there is in each a particular Principle." Thus the bricks have within themselves the Principle that pertains to bricks. (See Bodde, II, 535–536.)

[Feelings, or *ch'ing*, proceed from the mind, which is "the unifying agent between the nature and the feelings." Nature is non-concrete and good, but feelings pertain to the concrete world. (See Bodde, II, 556–557.) Tai Chen attacks Chu Hsi for setting up an opposition between the feelings and desires and the rational principle. Enlightenment (in Chu Hsi) is to be achieved by a sort of "apatheia" and suppression of feelings. This attack on natural instincts becomes as cruel a weapon in the hands of later rulers as was the draconic law code of the Legalists. — Tr.]

12*. *Tai-shih i-shu, chiu, fu-lu,* "Ta P'eng-chin-shih" [Tai's Posthumous Letter No. 9, "Letter of Reply to Dr. P'eng," Appendix].

13*. *Ibid.* [A somewhat different translation of this quotation may be found in Bodde, II, 651. — Tr.]

14. A somewhat different translation may be found in Bodde, II, 667.

15*. Quoted in *Tai Tung-yüan chi, chuan-shou,* "Tuan Yü-ts'ai hsü-yin" [Tuan Yü-ts'ai's Preface to the Collected Works of Tai Chen].

16*. This letter expounded the same thesis as the *Meng-tzu tzu-i shu-cheng* [Elucidation of the Meaning of Words in *Mencius*].

17*. *Han-hsüeh shih-ch'eng-chi* [Biographies of Leaders of the Present Dynasty], *chüan* 6.

18*. *Kuo-ch'ao hsüeh-an hsiao-shih* [Minor Observations on the Writings of the Reigning Dynasty].

19*. *Han-hsüeh shang-tui* [Discussions of Han Learning], *chüan* 1.

20. For more information about Tai Chen, cf. Hu Shih, "A Note on Ch'üan Tsu-wang, Chao I-ch'ing, and Tai Chen," in Arthur W. Hummel, ed., *Eminent Chinese of the Ch'ing Period* (Washington, 1944), II, 970–982.

12. Tuan Yü-ts'ai (1735–1815), Wang Nien-sun (1744–1832), and Wang Yin-chih (1766–1834)

1. *Hsiao-ch'en* is the correlation of the twelve months with the twelve lines of the *ch'ien* and *k'un* hexagrams, and *na-chia* is the correlation of the ten *kan-chih* with the hexagrams.

2. There were many interpretations of these Five Relationships and Six Feelings. According to one, the Five Relationships are those of prince and ministers, father and son, brothers, husband and wife, and friends; the Six Feelings are happiness, anger, melancholy, joy, love, and hatred.

3. For a discussion of the apocryphal and prognosticatory texts in the Han dynasty, cf. Bodde, II, Chap. III.

4*. *Ching-yün-lou chi,* "Yü chu t'ung-chih lun chiao-shu chi nan" [Collection of the Ching-yün-lou, "Letter to his Colleagues Discussing the Difficulties of Collating Texts"].

5*. *Han-hsüeh shang-tui* [Discussions of Han Learning], *chüan* 2, 2nd part.

6. This is a quotation from the "Airs of Pei" (*Pei-feng*) of the "Folk Songs" (*kuo-feng*) in the *Book of Odes*. My translation is taken from Arthur Waley, *The Book of Songs* (Boston, 1937), p. 93, because it is closer to Wang Nien-sun's explanation. Legge renders this quotation as "The wind blows and is fierce," in *The Chinese Classics*: Vol. IV, *The She King, or The Book of Poetry* (London, 1871), Part 2, p. 46. Ezra Pound renders this quotation as "cold parcheth the end wind," in *The Classic Anthology as Defined by Confucius* (Cambridge, Mass., 1954), p. 14.

13. Summary

1. This is a quotation from the *Tao-te-ching* by Lao-tzu, Chap. 11. My translation is taken from Arthur Waley, *The Way and Its Power* (Boston, 1935), p. 155.

2. Liang's quotation from *Chuang-tzu* is inaccurate, although correct in

meaning, and I have translated it directly from Liang. An accurate quotation, as translated by Feng Yu-lan, is as follows: "The efficiency of the salve to cure the chapped hand was in both cases the same; yet here it secured him a title, there, nothing more than a capacity for washing silk." The story behind this passage is as follows:

> There was a man of Sung who had a recipe for salve for chapped hands. From generation to generation, his family made silk-washing their occupation. A stranger heard of this and proposed to offer him one hundred ounces of gold for the recipe. The kindred all came together to consider this proposal. "We have," said they, "been washing silk for generations. What we gained is not more than a few ounces of gold. Now in one morning we can sell this art for one hundred ounces. Let us give it to the stranger." So the stranger got it. He went and informed the King of Wu. When Wu and Yüeh were at war, the King of Wu gave him the command of his fleet. In the winter he had a naval engagement with Yüeh, in which the latter was totally defeated [because he had no means of curing chapped hands]. The stranger was rewarded with a fief and a title.

Cf. Feng Yu-lan, trans., *Chuang Tzu* (Shanghai, 1933), Chap. 1, p. 39.

17. *Notation Book and Literary Style*

1*. *T'ing-lin wen-chi*, "Yü yu-jen lun men-jen shu" [Literary Collection of Ku Yen-wu, "Discussion with Friends on his Pupils"].

2*. *Ibid.*, "Yü yu-jen shu, shih" ["Letters to Friends," No. 10].

3*. The first careful observations of an object.

4*. Such as a list of items for comparison, together with the author's own opinion.

5*. Opinions which have been accepted as final after being confirmed by repeated evidence.

6. This is a quotation from the Appendix to the *Book of Changes* and appears in the following context, according to Legge's translation:

> "The appellations and names [of the diagrams and lines] are but small matters, but the classes of things comprehended under them are large. Their scope reaches far, and the explanations attached to them are elegant. The words are indirect, but to the point, the matters seem plainly set forth, but there is a secret principle in them. Their object is, in cases that are doubtful, to help the people in their conduct, and to make plain the recompenses of good and evil."

Cf. James Legge, *The Sacred Books of China*, Part II, *Yi King*. (Oxford, 1882), Appendix III, p. 396.

7. This is a quotation from *Tso Chuan*, in the 25th year of Duke Hsiang. The context, in Legge's translation, is as follows: "Without words, who would know one's thoughts; without elegant composition of the words, they will not go far." Cf. James Legge, *The Chinese Classics* (Oxford, 1893), vol. V, Part II, p. 517.

8. This is a quotation from the *Analects*, Book 8, *T'ai-po*, Chap. 4. My translation is from Legge, *Classics*, I, 209.

9. This means that style per se is neutral, and that it follows time. The style of an ancient age is ancient, and the style of a modern age is modern. In other words, each age has its own style.

10*. *Jih-chih-lu* [Record of Daily Knowledge], 19.

19. *The Ancient-Style Writers*

1*. *Tung-yüan chi*, "Yü Fang Hsi-yüan shu" [Collected Works of Tai Chen, "Letter to Fang Hsi-yüan"]. [Here *tao* (truth) probably means "great principles," "distilled ideas," and *i* (art), "literary skill," "craftsmanship." In Tai's opinion, any writing that expounds great ideas requires some skill in doing so. Therefore, no writing is all *tao* and no *i*. – Tr.]

2*. *Ch'ien-yen-t'ang chi*, "Yü mou yu-jen shu" [Collection of Ch'ien-yen-t'ang, "Letter to a Friend"], 33.

3. For a discussion of Chang Hsüeh-ch'eng's life and work, see the unpubl. diss. (Harvard University, 1953) by David S. Nivison, "The Literary and Historical Thought of Chang Hsüeh-ch'eng (1738–1801)."

4*. *Yüan-tao p'ien* [Chapter on the "*Origin of the Way*"]. [These two quotations and the following ones are not very exact, although their meanings are correct. Chang thought that because common people acted without knowing why they did so, whereas the sages acted only because they realized they had to do so, common people were closer to the Way (*tao*) than the sages. He who learned from the sages was a wise man, and he who learned from the common men was a sage, for the common men saw the Way unconsciously.

[The Duke of Chou learned from the ancient sages and discovered the underlying reasons for their actions. This was not due to his innate wisdom but to his time, opportunities, position, and the force of circumstances. He synthesized past knowledge without knowing why he did it, and Confucius learned from him. Therefore it was the Duke of Chou rather than Confucius who was the great synthesizer. Cf. Chang Hsüeh-ch'eng, *Wen-shih t'ung-i* (General Principles of Literature and Learning) (2nd ed.; Shanghai, 1934), *chüan* 2, pp. 32–34. – Tr.]

5*. *I-chiao, Shih-chiao, Ching-chieh, chu p'ien* [Chapters on the "Teachings of the *Book of Changes*," "Teachings of the *Book of Odes*," and the "Explanation of the Classics"]. [The Six Classics are the *Book of Odes*, the *Book of History*, the *Book of Rites*, the *Book of Music*, the *Book of Changes*, and the *Spring and Autumn Annals*. Chang believed that ancient men never talked about principle without factual basis. Since the Six Classics recorded ancient rulers' accomplishments, institutions, codes, and customs, they were history also. Philosophers of the past either transmitted or wrote commentaries on the Six Classics; therefore their writings could be regarded as having originated from the Six Classics. *Ibid.*, *chüan* 1, pp. 1, 25, 26. – Tr.]

6*. *Shih-chiao p'ien* [Chapter on the "Teachings of the *Book of Odes*"]. [Before the Warring States period (403–321 B.C.), officials and teachers transmitted knowledge by oral instruction only. Not until that time were bamboo slips used for writing, rather than relying on oral transmission. *Ibid.*, *chüan* 1, p. 20. – Tr.]

7*. *Yen-kung p'ien* [Chapter on the "Discussion of Public Affairs"]. [When ancient men spoke, they aimed at clarifing their ideas and attaining the Way (*tao*). Their intention was public. They were never proud of their literary skill and never regarded their works as private property. *Ibid.*, *chüan* 2, p. 49. – Tr.]

8*. *Shuo-lin p'ien* [Chapter on "Miscellaneous Things"]. [This quotation does not mean that whatever is ancient is always preferable to whatever is modern. It means that even the bad ancient works may contain information and citation of ancient source material that good modern works do not contain.

Thus the ancient "dregs" may spur modern man to discover the distilled "essence." *Ibid., chüan* 2, p. 5. – Tr.]

9*. *Chu-Lu p'ien* [Chapter on "Chu Hsi and Lu Chiu-yüan"]. [Later men surpass past men because they build their knowledge on that of past men. Those who attacked Chu Hsi did not know they were actually his epigones. *Ibid., chüan* 3, pp. 78–79. – Tr.]

10*. *Kan-yü p'ien* [Chapter on "Reflections and Feelings"]. [A man's chances of putting his learning into practice are influenced by a multitude of factors such as fate, force of circumstances, etc. Even though his knowledge is great and useful, he may still have the misfortune of non-recognition and non-appreciation. *Ibid., chüan* 3, pp. 96–97. – Tr.]

11*. *Wen-li p'ien* [Chapter on the "Principle of Writing"]. [The purpose of writing is to express one's ideas, feelings, etc. Therefore a writing must have substance. Just as a sick man, at a jovial party, cannot change his groaning into laughter, one cannot and need not sacrifice his own style to imitate others. *Ibid., chüan* 3, pp. 82–83. – Tr.]

12*. *Po-yüeh p'ien* [Chapter on "Erudition and Discipline"]. [This quotation is taken from Chang's reply to a friend who felt lost in the company of great scholars. Chang consoled him by saying that one must have specialization in learning and need not feel inadequate over matters outside his field, just as a merchant who sold cloth need not bother about cereals. *Ibid., chüan* 2, p. 45. – Tr.]

20. Division in the Ch'ing School of Learning

1. See Section 2, note 1, and Bodde, II, 8, 89, 106, 118.

21. Modern Texts versus Ancient Texts

1. For a discussion of the controversy over the Modern and Ancient Texts, cf. Levenson, *Liang Ch'i-ch'ao*, Appendix, "The Controversy over the Authenticity of the Confucian Classics," pp. 221–223, which draws largely from P. Pelliot, "Le Chou King en caractères anciens et le Chang Chou Che Wen," *Mémoires concernant l'Asie Orientale* (Paris, 1916), pp. 123–177.

22. The Kung-yang Commentary

1*. Ho Hsiu, *Kung-yang chuan-chu tzu-hsü* [Commentary on the *Kung-yang Commentary*, Preface].

2. Ho Hsiu (129–182 A.D.) was a great classical scholar of the Eastern Han period. His commentary on the *Kung-yang Commentary* on the *Spring and Autumn Annals*, which attaches to it an esoteric meaning, has been accepted as a standard work over the centuries. Cf. Woo Kang, *Les trois théories politiques du Tch'ouen, Ts'ieou, interprétées par Tong Tchong-chou* (*Tung Chung-shu*) *d'après les principes de l'école de Kong-yang* (Paris, 1932).

3. The "Three Epochs" and "Three Periods of Unity" are explained in the next section. The phrase "relegating the Chou Dynasty and entrusting the kingship to Lu" means that the Chou Dynasty had become too decadent to deserve the kingship, which should pass to Lu, the state of the Duke of Chou and Confucius. The phrase "receiving the Mandate to reform institutions" means that Confucius had actually received the Mandate from Heaven "to correct

the faults of the decadent Chou dynasty and establish the institutions of a new king and dynasty." Since only a king can receive the Mandate of Heaven, Confucius was canonized by the Modern Text School as the *su-wang*, uncrowned king. Cf. Bodde, II, 71 ff.; Liu Feng-lu, *Ch'un-ch'iu Kung-yang ching-chuan Ho-shih shih-li*, in Juan Yuan, ed., *Huang-Ch'ing ching-chieh* [Exegesis of the Classics in the Imperial Ch'ing Period], *chüan* 1285, p. 1.

4*. *Shih ku-wei*, "Ch'i Lu Han Mao i-t'ung lun," *chung* [The Ancient Hidden Meaning of the *Odes*, "On the Similarities and Differences of the Ch'i, Lu, Han, and Mao Schools of Odes," middle section].

5*. *Shih ku-wei*, "Fu-tzu cheng-yüeh lun" [The Ancient Hidden Meaning of the *Odes*, "On the Master Rectifying Music"], upper section.

6*. Not published.

23. K'ang Yu-wei (1858–1927)

1. In some versions, the phrase "pressured and bribed" is omitted.

2. *Po-shih* was an official title in the Han period, literally, "erudite scholar." In modern Chinese, *po-shih* denotes the holder of a doctoral degree.

3. It is interesting to note that all the reforms in China before K'ang were reforms within the Confucian framework, whereas K'ang wanted to introduce reform after the fashion of Japan's Meiji Restoration and Russia's westernization by Peter the Great. His attempts led to the *coup d'état* of 1898.

4. Here the word "nature" means "the nature of man and things," and not the "naturalistic world" as understood in the West. Neo-Confucianists spent much time contemplating the nature of bamboo trees.

24. K'ang's Ta-t'ung shu

1. A chapter of the *Book of Rites.*

2. Translation taken from James Legge, *The Sacred Books of China*, Part III, *The Li Ki* (Oxford, 1885), pp. 364–366.

3. This is a Chinese expression for "disorder," "calamity," and perhaps even the "state of nature."

4. Actually 1200–1300 scholars.

26. Contrast between K'ang and Liang

1*. *Hsin-min ts'ung-pao* [New People's Periodical], 1902.

2*. *Ibid.*

3*. *Kuo-feng pao* [Kuo-feng Newspaper], 1915.

4. This is an overstatement.

5. These phrases are the opening passages of the famous primer for Chinese children, *San-tzu-ching*, the Three-Character-Classic or Trimetrical Classic, composed by Wang Ying-lin (1223–1296), "arranged in 356 alternately rhyming lines of three characters to each, and containing about 500 different characters in all." See Herbert A. Giles' translation: *San Tzu-ching* (*Elementary Chinese*) (2nd ed.; Shanghai, 1910). Mr. Giles' translation of the opening passages, below, is less literal than mine:

Jen chih ch'u	Men at their birth
Hsing pen shan	are naturally good.
Hsing hsiang chin	Their natures are much the same.
Hsi hsiang yüan	Their habits become widely different.

6. What Liang probably meant to say was: before he himself had mastered a subject in full he already began to teach it to others.

7. Better known as Ch'en Sheng (d. 209 B.C.), who, together with Wu Kuang, rebelled against the Ch'in state. Though supported by a large following, he did not ultimately succeed in overthrowing the Ch'in.

8. Liang's life was marked by frequent excursions into politics, as well as lack of persistence and depth in literary pursuit.

27. T'an Ssu-t'ung (1866–1898)

1. *Vijñānāmātra* is "idealism, the doctrine that nothing exists apart from mind." Cf. William E. Soothill and Lewis Hodous, *A Dictionary of Chinese Buddhist Terms* (London, 1937), p. 344. *Avatamsaka* is also known as *Kegon sūtra*; it holds that "all phenomena are of the same essence as the noumenon." *Ibid.*, p. 270.

2*. *Jen-hsüeh* [The Book on Benevolence], *chüan* 1.

3*. *Ibid., chüan* 2.

4. One of the basic tenets of Confucianism is *cheng-ming*, or Rectification of Names. Confucius believed that disorder arose when the actualities of things did not correspond to their names, and that order might be restored when the actual was made to correspond to its name. He preached that the Emperor must carry out to the full his alloted duties, in accordance with the ideal image of the Emperor; the minister, in accordance with the ideal image of the minister; the father, with the image of the father; and the son, with that of the son. Thus the term *ming-chiao*, literally, "name-ethics," may be rendered into something like "the (objective) norms of social conduct." However, the word *ming* applies not only to social roles but also to patterns of behavior – to the proper relations which must obtain between people in various roles. For a discussion of the Rectification of Names, see Bodde, I, 59–62. Bodde translates *ming-chiao* as "morals and institution." *Ibid.*, II, 170.

5. The three bonds are those between sovereign and subject, between husband and wife, and between father and son. The five relationships are the above and two more: that between friends and that between brothers.

6. Here, *ming* seems to denote "notion" rather than "name" or "norm."

7*. His text we do not quote here.

8. Ch'en She, as noted earlier, was better known as Ch'en Sheng (d. 209 B.C.), who revolted against the state of Ch'in. Yang Hsüan-kan (d. 613 A.D.) was among the first to revolt against the Emperor Yang Ti (580–618 A.D.) of the Sui Dynasty.

9. The T'ung-meng Hui was a revolutionary party founded by Sun Yat-sen in 1905. The Kuang-fu Hui was a faction of it which later fused with a part of the Association to Prepare for the Establishment of Constitutional Government to become the United Party, the T'ung-i tang.

28. Chang Ping-lin (1868–1936)

1. Maitreya, also known as Maitreyanatha, is the name of an Indian Buddhist philosopher, not the future Buddha. Vasubandhu is the author of *Abidharmakośa*.

2. *Yoga* means "union, especially an ecstatic union of the individual soul with a divine being." Cf. Soothill, p. 407. The Yogācāra is an esoteric sect.

3*. *Tao-Han wei-yen* [Candid Opinions on the Great Han Learning], last *chüan.*

30. Buddhism in Late Ch'ing

1. The Dharmalaksana is a school of Mahayana Buddhist philosophy which holds that the ultimate reality is a transcendental consciousness (*alaya-vijñana*). The phenomenal forms of reality which we perceive arise out of "seeds" or potentialities inherent in this consciousness, hence they are simply "marks" or "characters" or "signs" (*lakṣana*) of this ultimate reality. This sect holds that all is consciousness "in its ultimate nature." Cf. Soothill, p. 344.

2*. *Tung-yüan chi* [Collection of Tai Chen].

3*. The Literary Collection of Kung Tzu-chen contains A Tribute to Chih-kuei-tzu; Chih-kuei-tzu was P'eng Shao-sheng.

4. The Buddhist commandments are (1) not to kill, (2) not to steal, (3) not to commit adultery, (4) not to speak falsely, (5) not to drink wine, and there are many others. Cf. Soothill, p. 239.

5. The chief tenet of the Sukhāvatī Sect is salvation by faith in Amitābha. The *Avatamsaka* comprised the sermons, according to the teaching of this sect, "first preached by Sākyamuni after enlightenment." *Ibid.*, p. 84. It holds that "all phenomena are of the same essence as the noumenon." *Ibid.*, p. 270.

6. Salvation by faith is contrasted with salvation by works. The former means dependence on "Another's strength, especially that of a Buddha, or Bodhisattva, obtained through faith in Mahayana salvation." *Ibid.*, p. 165. *Heng-ch'ao* (lit., "short cut") means "Happy salvation to Amitābha's paradise through trust in him." *Ibid.*, p. 447.

7*. Chiang Fang-chen, *Ou-chou wen-i fu-hsing shih-tai shih, tzu-hsü* [Preface to A History of the Renaissance Period in Europe].

31. Ch'ing Arts and Literature

1. According to the *Tz'u-yüan, ssu-k'ung ch'eng-tan* (here rendered as "legal document") is a Taoist expression which identifies the Confucian teachings with practical and utilitarian legal codes and regulations.

2. The "double-harness style," known as the *p'ien-wen*, is a kind of parallel prose which flourished during the Six Dynasties, especially during the Ch'i and Liang Dynasties (479–556 A.D.). It is "characterized by a tendency to use four- and six-word parallel phrases, a somewhat florid and artificial style, an emphasis on verbal parallelism, attention to tonal euphony, occasional rhyme, and frequency of allusion. . . . The *Anthology* (*Wen-hsüan*) of Hsiao T'ung (501–531) is the great repository of specimens." Cf. James R. Hightower, *Topics in Chinese Literature* (Cambridge, Mass., 1950), p. 38.

3*. *Jih-chih-lu,* 18.

33. General Conclusions

1*. *Kuang-yang tsa-chi* [Miscellaneous Records of Kuang-yang], *chüan* 5.

Index

REFERENCE MATTER

BIBLIOGRAPHY

GLOSSARY

BIBLIOGRAPHY

[Translator's Note: Sections 14, 15, and 16 in Liang Ch'i-ch'ao's Ch'ing-tai hsüeh-shu kai-lun (pp. 81-99) are bibliographical references to the School of Empirical Research of the middle Ch'ing period. The works cited in these sections do not give information on the dates of authors, volume numbers, and dates of publication. Wherever possible I have supplied this missing information in my translation, although it is not available in every case. My data, however, are not necessarily drawn from the first editions of these works, dependent as I have been on what is to be found in the Chinese-Japanese Library of Harvard University and the Library of Congress. Inaccuracies as to authorship and book titles have been corrected whenever discovered, but a few works are unidentifiable. Because much of my information comes from several major collectanea, I have found it expedient to use abbreviations as follows:

HCCC	Huang-Ch'ing ching-chieh 皇清經解 (Exegesis of the classics in the Imperial Ch'ing period). 1400 chüan; Canton, 1860; compiled by Juan Yüan 阮元 (1764-1849).
HCCCHP	Huang-Ch'ing ching-chieh hsüeh-pien 皇清經解續編 (Supplementary exegesis of the classics in the Imperial Ch'ing period). 1430 chüan; 1888; compiled by Wang Hsien-ch'ien 王先謙 (1842-1917).
KYTS	Kuang-ya ts'ung-shu 廣雅叢書 (Collectanea of Kuang-ya). 154 titles; Canton, 1920; compiled by Hsü Chao-ch'i 徐紹棨.
YYTTS	Yüeh-ya-t'ang ts'ung-shu 粵雅堂叢書 (Collectanea of the Graceful Cantonese Hall). 170 titles; Canton, Hsien-feng period (1851-1861); compiled by Wu Ch'ung-yao 伍崇曜.

References to works included in these collectanea indicate the volumes of the collectanea in which those works appear. Also, I have abbreviated chüan as "ch." throughout.]

[*81] Section 14. Bibliographical Notes on Empirical Research on Classical Studies, Chinese Traditional Linguistics Phonology, Government Regulations and Institutions, History, and Local Gazettes

The core of the Ch'ing school of learning was naturally classical studies, and its greatest contribution in this field was new sub-commentaries for almost all of the classics. For the Book of Changes, these were:

Hui Tung 惠棟 (1697-1758). Chou-I shu 周易述 [A narrative of the Chou Book of Changes]. 21 ch.; HCCC, 75-78.

Chang Hui-yen 張惠言 (1761-1802). Chou-I Yü-shih i 周易虞氏義 [Yu Fan's interpretation of the Chou Book of Changes]. 9 ch.; 1803.

Yao P'ei-chung 姚配中 (1792-1844). Chou-I Yao-shih hsüeh 周易姚氏學 [Mr. Yao's studies of the Chou Book of Changes]. 6 ch.; HCCCHP, 200-202.

With respect to the Book of History, there were:

Chiang Sheng 江聲 (1721-1799). Shang-shu chi chu-yin-shu 尚書集注音疏 [Book of History with selected commentaries, glossaries, and sub-commentary]. 14 ch.; HCCC, 85-90.

Sun Hsing-yen 孫星衍 (1753-1818). Shang-shu chin-ku wen chu-shu 尚書今古文注疏 [Commentary and sub-commentary on the Book of History in ancient and modern texts]. 30 ch.; 1885.

Tuan Yü-ts'ai 段玉裁 (1735-1815). Ku-wen Shang-shu chuan-i 古文尚書撰異 [Philological discriminations of the ancient text of the Book of History]. 3 ch.; HCCC, 134-139.

Wang Ming-sheng 王鳴盛 (1722-1798). Shang-shu hou-an 尚書後案 [Latest study of the Book of History]. 31 ch.; HCCC, 91-102.

With respect to the Book of Odes, there were:

Ch'en Huan 陳奐 (1786-1863). Shih Mao-shih chuan shu 詩毛氏傳疏 [Sub-commentary on Mao's commentary on the Book of Odes]. 30 ch.; Tao-kuang period.

Ma Jui-ch'en 馬瑞辰 (1782-1853). Mao-shih chuan-chien t'ung shih 毛詩傳箋通釋 [A general interpretation of Cheng Hsüan's commentaries on Mao's Book of Odes]. 32 ch.; HCCCHP, 94-102.

Hu Ch'eng-kung 胡承珙 (1776-1832). Mao-shih hou-chien 毛詩後箋 [Restudy of Mao's Book of Odes]. 30 ch.; HCCCHP, 103-115.

With respect to the Officials of Chou 周官 , there was:

Sun I-jang 孫詒讓 (1848-1908). Chou-li cheng-i 周禮正義 [True meaning of the Rites of Chou]. 12 ts'e; 1907.

With respect to Ceremony and Ritual 儀禮, there were:

Hu Ch'eng-kung 胡承珙 (1776-1832). I-li chin-ku-wen shu-i 儀禮今古文疏義 [Elucidation of the meaning of the Ceremony and Ritual in ancient and modern texts]. 17 ch.; HCCCHP, 116-117.

Hu P'ei-hui 胡培翬 (1782-1849). I-li cheng-i 儀禮正義 [True meaning of the Ceremony and Ritual]. 40 ch.; Shanghai, 1934.

With respect to the Tso Commentary [on the Spring and Autumn Annals], there was:

Liu Wen-ch'i 劉文淇 (1789-1854). Ch'un-ch'iu Tso-shih-chuan cheng-i 春秋左氏傳正義 [Correct interpretation of the Tso Commentary on the Spring and Autumn Annals].

With respect to the Kung-yang Commentary [on the Spring and Autumn Annals], there were:

K'ung Kuang-sen 孔廣森 (1752-1786). Ch'un-ch'iu Kung-yang t'ung-i 春秋公羊通義 [A general treatise on the Kung-yang Commentary on the Spring and Autumn Annals]. 13 ch.; HCCC, 171-174.

Ch'en Li 陳立 (1810-1882). Kung-yang i-shu 公羊義疏 [Elucidation of the ideas in the Kung-yang Commentary]. 76 ch.; Shanghai, 1934.

With respect to the Analects, there was:

Liu Pao-nan 劉寶楠 (1791-1855). Lun-yü cheng-i 論語正義 [True meaning of the Analects]. 24 ch.; 1934.

With respect to the Classic of Filial Piety 孝經, there was:

P'i Hsi-jui 皮錫瑞 (1850-1908). Hsiao-ching Cheng-shih Chu 孝經鄭氏注 [Sub-commentary on the Cheng Commentary on the Classic of Filial Piety]. 2 ch.; 1907.

[*82] With respect to the Erh-ya 爾雅 [A classified glossary], there were:

Shao Chin-han 邵晉涵 (1743-1796). Erh-ya cheng-i 爾雅正義 [True meaning of the Erh-ya]. 20 ch.; HCCC, 118-121.

Hao I-hsing 郝懿行 (1757-1825). Erh-ya i-shu 爾雅義疏 [Commentary on the meaning of the Erh-ya]. 20 ch.; HCCC, 286-289.

With respect to the Mencius, there was:

Chiao Hsün 焦循 (1763-1820). Men-tzu cheng-i 孟子正義 [True meaning of the Mencius]. 30 ch.; HCCC, 247-252.

Among the above works, only those by Ma Jui-ch'en and Hu Ch'eng-kung on the Book of Odes were not treatises on the complete text and [only those], therefore, cannot virtually be called new sub-commentaries. The various writers on the Book of Changes merely echoed the views of Han scholars and did not speak as philologists. The one Ch'ing scholar who was truly expert in expounding the Changes was Chiao Hsün, whose works--I-t'ung shih 易通釋 [General interpretation of the Changes, 20 ch.; HCCC, 241-245], I-t'u-lüeh 易圖略 [An outline of diagrams in the Changes, 8 ch.; HCCC, 246], and I-chang-chü 易章句 [An annotated text of the Changes, 12 ch.; HCCC, 240] -- were quite lucid, perspicuous, excellent, and subtle, but were not in the style of the new sub-commentaries. For the Book of History, the works by the two writers Tuan Yü-ts'ai and Wang Ming-sheng were somewhat crude and superficial; and for the Kung-yang Commentary, except for K'ung Kuang-sen's work which was deficient in knowledge of methodology 家法, all the rest were extensive and comprehensive works of excellence, unsurpassed by those of the ancients. In particular, Chien Chao-liang 簡朝亮 (1851-1933), who came from my area, wrote Shang-shu chi-chu shu-shu 尚書集注述疏 [A narrative sub-commentary on the collected commentaries on the Book of History, 32 + 3 ch.; 1907] and Lun-yü chi-chu pu-cheng shu-shu 論語集注補正述疏 [A narrative sub-commentary to supplement and correct the collected commentaries on the Analects, 10 + 1 ch.], intending to link up the Han and Sung [schools of learning]. Although his method was not that of the Orthodox School, he made many excellent points.

All the Thirteen Classics, except for the Book of Rites and the Ku-liang Commentary, had one or more new sub-commentaries, and the Book of Rites of the Elder Tai had a pu-chu 補注 [supplementary commentary] by K'ung Kuang-shen and a chieh-ku 解詁 [annotation] by Wang P'in-chen 王聘珍. As a rule, these new sub-commentaries captured the essence of the age's classical studies, which were selected and edited with discrimination; they may be called great synthetic works.

As for the remaining specialized works of research, the most famous were:

Hui Shih-ch'i 惠士奇 (1671-1741). Li shuo 禮說 [On rites]. 14 ch.; HCCC, 47-50.

Hu Wei 胡渭 (1633-1714). Yü-kung chui-chih 禹貢錐指 [Guide to the "Yü-kung" gazetteer]. 21 ch.; HCCC, 9-17.

Hui Tung 惠棟 (1697-1758). I-Han-hsüeh 易漢學 [Commentaries on the Changes by scholars of the Han dynasty]. 8 ch.

----- Ku-wen Shang-shu k'ao 古文尚書考 [A study of the Book of History in ancient text]. 2 ch.; 1768.

----- Ming-t'ang ta-tao lu 明堂大道錄 [Principal teachings concerning the Luminous Hall]. 8 ch.; HCCCHP, 38-39.

[*83] Chang Hui-yen 張惠言 (1761-1802). Chou-I Cheng-shih i 周易鄭氏義 [Cheng Hsüan's annotation of the Chou Changes]. 2 ch.; HCCC, 277.

----- (Chou-I) Hsün-shih chiu-chia (周易) 荀氏九家 [Interpretation of the Chou Changes by the Nine Commentators of the Hsün Shang School]. 3 ch.

----- I-i pieh-lu 易義別錄 [A supplementary record of the interpretations of the Changes]. 14 ch.; HCCC, 278-279.

Ch'en Shou-ch'i 陳壽祺 (1771-1834) [and Ch'en Ch'iao-tsung 陳喬樅 (1809-1869)]. San-chia-shih i-shuo k'ao 三家詩遺說考 [A study of the legacy of the three schools of Odes]. 14 ch.; HCCCHP, 245-256.

Chiang Yung 江永 (1681-1762). Chou-li i-i chü-yao 周禮疑義舉要 [Essential questions concerning certain doubtful passages in the Rites of Chou]. 7 ch.; HCCC, 56.

Tai Chen 戴震 (1724-1777). K'ao-kung-chi t'u 考工記圖 [Empirical study of the chapter on ancient craftsmanship in the Book of Rites, with illustrations]. 2 ch.; HCCC, 132.

Tuan Yü-ts'ai 段玉裁 (1735-1815). Chou-li I-li Han-tu k'ao 周禮儀禮漢讀考 [An examination of the Han reading of the Rites of Chou and Ceremony and Ritual]. 6 + 1 ch.; HCCC, 143-144.

Chang Hui-yen 張惠言 (1761-1802). I-li-t'u 儀禮圖 [Pictorial illustrations of Ceremony and Ritual]. 6 ch.; HCCCHP, 75-77.

Ling T'ing-k'an 凌廷堪 (1755-1809). Li-ching shih-li 禮經釋例 [Explanation of the Ceremony and Ritual]. 13 ch.; HCCC, 188-191.

Chin Pang 金榜 (1735-1801). Li-chien 禮箋 [Commentary on the Rites]. 3 ch.; HCCC, 130.

K'ung Kuang-sen 孔廣森 (1752-1786). Li-hsüeh chih-yen 禮學卮言 [Empirical studies of the Rites from all angles]. 6 ch.

Wu I 武億 (1745-1799). San-li i-cheng 三禮義證 [Textual research on the meaning of the three Rites]. 12 ch.

Chin O 金鶚. Ch'iu-ku-lu li-shuo 求古錄禮說 [Antiquarian researches: on Rites]. HCCCHP, 144-148.

Huang I-chou 黃以周. Li-shu t'ung-ku 禮書通故 [Comprehensive study of ancient literature relating to the Book of Rites]. 100 ch.; 1893.

Wang Yin-chih 王引之 (1766-1834). Ch'un-ch'iu ming-tzu chieh-ku 春秋名字解詁 [A philological interpretation of names and derived names in the Spring and Autumn Annals]. 2 ch.

Hou K'ang 侯康 (1798-1837). Ku-liang li-cheng 穀梁禮證 [Textual research on the Rites according to the Ku-liang Commentary]. 2 ch.; HCCCHP, 211.

Chiang Yung 江永 (1681-1762). Hsiang-tang-t'u-k'ao 鄉黨圖考 [On the tenth chapter of the Analects, with plates]. 10 ch.; HCCC, 59-61.

Wang Yin-chih 王引之 (1766-1834). Ching-i shu-wen 經義述聞 [Interpretation of the classics heard (from my father)]. 32 ch.; 1797.

Ch'en Shou-ch'i 陳壽祺 (1771-1834). Tso-hai ching-pien 左海經辨 [Examination of the classics by Ch'en Shou-ch'i]. 2 ch.; HCCC, 283.

Ch'eng Yao-t'ien 程瑤田 (1725-1814). T'ung-i lu 通藝錄 [Collection of classical studies]. 24 titles; 1933.

Chiao Hsün 焦循 (1763-1820). Ch'ün-ching kung-shih t'u 羣經宮室圖 [Diagrammatic reconstruction of classical buildings]. 2 ch.; HCCCHP, 85.

There were no less than several hundred excellent pieces of work like the above.

Ch'ing scholars looked upon linguistics as a gateway to the study of the classics and were profoundly devoted to it; thus, this ancillary subject grew into a major field. With respect to the Shuo-wen 說文 [Explanation of script], there were:

Tuan Yü-ts'ai 段玉裁 (1735-1815). Shuo-wen (chieh-tzu) chu 說文(解字)注 [Annotations on the Explanation of Script]. 15 ch.; HCCC, 145-159.

Kuei Fu 桂馥 (1736-1805). Shuo-wen i-cheng 說文義證 [Textual study of the ideas in the Explanation of Script].

Wang Yün 王筠 (1784-1854). Shuo-wen shih-li 說文釋例 [Explanation of the Explanation of Script]. 20 ch.; 1883.

-----Shuo-wen chü-tu 說文句讀 [Philological studies of the syntax of the Explanation of Script]. 14 ts'e; 1865.

Chu Chün-sheng 朱駿聲 (1788-1858). Shuo-wen t'ung hsün ting-sheng 說文通訓定聲 [Ascertaining the sound and meaning of the Explanation of Script]. 19 ch.; 1848.

With respect to works in the ancient script, in addition to the Explanation of Script, there were:

Tai Chen 戴震 (1724-1777). Fan-yen shu-cheng 方言疏證 [Commentary on the Dialects]. 13 ch.; 1933.

Chiang Sheng 江聲 (1721-1799) and Pi Yüan 畢沅 (1730-1797). Shih-ming shu-cheng 釋名疏證 [Textual research on the Explanation of Names]. 8 ch.; 1790.

[*84] Sung Hsiang-feng 宋翔鳳. Hsiao-erh-ya hsün-ts'uan 小爾雅訓纂 [Philological compilation of the Small Erh-ya]. 6 ch.; HCCCHP, 92.

Hu Ch'eng-kung 胡承珙 (1776-1832). Hsiao-erh-ya i-cheng 小爾雅義證 [Textual research on the meaning of the Small Erh-ya]. 13 ch.; 1903.

Wang Nien-sun 王念孫 (1744-1832). Kuang-ya shu-cheng 廣雅疏證 [Textual research on the Kuang-ya]. 10 ch.; HCCC, 163-170.

These works were somewhat similar in style to the two sub-commentaries [cited above] by Shao Chin-han and Hao I-hsing. To have access to them is to dissolve almost all problems and obstacles in the use of the dictionaries written prior to the Six Dynasties (221-589). But the best and most incisive works, which applied extremely rigorous philological methods to a number of books thoroughly and reached a comprehensive mastery of them, were Wang Nien-sun's Ching-chuan shih-tz'u 經傳釋詞 [Explanation of the particles in the classics and commentaries, 10 ch.; 1819] and Yü Yüeh's 俞樾 (1821-1907) Ku-shu i-i chü-li 古書疑義舉例 [Inquiry into ancient works, with examples]. In modern times, Chang Ping-lin's 章炳麟 (1868-1936) Hsiao-hsüeh wen-ta 小學問答 [Questions and answers in linguistics] had even more new insights and interpretations. Ma Chien-chung 馬建忠 (1844-1900), in a spirit of emulation [of these scholars], wrote Wen-t'ung 文通 [A grammar of composition] and Yen Fu 嚴復 (1853-1921) did likewise, writing Ying-wen Han-ku 英文漢詁 [English grammar in Chinese], which became the embryo of [Chinese] grammatical studies, 文典學. In addition, Liang Ch'i-ch'ao's 梁啟超 (1873-1929) Kuo-wen yü-yüan chieh 國文語原解 [Explanation of the etymology of our national language] frequently reflected [principles of] sociology.

Phonology was, in turn, an adjunct of linguistics particularly flourishing during the Ch'ing period, beginning with:

Ku Yen-wu 顧炎武 (1613-1682). Yin-lun 音論 [Phonology]. 1 ch.; HCCC, 1.

----- Ku-yin piao 古音表 [Tables of ancient phonology]. 3 ch.; 1667.

----- T'ang-yün cheng 唐韻正 [Rectification of the T'ang rhymes]. 20 ch.; 1667.

Chiang Yung 江永 (1681-1762). Yin-hsüeh pien-wei 音學辨微 [Detailed study of phonology]. 1 ch.; 1934.

----- Ku-yün piao-chun 古韻標準 [Standards of ancient phonology]. 4 ch.; 1789.

Tai Chen 戴震 (1724-1777). Sheng-yün k'ao 聲韻考 [Study of phonetics]. 4 ch.; 1936.

----- Sheng-lui piao 聲類表 [Classified tables of initials]. 9 ch.; 1936.

Tuan Yü-ts'ai 段玉裁 (1735-1815). Liu-shu yin-yün piao 六書

音韻表 [Phonetic tables of the Six Scripts]. 5 ch.; HCCC, 160.

Yao Wen-t'ien 姚文田 (1758-1827). Shuo-wen sheng-hsi 說文聲系 [Rhymed grouping of characters in the Explanation of Script]. 14 ch.; 1821-1874.

Miao K'uei 苗夔. Shuo-wen sheng-tu piao 說文聲讀表 [Tables of the pronunciation of sounds in the Explanation of Script]. 17 ch.; HCCCHP, 212.

Yen K'o-chün 嚴可均 (1762-1843). Shuo-wen sheng-lui 說文聲類 [Classification of rhymes in the Explanation of Script]. 17 ch.; HCCCHP, 87.

Ch'en Li 陳澧 (1810-1882). Ch'ieh-yün-k'ao 切韻考 [A study of sound combinations]. 9 ch.; 1856, 1884.

The various chapters on phonology in Chang Ping-lin's Kuo-ku lun-heng 國故論衡 [Essays on traditional learning] are all uniquely excellent. The original intention of these [phonological] studies was the investigation of ancient sounds, but the more they extended in range, the [*85] more minute they became, and finally reached the ultimate goal of studying the structure of the human vocal organs and the formulations of laws of sound-inflection. Liu Hsien-t'ing's 劉獻廷 (1648-1695) Hsin-yün p'u 新韻譜 [Characters arranged by rhyme according to modern pronunciation] created alphabets, but [unfortunately] this book was not transmitted. More recently, a general agreement has been reached after collective discussion among scholars in this field, and the result was the promulgation of the Phonetic Symbols.

The study of government regulations and institutions was also a unique achievement of the Ch'ing period, motivated at first by the examination of the three Rites but afterward extended far more widely. Hui Tung 惠棟 (1697-1758) wrote the Ming-t'ang ta-tao lu 明堂大

道錄 [Principle teachings concerning the Luminous Hall], marking the beginning of monographic works which examined a single aspect of ancient institutions exclusively. Hsü Ch'ien-hsüeh 徐乾學 (1631-1694) compiled the Tu-li t'ung-k'ao 讀禮通考 [A general inquiry into the study of the Rites] and Ch'in Hui-t'ien 秦蕙田 (1702-1764) compiled the Wu-li t'ung-k'ao 五禮通考 [A general inquiry into the five Rites]; most parts of these works came from the hands of famous scholars of that time. Later writings were:

Hu K'uang-chung 胡匡衷. I-li shih-kuan 儀禮釋官 [Explanation of the functionary system in the various principalities as mentioned in Ceremonies and Rites]. 9 ch.; HCCC, 186-187.

Tai Chen 戴震 (1724-1777). K'ao-kung chi t'u chu 考工記圖注 [Empirical study of the chapter on ancient craftsmanship in the Rites of Chou, with pictures]. 3 ch.; HCCC, 132.

Shen T'ung 沈彤 (1688-1752). Chou-kuan lu-t'ien k'ao 周官祿田考 [A study of emolument-land in the Rites of Chou]. 3 ch.; HCCC, 72.

Wang Ming-sheng 王鳴盛 (1722-1798). Chou-li chün-fu shuo 周禮軍賦說 [An explanation of military taxes in the Rites of Chou]. 4 ch.; HCCC, 103.

Hung I-hsüan 洪頤煊 (1765-1837). Li-ching kung-shih ta-wen 禮經宮室答問 [Questions and answers about palace chambers in Ceremony and Ritual].

Jen Ta-ch'un 任大椿 (1738-1789). Pien-fu shih-li 弁服釋例 [Explanation and illustration of hats and attires]. 8 ch.; HCCC, 116-117.

-----Shen-i shih-li 深衣釋例 [Explanation of sacrificial uniform]. 2 ch.; HCCCHP, 44.

All the above works were annotations to the Rites only, but Chiao

Hsün's Ch'ün-ching kung-shih t'u and Ch'eng Yao-t'ien's T'ung-i lu [cited above] covered various classics. In the late Ch'ing, Huang I-chou's 黄以周 Li-shu t'ung-ku 禮書通故 [Understanding the past through the Book of Rites] had particularly wide scope and incisive judgment; he was truly a vigorous later exponent of the study of the Rites in the Ch'ing period.

The study of the "principle of music" almost developed into a major field too, beginning with Mao Ch'i-ling's 毛奇齡 (1623-1716) Ching-shan yüeh-lu 竟山樂錄 [A record of (my father) Ching-shan's music, 4 ch.; 1776]. It was followed by:

[*86] Chiang Yung 江永 (1681-1762). Lü-lü hsin-lun 律呂新論 [New discourse on musical principles]. 2 ch.; 1843.

----- Lü-lü ch'an-wei 律呂闡微 [Exposition of the abstruse musical principles]. 10 ch.

Chiang Fan 江藩 (1761-1831). Yüeh-hsien k'ao 樂縣考 [A study of ancient musical bells]. 2 ch.; Hsien-feng period (1851-1861); YYTTS, 206.

Ling T'ing-k'an 凌廷堪 (1757-1809). Yen-yüeh k'ao-yüan 燕樂考原 [An inquiry into the origin of sacrificial music]. 6 ch.; YYTTS, 94-96.

Ch'en Li 陳澧 (1810-1882). Sheng-lü t'ung-k'ao 聲律通考 [General examination of the principles of rhymes]. 10 ch.; 1860.

[The last named] was the latest and the best.

All of them were sufficiently good material for the writing of a future history of Chinese music. Chiao Hsün wrote On Drama 劇說 which emphasized the study of the historical background of modern music; it is eminently practical and useful.

The various masters of the early Ch'ing all studied history with the intent of using it in governing the nation. Wang Fu-chih 王夫之

(1619-1692) was skilled in historical discourse; his Tu T'ung-chien lun 讀通鑑論 [Remarks on reading the Comprehensive Mirror, 30 ch.] and Sung lun 宋論 [Remarks on the (Chao) Sung, 15 ch.] both revealed extraordinary insight, although later historians did not follow his model. Huang Tsung-hsi 黃宗羲 (1610-1695) and Wan Ssu-t'ung 萬斯同 (1638-1702) assigned to themselves the task of writing the history [for the Ming dynasty] and they were, in fact, the direct heirs of the traditional historical learning. In the K'ang-hsi period (1662-1722), the Ch'ing court set up the Bureau for the Compilation of Ming History, 明史館, to attract scholars remaining [from the Ming dynasty]. Although the various masters did not accept appointments in it, still, because of their ready knowledge and a desire to express their nostalgia for the "ancien regime," they participated in its functions indirectly, by collectively discussing the style and structure [of the Ming History] as well as the selection of material. Therefore, of all the officially compiled histories since the T'ang, the Ming History was exceptionally complete and superb. After the Ch'ien-lung period (1736-1796), the most outstanding scion of this school was Ch'üan Tsu-wang 全祖望 (1705-1755). Ku Yen-wu's historical studies frequently discussed the merits and failings of government regulations, institutions, and customs, although he was also partial to textual research.

From the Ch'ien-lung and Chia-ch'ing periods (1736-1820), the School of Empirical [Textual] Research held sway over the academic world, and its powerful surge could not fail to reach historical studies, to wit:

Chao I 趙翼 (1727-1814). Nien-erh-shih cha-chi 廿二史劄記 [Notes on the Twenty-Two Histories]. 36 ch.; 1894.

Wang Ming-sheng 王鳴盛 (1722-1798). Shih-ch'i-shih shang-chüeh 十七史商榷 [Discussions of the Seventeen Histories]. 100 ch.; preface, 1789.

[*87] Ch'ien Ta-hsin 錢大昕 (1728-1804). Erh-shih-erh-shih k'ao-i 二十二史考異 [An inquiry into the errors among the Twenty-Two Histories]. 100 ch.; 1782.

Hung I-hsüan 洪頤煊 (1765-1837). Chu-shih k'ao-i 諸史考異 [An inquiry into the errors among the various histories]. 18 ch.; 1920.

All of these works were influenced by [textual research], and all four were somewhat similar in style and structure, as they all had the common aim of investigating historical vestiges empirically and collating and correcting errors. Chao's work, however, frequently listed a number of historical episodes at the end of [his treatment of] each dynasty for an inductive comparative study, in order to discover the causes of [dynastic] vitality and decadence, order and disorder; this was its outstanding feature. As for works of empirical research on the history of a single period, the more famous were:

Hui Tung 惠棟 (1697-1758). Hou-Han-shu pu-chu 後漢書補注 [Supplementary commentary on the History of the Later Han]. 24 ch.; KYTS, 186-197.

Liang Yü-sheng 梁玉繩 (1745-1819). Shih-chi chih-i 史記志異 [Notes on ambiguous points in the Historical Records]. 36 ch.; 1787; KYTS, 144-157.

----- Han-shu jen-piao k'ao 漢書人表考 [A study of the "Tables of Persons" in the History of the Han]. 9 ch.; KYTS, 181-184.

Ch'ien Tao-chao 錢大昭 (1744-1813). Han-shu pien-i 漢書辨疑 [An anatomy of the doubtful points in the History of the Han]. 22 ch.; KYTS,164-168.

----- Hou-Han-shu pien-i 後漢書辨異 [An anatomy of the doubtful points in the History of the Later Han]. 11 ch.; KYTS, 198-199.

-----Hsü-Han-shu pien-i 續漢書辨疑 [An anatomy of the doubtful points in the Supplementary History of the Han]. 9 ch.; KYTS, 200.

Liang Chang-chü 梁章鉅 (1775-1849). San-kuo-chih p'ang-cheng 三國志旁證 [Indirect evidence with respect to the Record of the Three Kingdoms]. 30 ch.; KYTS, 209-214.

Chou Shou-ch'ang 周壽昌 (1814-1884). Han-shu-chu chiao-pu 漢書注校補 [Collation and supplement to the Commentary on the History of the Han].

-----Hou-Han-shu-chu pu-cheng 後漢書註補正 [Supplementary correction of the Commentary on the History of the Later Han]. 8 ch.; KYTS, 201.

Hang Shih-chün 杭世駿 (1696-1773). San-kuo-chih pu-chu 三國志補注 [Supplementary commentary on the Record of the Three Kingdoms]. 6 ch.; YYTTS, 293-294.

Since Wan Ssu-t'ung emphatically proclaimed the importance of tables and monographs and wrote Li-tai shih-piao 歷代史表 [Historical tables of the various dynasties], there have been quite a number of readable specialized works on tables and monographs:

Ku Tung-kao 顧棟高 (1679-1759). Ch'un-ch'iu ta-shih piao 春秋大事表 [Tables of major events in the Spring and Autumn period]. 67 ch.; HCCCHP, 18-34.

Ch'ien Ta-chao 錢大昭 (1744-1813). Hou-Han-shu pu-piao 後漢書補表 [Supplementary tables of the History of the Later Han]. 8 ch.; KYTS, 253-255.

Chou Chia-yu 周嘉猷 (1751-1796). Nan-pei shih-piao 南北史表 [Historical tables of Southern and Northern dynasties]. 7 ch.; KYTS, 287-290.

-----San-kuo chi-nien piao 三國紀年表 [Chronological

tables of the Three Kingdoms]. 1 ch.; KYTS, 264.

-----Wu-tai chi-nien piao 五代紀年表 [Chronological tables of the Five Dynasties]. 1 ch.

Hung I-sun 洪飴孫 (1773-1816). San-kuo chih-kuan piao 三國職官表 [Tables of official posts in the Three Kingdoms]. 3 ch.; KYTS, 261-263.

Ch'ien Ta-hsin 錢大昕 (1728-1804). Yüan-shih shih-tsu piao 元史氏族表 [Tables of clans and tribes in the History of Yüan]. 3 ch.; KYTS, 297-298.

Ch'i Chao-nan 齊召南 . Li-tai ti-wang nien-piao 歷代帝王年表 [Chronological tables of the emperors and kings of the various dynasties]. 3 ch.; YYTTS, 137-139.

[*88] Lin Ch'un-p'u 林春溥 (b. 1775). Chu-po shan-fang shih-wu-chung 竹柏山房十五種 [Fifteen works of the Mountain-House amidst Bamboos and Cedars]; 1855. All of these [fifteen works] studied ancient history, and its chapters on the "Chronology of the Warring States," 戰國紀年, and "Chronological Tables of Confucius and Mencius," 孔孟年表, had particularly excellent judgment.

As regards officially sponsored work, there were:

Li-tai chih-kuan piao 歷代職官表 [Tables of government posts in successive dynasties]. 72 ch.; 1784.

Hung Liang-chi 洪亮吉 (1746-1809). Pu San-kuo chiang-yü chih 補三國疆域志 [Monograph on the territorial boundaries of the Three Kingdoms]. 2 ch.; KYTS, 260.

----- Tung-Chin chiang-yü chih 東晉疆域志 [Monograph on the territorial boundary of Eastern Chin]. 4 ch.; KYTS, 268-269.

----- Shih-liu kuo chiang-yü chih 十六國疆域志 [Mono-

graph on the territorial boundaries of the Sixteen States].
16 ch.; KYTS, 270-273.

Hung Ch'i-sun 洪齮孫 (1804-1859). Pu Liang chiang-yü chih 補梁疆域志 [Supplementary monograph on the territorial boundary of Liang]. 4 ch.; KYTS, 284-285.

Ch'ien I-chi 錢儀吉 (1783-1850). Pu Chin ping-chih 補晉兵志 [Supplementary monograph on the military of Chin]. 1 ch.; KYTS, 265.

Hou K'ang 侯康 (1798-1837). Pu San-kuo i-wen-chih 補三國藝文志 [Supplementary bibliography on the Three Kingdoms]. 4 ch.; 1877.

Ni Ts'an 倪燦 (1627-1688). Sung-shih i-wen-chih pu 宋史藝文志補 [Supplementary bibliography on the History of Sung]. 1 ch.; KYTS, 293.

----- Pu Liao-Chin-Yüan san-shih i-wen-chih 補遼金元三史藝文志 [Supplementary bibliography on the Three Histories of Liao, Chin, and Yüan]. 1 ch.; KYTS, 294.

Ku Huai-san 顧懷三 . Pu Wu-tai-shih i-wen-chih 補五代史藝文志 [Supplementary bibliography on the Histories of the Five Dynasties]. 1 ch.; 1897.

Ch'ien Ta-hsin 錢大昕 (1728-1804). Pu Yüan-shih i-wen-chih 補元史藝文志 [Supplementary bibliography on the History of Yüan]. 4 ch.; 1936-1937.

Hao I-hsing 郝懿行 (1757-1825). Pu Sung-shu hsing-fa-chih shih-huo-chih 補宋書刑法志食貨志 [Supplementary monographs on punishment and finance in the History of the (Liu) Sung]. 2 ch.; 1936-1937.

All these can be considered good works. As to the unofficial and miscellaneous histories, 別史雜史 , of ancient periods, there were also many works of textual research and commentaries:

Ch'en Feng-heng 陳逢衡 (1778-1855). I Chou-shu pu-chu 逸周書補注 [Supplementary commentary on the Lost Book of Chou]. 22 ch.; 1825.

Chu Yu-tseng 朱右曾 . I Chou-shu chi-hsün chiao-shih 逸周書集訓校釋 [Collected philological collation and interpretation of the Lost Book of Chou]. 10 ch.

Ting Tsung-lo 丁宗洛 . I Chou-shu kuan-chien 逸周書管箋 [Commentary on the Lost Book of Chou]. 10 ch.; 1830.

Hung Liang-chi 洪亮吉 (1746-1809). Kuo-yü chu-shu 國語注疏 [Commentary on the famous discourses of the Various States of the Tso-chuan].

Huang P'ei-lieh 黃丕烈 (1763-1825). Kuo-yü cha-chi 國語札記 [Notes on Kuo-yü]. 1 ch.

----- Chan-kuo ts'e cha-chi 戰國策札記 [Notes on the Strategies of the Warring States]. 3 ch.

Ch'eng En-tse 程恩澤 (1785-1837). Kuo-ts'e ti-ming k'ao 國策地名考 [A study of place names in the Strategies of the Warring States].

Hao I-hsing 郝懿行 (1757-1825). Shan-hai-ching chien-shu 山海經箋疏 [Commentary on the Classic of Mountains and Seas]. 18 ch.; 1879-1884.

Ch'en Feng-heng 陳逢衡 (1778-1885). Chu-shu chi-nien chi-cheng 竹書記年集証 [Collected commentary on the Bamboo Annals]. 48 ch.; 1813.

Coming down to the late Ch'ing, the study of the History of the Yüan suddenly became a vogue of the time:

Ho Ch'iu-t'ao 何秋濤 (1824-1862). Yüan Sheng-wu ch'in-cheng-lu 元聖武親征錄 [Records of imperial expeditions during the Yüan period]. 1 ch.; 1896.

Li Wen-t'ien 李文田 (1834-1895). Yüan-mi-shih chu 元秘史注 [Commentary on the Secret History of Yüan]. 15 ch.

Because all of these works transferred the methods of textual research used for the classics to the study of history, they can fittingly be termed works of textual research rather than historical works. The only [*89] one that concentrated exclusively on historical methods was Chang Hsüeh-ch'eng's 章學誠 (1738-1801) Wen-shih t'ung-i 文史通義 [General principles of literature and history], which is as valuable as Liu Chih-chi's 劉知幾 (661-721) Shih-t'ung 史通 [Study of historiography].

Since the T'ang period, a private individual has seldom written a dynastic history single-handed, but Wan Ssu-t'ung's Draft History of the Ming was a great masterpiece, and Wei Yüan 魏源 (1794-1856), also unaided, rewrote the History of the Yüan. K'o Shao-min's 柯劭忞 (1850-1933) Hsin Yüan-shih 新元史 [New history of the Yüan] was another masterpiece of more recent origin, and Wei Yüan also wrote Sheng-wu chi 聖武記 [Records of the imperial military exploits, 14 ch.; 1842], which systematically recorded the major events of the Ch'ing dynasty. Pi Yüan's 畢沅 (1730-1797) Hsü Tzu-chih t'ung-chien 續資治通鑑 [Supplementary comprehensive mirror for the aid of government] is another piece of good work.

Huang Tsung-hsi first wrote the Ming-ju hsüeh-an 明儒學案 [Collected writings of the Ming Confucianists] which became the progenitor of [Chinese] intellectual history, 學史 . His Sung-Yüan hsüeh-an 宋元學案 [Collected writings of Sung and Yüan philosophers] was supplemented and completed by his son Po-chia 百家 (b. 1643) and Ch'üan Tsu-wang, in turn. These were all shining beacons in Ch'ing historical studies.

A local gazetteer may be regarded as a miniature history. At the height of the Ch'ing period, all provinces, prefectures, and counties prided themselves on the compilation of gazetteers, most of which were accomplished by learned hands. For the various provincial gazetteers, Juan Yüan 阮元 (1764-1849) was the editor-in-chief of the Chekiang Gazetteer, the Kwangtung Gazetteer, and the Yünnan Gazetteer, and Hsieh Ch'i-k'un 謝啟昆 (1737-1802) of the Kwangsi Gazetteer. The Hupei Gazetteer was originally drafted by Chang Hsüeh-ch'eng. Among the prefecture and county gazetteers, there were:

Tai Chen 戴震 (1724-1777). Fen-chou Prefecture Gazetteer 汾州府志. 34 ch.; 1771.

[*90] Hung Liang-chi 洪良吉 (1746-1809). Ching County Gazetteer 涇縣志. 40 ch.; 1914.

----- Ch'un-hua County Gazetteer 淳化縣志. 30 ch.; 1784.

Sun Hsing-yen 孫星衍 (1753-1818). San-shui County Gazetteer 三水縣志. 11 ch.; 1785.

Ch'ien Tien 錢坫 (1744-1806). Chao-i County Gazetteer 朝邑縣志. 11 ch.; 1780.

Sung Hsing-yen and T'ang Yü-tso 湯毓倬. Yen shih Gazetteer 偃師縣志. 30 ch.

Wu I 武億 (1745-1799). An-yang Gazetteer 安陽縣志. 14 ch.; 1799.

Tuan Yü-ts'ai 段玉裁 (1735-1815). Fu-shun County Gazetteer 富順縣志. 5 ch.; 1882.

Chang Hsüeh-ch'eng 章學誠 (1738-1801). Ho-chou Gazetteer 和州志. 8 ch.

Jen Shou-shih 任壽世. Po-chou Gazetteer 亳州志. 44 ch.; 1825.

Chang Hsüeh-ch'eng 章學誠 (1738-1801). Yung-ch'ing County Gazetteer 永清縣志. 25 ch.; 1779.

-----T'ieh-men County Gazetteer 天門縣志. 24 ch.; 1765.

Li Chao-lo 李兆洛 (1769-1841). Feng-t'ai County Gazetteer 鳳台縣志. 10 ch.

Chang Yu-ch'eng 章祐誠. Changsha Gazetteer 長沙縣志.

Cheng Chen 鄭珍 (1806-1864) and Mo Yu-chih 莫友芝 (1811-1871). Tsun-i Prefecture Gazetteer 遵義府志. 49 ch.; 1841.

All these authors were the élite of their time, and their works possessed rare organization and incisive judgment. Their discussions of [the gazetteer] style and structure were quite complete and minute, and may be seen in their respective literary collections. He who wants to know the characteristics of the Ch'ing historians should look for them here.

Section 15. Bibliographical Notes on Empirical Research on Geography, Astronomy, and Mathematics

Ku Yen-wu and Liu Hsien-t'ing were addicted to geography, although their writings [on this subject] were never completed. Ku Tsu-yü's 顧祖禹 (1631-1692) Tu-shih fang-yü chi-yao 讀史方輿紀要 [Essentials of historical geography, 30 ch.] gave an exhaustive description of [Chinese] topography and strategic places and was unsurpassed by later writers. Thus, geographical studies in the middle Ch'ing tended to emphasize the antiquarian aspect also. After Tai Chen wrote Shui-ti-chi 水地記 [A record of waterways and topography, 1 ch.] and collated [texts of] the Shui-ching chu 水經注 [Commentary on the Water Classic], the Water Classic became the central topic of studies:

K'ung Chi-han 孔繼涵 (1739-1784). Shui-ching shih-ti 水經釋地 [The Water Classic as a geographical guide]. 8 ch.; Kuang-hsü period.

Ch'üan Tsu-wang 全祖望 (1705-1755). Ch'i-chiao shui-ching-chu 七校水經注 [Seven-times collated Commentary on the Water Classic]. 40 ch.; 1888.

[*91] Chao I-ch'ing 趙一清 (1710?-1764?). Shui-ching-chu shih 水經注釋 [Interpretation of the Commentary on the Water Classic]. 40 ch.; 1794.

Chang K'uang-hsüeh 張匡學. Shui-ching-chu shih-ti 水經注釋地 [Study of geography in terms of the Commentary on the Water Classic]. 43 ch.; 1897.

More recently, Yang Shou-ching's 楊守敬 (1839-1915) Shui-ching-chu shu Yao-shan 水經注疏要刪 [Sub-commentary on the Commentary on the Water Classic, 40 ch.; 1895] was distinctive for its great synthesis of all these studies (not published entirely; what was published was only an outline of this work, 注疏要刪), and Ch'i Shao-nan's 齊召南 (1706-1768) Shui-tao t'i-kang 水道提綱 [An outline of waterways] undertook to study modern geography in terms of waterways, while both Hung I-hsüan's 洪頤煊 (1765-1837) Han-chih shui-tao shu-cheng 漢志水道疏証 [Elucidation on the waterways as discussed in the History of the Han] and Ch'en Li's 陳澧 (1810-1882) Han-shu ti-li-chih shui-tao t'u-shuo 漢書地理志水道圖說 [Maps and explanations of waterways as discussed in the monograph on geography in the History of the Han] also studied the Han geography in terms of waterways.

The following are works of empirical studies of the pre-Ch'in geography:

Yen Jo-chü 閻若璩 (1636-1704). Ssu-shu shih-ti 四書釋地 [Elucidation of geographical names in the Four Books]. 4 ch.; HCCC, 5-7.

Hsü Shan 徐善. Ch'un-ch'iu ti-ming k'ao-lüeh 春秋地名考略 [A brief study of place names in the Spring and Autumn Annals].

Chiang Yung 江永 (1681-1762). Ch'un-ch'iu ti-ming k'ao-shih 春秋地名考實 [Verification of place names in the Spring and Autumn Annals]. 4 ch.; HCCC, 57.

Chiao Hsün 焦循 (1763-1820). Mao-shih ti-li shih 毛詩地理釋 [Elucidation of geography according to the Mao Odes].

Ch'eng En-tse 程恩澤 (1785-1837). Kuo-ts'e ti-ming k'ao 國策地名考 [A study of place names in the Strategies of the Warring States]. 20 ch.; YYTTS, 199-203.

As for empirical studies of geography as contained in the various dynastic histories, the best comprehensive works were:

Wu Cho-hsin 吳卓信 (1755-1823). Han-shu ti-li-chih pu-chu 漢書地理志補注 [A supplementary commentary on the monograph on geography in the History of the Han]. 103 ch.; 1936-1937.

Yang Shou-ching 楊守敬 (1839-1914). Sui-shu ti-li-chih k'ao-cheng 隋書地理志考證 [A documentary study of the monograph on geography in the History of the Sui]. 10 ch.; 1936-1937.

General studies [of the geography] of the successive dynasties included:

Ch'en Fan-chi 陳芳績. Li-tai ti-li yen-ko piao 歷代地理沿革表 [Evolutionary tables of the geography of the successive dynasties]. 47 ch.; 1668; KYTS, 374-391.

Li Chao-lo 李兆洛 (1769-1841). Li-tai ti-li-chih yün-pien chin-shih 歷代地理志韵編今釋 [Geographical names from the monographs on geography of the successive dynasties arranged according to rhymes, with modern identifications]. 20 ch.; 1870.

The above two works are convenient to use. [Other general studies are:]

Yang Shou-ching 楊守敬 (1839-1915). Li-tai chiang-yü-chih 歷代疆域志 [Monograph on the territorial boundaries of the successive dynasties].

----- Li-tai ti-li yen-ko-t'u 歷代地理沿革圖 [Evolutionary maps of the geography of the successive dynasties].

These two works are highly synthetic, but it is regrettable that their map-making techniques fell short of excellence. Therefore it is difficult to speak of their reliability.

Because of the frequent border-incidents after the Ch'ien-lung period (1737-1796), scholars of the Chia-ching and Tao-kuang periods (1796-1850) began to focus their attention on the geography of the Northwest border regions like Sinkiang, Tsinghai, Tibet, and Mongolia, the best known among them being Hsü Sung 徐松 (1781-1848), Chang Mu 張穆 (1805-1849), and Ho Ch'iu-t'ao 何秋濤 (1824-1862). [Their works are these:]

Hsü Sung. Hsi-yü shui-tao chi 西域水道記 [A record of waterways in the western region (Sinkiang)]. 5 ch.; 1823.

----- Han-shu Hsi-yü-chuan pu-chu 漢書西域傳補注 [Supplementary commentary on the chapter on the western region (Sinkiang) in the History of the Han]. 2 ch.; 1829.

----- Hsin-chiang fu 新疆賦 [A song-poem on Sinkiang]. 1 ch.; pub. date unknown.

[*92] Chang Mu. Meng-ku yu-mu chi 蒙古遊牧記 [An account of pastoral clans in Mongolia]. 16 ch.; 1867.

Ho Ch'iu-t'ao. Shuo-fang pei-cheng 朔方備乘 [A manual of the northern frontiers]. 80 ch.; 1881.

[Out of these studies] gradually grew an interest in studying the History of the Yüan, 元史, which reached a particularly flourishing state in the late Ch'ing.

As for [the study of] the geography of foreign countries, a start had been made with Hsü Chi-yü's (1793-1873) Ying-huan chih-lüeh 瀛環志略 [A brief description of the world, 10 ch.; 1850] and Wei Yüan's Hai-kuo t'u-chih 海國圖志 [An illustrated gazetteer of the maritime countries, 100 ch.; 1852], but unfortunately it never developed to any height. A more recent man, Ting Ch'ien 丁謙 , has done extensive textual research on such ancient works as Ko-shih wai-i chuan 各史外夷傳 [Biographies of the outlandish barbarians in the various dynastic histories], Mu-t'ien-tzu chuan 穆天子傳 [Biography of the Emperor Mu, 6 ch.; 1915], Fo-kuo chi 佛國記 [Notes on India, 1 ch.; 1915], and Ta-T'ang Hsi-yü chi 大唐西域記 [Notes on the western region (Sinkiang) of the Great T'ang, 1 ch.; 1915]. He completed more than twenty works (no general title for them; recently, they were edited and published by the Chekiang Provincial Library); all of them [were] quite excellent and incisive.

To sum up, Ch'ing geographical studies were overly inclined to antiquarian research and so turned a living subject into a dead one. However, according to Ch'üan Tsu-wang's Biography of Liu Hsien-t'ing, we know that Liu had intended to study "human geography." It is a matter of regret that he did not complete his work and that he had no followers.

After Hsü Kuang-ch'i 徐光啟 (1562-1633) of the Ming period (1368-1644), scholars and officials began to develop an interest in studying astronomy and mathematics. During the early Ch'ing, Wang Hsu-shan and Mei Wen-ting were the most accomplished specialists [in these fields], and great scholars like Huang Tsung-hsi and Chiang Yung all promoted these subjects. The Emperor K'ang-hsi, in particular, took a profound interest in them and summoned a Western scholar, Johannes Adam Schall von Bell, to serve in the inner court. As this trend became wide-spread, admirers [of these subjects] multiplied increasingly.

Emperor K'ang-hsi 康熙 (1654-1722). Shu-li ching-yün 數理精蘊 [Essentials of mathematics]. 53 ch.

----- Li-hsiang k'ao-ch'eng 曆象考成 [Examination of the astronomical figures]. 42 ch.; 1724.

Wang Hsi-shan 王錫闡 (1628-1682). Hsiao-an hsin-fa 曉菴新法 [New methods of Wang Hsi-shan]. 6 ch.; 1843.

Mei Wen-ting 梅文鼎 (1633-1721). Mei Wu-an li-suan ch'üan-shu 梅勿菴曆算全書 [Complete works on astronomy and mathematics of Mei Wen-ting]. 74 ch., totaling twenty-nine works; 1723.

[*93] Chiang Yung 江永 (1681-1762). Shu-hsüeh 數學 [Mathematics]. 9 ch., totaling nine works.

Tai Chen edited ten mathematical works, ranging from the Chou Gnomon 周髀 to works by men of the Six Dynasties and the T'ang, under the title Suan-ching 算經 [Classics of mathematics]. From that time on, nine out of ten classicists studied astronomy and mathematics concurrently, and the particularly knowledgeable persons in these fields included Li Jui 李銳 (1765-1814), Tung Yu-ch'eng 董祐誠 (179?-1823), Chiao Hsün 焦循 (1763-1820), Lo Shih-lin 羅士琳 (d. 1853), Chang Tso-nan 張作楠, Liu Heng 劉衡 (1776-1841), Hsü Yu-jen 徐有壬 (1800-1860), Tsou Po-ch'i 鄒伯奇 (1819-1869), Ting Ch'ü-chung 丁取忠, Li Shan-lan 李善蘭 (1810-1882), and Hua Heng-fang 華蘅芳 (1833-1902). [Their works included:]

Li Jui. Li-shih i-shu 李氏遺書 [Posthumous publications of Mr. Li]. 18 ch.; 1823.

Tung Yu-ch'eng. Tung Fang-li i-shu 董方立遺書 [Posthumous publication of Tung Yu-ch'eng]. 10 titles; 1869.

Chiao Hsün. Li-t'ang hsüeh-suan chi 里堂學算記 [An account of my learning of mathematics]. 5 titles.

Chang Tso-nan. Ts'ui-wei shan-fang suan-ts'ao 翠微山房算草 [Mathematics of the Ts'ui-wei (Subtly-Green) Mountain Studio].

Liu Heng. Liu-chiu-hsüan suan-shu 六九軒算書 [Mathematical works of the Six-Nine Chamber]. 1850-1851.

Hsü Yu-jen. Wu-min i-chai suan-hsüeh 務民義齋算學 [Mathematics of the Serving-the-People Righteous Studio]. 11 ch.

Tsou Po-ch'i. Tsou-cheng-chün i-shu 鄒徵君遺書 [Posthumous publication of Tsou Po-ch'i]. 1873.

Ting Ch'ü-chung. Pai-fu-t'ang suan-hsüeh ts'ung-shu 白芙堂算學叢書 [Collected works on mathematics in the White Lotus Studio]. 23 titles; 1874.

Li Shan-lan. Tse ku-hsi-chai suan-hsüeh 則古昔齋算學 [Mathematics of the Emulating-the-Antiquity Studio]. 13 titles; 1867.

Tseng Kuo-fan 曾國藩 (1811-1872) established the Kiangnan Arsenal in Shanghai, which translated considerable [amounts of] Western scientific works, with most of the more famous works on mathematics done by Li Shan-lan and Hua Heng-fang. [Li joined the staff of Tseng Kuo-fan in 1863, but I am not certain whether he worked in the Arsenal's translation bureau. -- Tr.] From that time forth, the so-called "Western learning" gradually came into prominence. Juan Yüan wrote Ch'ou-jen chuan 疇人傳 [Biographies of mathematicians, 46 ch.; 1799; HCCC, 237], and Lo Shih-lin 羅士琳 (d. 1853) supplemented it, giving an outline of the development of this type of study [science] in the Ch'ing period. Actually, this subject in China had begun quite early, but it was not until the Ch'ing period that it really grew to prominence. It was then that scholars studied it intensively, in a spirit of humility, each making a creative accomplishment. They were quite capable of absorbing Western methods. It is here that the potential capacity of our people may be seen.

[*94] Section 16. Bibliographical Notes on Empirical Research on Bronze and Stone Inscriptions and Collation and Assembling of Lost Texts

Another outstanding subject of study during the Ch'ing period was the bronze and stone inscriptions. With Ku Yen-wu's Chih-shih wen-tzu chi 金石文字記 [Notes on bronze and stone inscriptions, 6 ch.; 1888], a beginning of this study was virtually made, and it was followed by:

Ch'ien Ta-hsin 錢大昕 (1728-1804). Chin-shih wen pa-wei 金石文跋尾 [Postscripts to bronze and stone inscriptions]. 25 ch.; 1884.

Wu I 武億 (1745-1799). Chin-shih san-pa 金石三跋 [Three collections of postscripts to the bronze and stone inscriptions]. 10 ch.

Hung I-hsüan 洪頤煊 (1765-1837). P'ing-chin-kuan tu-pei chi 平津館讀碑記 [Notes on reading (inscriptions on) the monuments in the P'ing-chin Hall]. 9 ch.; 1888.

Yen K'o-chün 嚴可均 (1762-1842). T'ieh-ch'iao chin-shih pa 鐵橋金石跋 [Postscripts to bronze and stone inscriptions by Yen K'o-chün]. 4 ch.; 1903.

Ch'en Chien-ch'i 陳介祺 (1813-1884). Chin-shih wen-tzu k'ao shih 金石文字考釋 [Explanation of bronze and stone inscriptions]. 1 ch.

All of these were extremely high-quality works of textual studies. Wang Ch'ang's 王昶 (1725-1807) Chin-shih ts'ui-pien 金石萃編 [Miscellaneous collection of bronze and stone inscriptions, 160 ch.; 1805] assembled the different interpretations, [producing something]

like a collectanea, while Sun Hsing-yen 孫星衍 (1753-1818) and Hsing Chu's 邢澍 Huan-yü fang-pei-lu 寰宇訪碑錄 [An account of visits to monuments in the world, 12 ch.; 1820) was exclusively a catalogue. Later, as more and more monuments and tablets were excavated, works like the [above-mentioned] Miscellaneous Collection and Visit to the Monuments could not exhaust them, even though supplemented repeatedly.

The school of Ku Yen-wu and Ch'ien Ta-hsin specialized in the use of bronze and stone inscriptions as raw material for textual research on the classics and histories, while Huang Tsung-hsi's school used them to study literary and historical style and themes. Huang wrote Chin-shih yao-li 金石要例 [Essential composition rules of bronze and stone inscriptions]; after him came Liang Yü-sheng 梁玉繩 (1745-1819), Wang Ch'i-sun 王芑孫 (1755-1818), Kuo Lin 郭麐, Liu Pao-nan 劉寶楠 (1791-1855), Li Fu-sun 李富孫 (1764-1843), and Feng Teng-fu 馮登府 (1783-1841), who had all produced works one after the other.

There was another school, led by Weng Fang-kang 翁方綱 (1733-1818) and Huang I 黃易, which specialized in determining the authenticity of [such objects]; hence this school's researches did not purport to assist in [the study of] the classics and histories. Pao Shih-[*95] -ch'en's 包世臣 (1775-1855) school concentrated on the study of calligraphic style, an aesthetic occupation, while Yeh Ch'ang-ch'ih 葉昌熾 (1847-1917) wrote Yü-shih 語石 [On stone inscriptions, 10 ch.; 1908], which synthesized quite well the forte of these various schools. The above were studies of stone inscriptions.

The "study of bronze inscriptions," 金文學, promoted textual studies on Shang and Chou bronze artifacts, which at first had been assembled only in the imperial palaces. Hsi-Ch'ing ku-chien 西清古鑑 [Illustration of ancient objects in the Western Ch'ing Palace,40 + 16 ch.] and Ning-shou chien-ku 寧壽鑑古 [Illustration of ancient objects in the Palace of Tranquility and Longevity, 16 ch.]were such official works, but the script of these books had been copied fancifully and their original form had been lost; there were no explanatory notes either or, if there were, they were nothing but speculative guesswork. However, beginning with such high provincial grandees as Juan Yüan and Wu Jung-kuang 吳榮光 (1773-1843), who had the power and means to pursue their antiquarian interest, the [bronze] collection gradually grew richer, and subsequently there emerged writings and records about it. Juan wrote the Chi-ku-chai chung-ting i-ch'i k'uan-shih 積古齋鐘鼎彝器款識 [Inscriptions of the bronze bells, tripods, and other ritual bronzes of the Studio for Antiquarian Collections, 10 ch.; 1883], and Wu wrote the Yün-ch'ing kuan chin-wen 筠清館金文 [Bronze inscriptions of the Yün-ch'ing Studio, 5 ch.; 1840], thereby initiating the study of bronze inscriptions, which became the more popular after the Tao-kuang and Hsien-feng periods (1820-1861), with such renowned scholars as Liu Hsi-hai 劉喜海 (d. 1853), Wu Shih-fen 吳式芬 (1796-1856), Ch'en Chieh-ch'i 陳介祺 (1813-1884), Wang I-jung 王懿榮 (1845-1900), P'an Tsu-yin 潘祖蔭 (1830-1890), Wu Ta-ch'eng 吳大澂 (1835-1902), and Lo Chen-yü 羅振玉 (1866-1940). Wu Shih-fen wrote Chün-ku-lu chin-wen 攈古錄金文 [Collected ancient records: bronze inscriptions, 3 ch.; 1895], P'an Tsu-yin wrote P'an-ku-lou i-ch'i k'uan-shih 攀古樓彝器款識 [Inscriptions of the ritual bronze pieces of the Studio for Antiquarian Pursuits, 2 ts'e; 1871], and Wu Ta-ch'eng wrote K'e-chai chi-ku-lu 愙齋集古錄 [Antiquarian collection of Wu Ta-ch'eng, 28 ts'e; 1930], all of which were considered extensive works of excellent quality; the findings of these textual studies proceeded for the most part from group consultation and analysis between [the author's] teachers and friends, and not necessarily from the author's private opinion alone.

The rise of interest in bronze inscriptions caused a revolution in traditional linguistics. Whereas before that time men had exalted the Explanation of Script, 說文, as if it had been one of the Six Classics and ranked [its author] Hsü Shen 許慎 (ca. A.D. 100) with Confucius, they now cited ancient script and big-seal writing to criticize him endlessly, and the most outstanding of these [attacks] were Chuang Shu-tsu's [*96] 莊述祖 (1750-1816) Shuo-wen ku-chou shu-cheng 說文古籀疏證 [A commentary on the ancient and big-seal scripts in the Explanation of Script, 1 ch.] and Sun I-jang's 孫詒讓 (1848-1908) Ku-chou shu-cheng 古籀疏證 [Commentary on the ancient and big-seal scripts].

After the inscriptions on the bronze pieces became intelligible, many historical events that had been outside the scope of the ancient classics were revealed, thereby adding an immeasurable amount of [new] historical material. The study of the designs and carving [of these pieces] should add valuable material to art history also, but it is deplorable that no one has as yet undertaken it. Lately, a study was made of oracle-bone inscriptions excavated in 1899 in the T'ang-yin county, 湯陰縣, of Honan Province and amounting to several thousand pieces, having unintelligible inscriptions whose dates nobody could determine. But later, Lo Chen-yü examined and found them to be Yin 殷 [Shang] writings, and wrote Yin-shang Chen-po wen-tzu k'ao 殷商貞卜文字考 [A study of the divination-writing of the Shang period, 1 ts'e; 1909], Yin-hsü shu-ch'i k'ao-shih 殷虛書契考釋 [Critical explanation of oracle-bone inscriptions of the Shang ruins, 3 ch.; 1927], and Yin-hsü wen-tze tai-wen p'ien 殷虛文字待問篇 [Unknown characters from the oracle-bone inscriptions of the Shang ruins, 1 ts'e; 1923]. Sun I-jang, also, based his Ming-yüan 名原 [Origins of writing] to a large degree on these oracle-bone inscriptions. Lately some people have gone further to assert that the raw material [of these artifacts] was not tortoise shell but bamboo slip. It is unfortunate that the inscriptions were too simple and that little historical data could be derived from them. Nevertheless, traces of linguistic evolution and differences are discernible here.

Ch'ing scholars made another contribution to historical studies by collating [texts]. The less was the dissemination of ancient books, the greater was the number of errors when they were transmitted and reprinted, until a point was reached where these books became simply unintelligible and hence useless. Ch'ing scholars made extensive searches for good editions for comparative study, and collation of texts thus became a specialized branch of learning in its own right. Competent works [of collation] that deserve mention are:

Wang Chung 汪中 (1745-1794) and Pi Yüan 畢沅 (1730-1797). Ta-Tai Li-chi cheng-wu 大戴禮記正誤 [Correction of mistakes in the Book of Rites of the Elder Tai]. 1 ch.; HCCC, 193.

Chou T'ing-ts'ai 周廷寀 and Chao Huai-yü 趙懷玉 (1747-1823). Han-shih wai-chuan 韓詩外傳 [Han Ying's illustrations of the didactic applications of the Odes]. 10 ch.; 1917.

[*97] Lu Wen-shao 盧文弨 (1717-1795). I-Chou-shu 逸周書 [Lost history of Chou]. 10 ch.; 1923.

Wang Chung, Pi Yüan, and Sun I-jang 孫詒讓 (1848-1908). Mo-tzu 墨子. 16 ch.

Hsieh Yung 謝墉 (1719-1795). Hsün-tzu 荀子.

Sun Hsing-yen 孫星衍 (1753-1818). Sun-tzu 孫子. 13 ch.; 1927.

-----Wu-tzu 吳子.

Wang Chi-p'ei 汪繼培 (b. 1775), Jen Ta-ch'un 任大椿 (1738-1789), and Ch'in En-fu 秦恩復 (1760-1843). Lieh-tzu 列子.

Ku Kuang-ch'i 顧廣圻 (1776-1835). Kuo-yü 國語 [Famous discourses of the various states of the Tso-chuan].

-----Chan Kuo-ts'e 戰國策 [Strategies of the Warring States].

-----Han-fei tzu 韓非之. 20 ch.; 1901.

Pi Yüan 畢沅 (1730-1797) and Liang Yü-sheng 梁玉繩 (1745-1819). Lü-shih Ch'un-ch'iu 呂氏春秋 [Lu Pu-wei's Spring and Autumn Annals].

Yen K'o-chün 嚴可均 (1762-1842). Shen-tzu 慎子 .

----- Shang-chün shu 商君書 [The book of the Lord of Shang]. 5 ch.; 1901.

Pi Yüan. Shan-hai-ching 山海經 [The Classic of Mountains and Seas]. 18 ch.; 1901.

Hung I-hsüan 洪頤煊 (1765-1837). Chu-shu chi-nien 竹書紀年 [The bamboo annals]. 2 ch.

----- Mu-t'ien-tzu chuan 穆天子傳 [Biography of the Emperor Mu]. 6 ch.

Ting Ch'ien 丁謙 . Mu-t'ien-tzu chuan 穆天子傳 [Biography of the Emperor Mu]. 7 ch.; 1915.

Tai Chen 戴震 (1724-1777) and Lu Wen-shao 盧文弨 (1717-1795). Ch'un-ch'iu fan-lu 春秋繁露 [On Tung Chung-shu's ramifications of the principles of the Spring and Autumn Annals].

Wang Chung 汪中 (1745-1794). Chia I hsin-shu 賈誼新書 [New book of Chia I].

Tai Chen 戴震. Suan-ching shih-shu 算經十書 [Ten mathematical classics]. 40 ch.; 1775.

Tai Chen and Ch'üan Tsu-wang 全祖望 (1705-1755). Shui-ching chu 水經注 [Commentary on the Water Classic]. 40 ch.

Ku Kuang-ch'i 顧廣圻 (1776-1835). Hua-yang kuo-chih 華陽國志 [A geographical account of Hua-yang (in West China)]. 1 ch.; 1883.

These works of collation either followed good texts, or used the citations of other books as a basis, or cross-referenced earlier and later passages within a single text, or corrected the language [of the texts], or established the [proper] reading for the sentences, or elucidated and confirmed their thematic and didactic [implications]. Often, phrases hitherto unintelligible suddenly became unveiled and transparent. A particularly great contribution was made by these Ch'ing scholars in stimulating an interest in the study of the various pre-Ch'in philosophers, since the majority of the collated works belonged to these philosophers. From the time that Emperor Wu of the Han had condemned and banned the Hundred Schools until the middle of the Ch'ing period, the study of these philosophers could be called virtually non-existent. Mention of men like Hsün-tzu and Mo-tzu, who had offended Mencius, was avoided by almost everyone. But with the rise of textual research, which respected [*98] only ancient evidence, scholars began to take cognizance of the fact that there were so many other valuable works besides the Six Classics. Thus, Wang Nien-sun's Tu-shu tsa-chih 讀書雜誌 [Miscellaneous notes on reading, 82 ch.; 1812-1831] had already reached out to examine the various philosophers; later, Yü Yüeh 俞樾 (1821-1906) gave his Chu-tzu p'ing-i 諸子平議 [Critiques of the various philosophers, 35 ch.; 1870] the same status as [his] Ch'ün-ching p'ing-i 群經平議 [Critiques of the various classics, 35 ch.; 1867]. Various scholars such as Wang Chung, Tai Chen, Lu Wen-shao, Sun Hsing-yen, and Pi Yüan also made a wide selection of ancient works for collation.

In collating texts it is necessary to fix on their meaning, and from this finding new interpretations will emerge. Hence, there were:

Wang Chung 汪中 (1745-1794). Hsün-ch'ing-tzu t'ung-lun 荀卿子通論 [A general explication of Hsün-tzu].
----- Mo-tzu hsü 墨子序 [Preface to the Mo-tzu].
----- Mo-tzu hou-hsü 墨子後序 [Postscript to the Mo-tzu].
(All of these are available in Shu-hsüeh 述學 [A description of learning].)

Sun Hsing-yen 孫星衍 (1753-1818). Mo-tzu hsü 墨子序 [Preface to

the Mo-tzu]. (The Mo-tzu, in Collected Works of the P'ing-chin Hall 平津館叢書本墨子 .)

When we read these today, we feel that they are quite plain and easy, but at that time they in fact elucidated what had not been elucidated, and even more, they asserted what no one else had dared to assert. Later on [there appeared]:

Hung I-hsüan 洪頤煊 (1765-1837). Kuan-tzu i-cheng 管子義證 [Textual studies of the meaning of the Kuan-tzu]. 8 ch.; 1893.

Sun I-jang 孫詒讓 (1848-1908). Mo-tzu chien-ku 墨子間詁 [Philological studies of Mo-tzu]. 19 ch.; 1935.

Wang Hsien-ch'ien 王先謙 (1842-1918). Han-fei-tzu chi-chieh 韓非子集解 [Collected interpretations of the Han-fei-tzu]. 1933.

[All of these studies] elevated [the philosophers' works] to the ranks of classics and [made them worthy] of commentaries. Today, the more liberal and enlightened scholars all regard philosophy and classics as equally important. These examples show that the forces producing the metamorphosis of thought may come from one direction, while the effect may be found in quite another direction.

We owe a debt of gratitude to the Ch'ing scholars for still another accomplishment, that is, the assembling of lost texts. Over a long time, books will undoubtedly become dispersed or lost, and this is readily seen when we compare the lost and extant texts from the various monographs [*99] on bibliography in the dynastic histories. The presence or absence of shallow and poor-quality works is of course immaterial, but the disappearance of well-known masterpieces represents a loss to our national heritage. The Complete Works of the Four Treasuries, compiled during the Ch'ien-lung period, adopted hundreds of books from the Great Yung-lo Encyclopedia, 永樂大典, becoming a harbinger of the [profession of] assembling lost texts which, from that time on, became more popular every day. No effort was spared to collect and record even a single phrase, if it existed, of the Chou and Ch'in philosophers, the Han commentaries on the classics, and the unofficial histories and collected works of the Wei, the Chin, and the Six Dynasties. Their source material came largely from the several large collectanea of the T'ang and Sung; for example, the I-wen lui-chü 藝文類聚 [Collected works on literature and the arts, 100 ch.; compiled by Ou-yang Hsün 歐陽洵 (557-641)], Ch'u-hsüeh chi 初學記 [Collection of the essentials of the classics, history, and literature for the beginner, 30 ch.; 1531; compiled by Hsü Chien 徐堅 (659-729), et al.], and the T'ai-p'ing yü-lan 太平御覽 [Imperial collection of the Sung T'ai-p'ing hsing-kuo period, 976-984, 1000 ch.; reprinted in 1892; compiled by Li Fang 李昉 (925-996), et al.]; and no discoverable classics, their commentaries, or other works were left out. There were quite a number of scholars at the time who engaged in this type of work, and I will not list them all, but Ma Kuo-han's 馬國翰 (1794-1857) Yü-han shan-fang chi-i-shu 玉函山房輯佚書 [Fragments of lost works assembled at the Yü-han Mountain Studio, 80 ch.; 1853], which had a tripartite division of classics, history, and philosophy, was a collection of several hundred assembled works. Other [such collections] may be inferred from this. Thus, the various monographs [on bibliography] in the Histories of the Han, Sui, and T'ang, as well as other books which had long been considered lost, were now to appear all at once in our catalogue of book collections. Even though only fragments [of such lost works] were recovered, we have already profited considerably from this.

ch'an 禪
Chang Erh-ch'i 張爾岐
Chang Hsüeh-ch'eng 章學誠
Chang Hui-yen 張惠言
Chang K'uang-hsüeh 張匡學
Chang Li-hsiang 張履祥
Chang Mu 張穆
Chang Ping-lin 章炳麟
Chang Ts'ang 張蒼
Chang-tzu cheng-meng chu 張子正蒙注
Chang Yin-lin 張蔭麟
Chang Yu-ch'eng 章祐誠
Ch'ang-sheng-tien 長生殿
Chao Chung-han 趙仲涵
Chao Ho-shou 趙鶴壽
Chao Huai-yü 趙懷玉
Chao I 趙翼
Chao-yü-chih 肇域志
Chen Kao-huang 箴膏肓
Ch'en Ch'iao-ts'ung 陳喬樅
Ch'en Chieh-ch'i 陳介祺
Ch'en Ch'ien-ch'iu 陳千秋
Ch'en Fang-chi 陳芳績
Ch'en Li 陳立
Ch'en Li 陳澧
Ch'en She, see Ch'en Sheng
Ch'en Sheng 陳勝 (Ch'en She 陳涉)
Ch'en Shou-ch'i 陳壽祺
Ch'en Tu-hsiu 陳獨秀
Ch'en T'uan 陳摶
Cheng Chen 鄭珍
Cheng Ch'iao 鄭樵
Cheng Hsüan 鄭玄
Cheng-hsüeh t'ung-i 政學通議
Cheng-i 正義
Cheng-meng 正蒙
Cheng-meng chu 正蒙注
cheng-ming 正名
Cheng Wen-cho 鄭文焯
Ch'eng Hao 程顥
Ch'eng I (Ch'eng Yi) 程頤
Ch'eng-kuan 承貫
Ch'eng Yao-t'ien 程瑤田
Chi-ch'i-t'ing chi 鮚埼亭集
Chi Yün 紀昀
Ch'i 齊
Ch'i fei-chi 起廢疾
"Ch'i Lu Han Mao i-t'ung lun" 齊魯韓毛異同論
Ch'i-lüeh 七略
Ch'i-shih I-shih hsüeh 齊詩翼氏學
Ch'i-shih I-shih-hsüeh shu-cheng 齊詩翼氏學疏證
Ch'i-wu-lun shih 齊物論釋
Chia-ch'ing 嘉慶
chia-fa 家法
Chia k'uei 賈逵

Chia Kung-yen 賈公彥
Chiang Fan 江藩
Chiang Fang-chen 蔣方震
Chiang Sheng 江聲
Chiang Shih-ch'üan 蔣士銓
Chiang T'ai-kung 姜太公
Chiang Yung 江永
Chiao-li-t'ang chi 校禮堂集
Chiao-shih ts'ung-shu 焦氏叢書
Chiao Shui-ching chu 校水經注
Chien-lun 檢論
ch'ien 乾
Ch'ien-ch'iu cha-chi 潛邱劄記
Ch'ien-Han shu 前漢書
Ch'ien-lung 乾隆
Ch'ien-ming 褰冥
Ch'ien Mu 錢穆
Ch'ien Ta-hsin 錢大昕
Ch'ien-yen-t'ang chi 潛研堂集
Chih-hsin-chi 知新記
Chih-kuei-tzu 知歸子
Chihli ho-ch'ü shu 直隸河渠書
Chin 晉
Chin Ho 金和
Chin Pang 金榜
Chin-t'an 金壇
Chin-wen Shang-shu ching-shuo k'ao 今文尚書經說考
Chin wu-shih-nien Chung-kuo ssu-hsiang shih 近五十年中國思想史
Ching-chieh p'ien 經解篇
Ching-chuan shih-tz'u 經傳釋詞
Ching Fang 京房
Ching-i shu-wen 經義述聞
Ching-i tsa-chi 經義雜記
ching-shih chih-yung 經世致用
Ching-yün-lou chi 經韻樓集
ch'ing 情
Ch'ing-ju p'ien 清儒篇
Ch'ing P'u 慶普
Ch'ing-shih 清史
Ch'ing-tai t'ung-shih 清代通史
ch'ing-t'an 清談
Chiu-ching ku-i 九經古義
Chiu-ching ku-i shou-su 九經古義首述
Chou-i-shu 周易書
Chou-t'i 周惕
Chou T'ing-ts'ai 周廷寀
Chu Hsi 朱熹
Chu Kuei 朱珪
Chu-Lu p'ien 朱陸篇
Chu Tsu-mou 朱祖謀
Chu-tzu wan-nien ting-lun 朱子晚年定論
Chu-tzu yü-lei 朱子語類
Chu Tz'u-ch'i 朱次琦
Ch'u Tz'u 楚辭
Chuang Ts'un-yü 莊存與

Chuang-tzu 莊子

Chuang-tzu chieh 莊子解

Ch'un-ch'iu fu-shih 春秋復始

Ch'un-ch'iu Kung-yang ching-chuan Ho-shih shih-li 春秋公羊經傳何氏釋例

Ch'un-ch'iu Kung-yang chuan 春秋公羊傳

Chung-Hsi chiao-t'ung shih 中西交通史

Chung-kuo che-hsüeh shih 中國哲學史

Chung-kuo chin-san-pai-nien hsüeh-shu shih 中國近三百年學術史

Chung-kuo chin-tai-shih lun-ts'ung 中國近代史論叢

Chung-li 中立

Chung Ling 鍾錂

Chung-shan cha-chi 鍾山札記

Chung-yung pu-chuan yen 中庸補傳衍

Chü-yeh-t'ang chi 居業堂集

ch'ü 曲

Ch'üan-hsüeh p'ien 勸學篇

Ch'üan Tsu-wang 全祖望

Ch'ün-ch'iao 春喬

Ch'ün-chiu 春秋

Ch'ün-ch'iu Tso-shih-chuan 春秋左氏傳

Erh-ya wen-tzu k'ao 爾雅文字考

Fa mo-shou 發墨守

Fan Ch'in 范欽

Fang Hao 方豪

Fang Pao 方苞

Fang Tung-shu 方東樹

Fang-yen shu-cheng 方言疏證

Fei Chih 費直

fei-fu 飛伏

Feng Ch'üan 馮銓

Feng-shan-shu 封禪書

Feng Teng-fu 馮登府

fou-kuang lüeh-ying 浮光掠影

Fu Ch'ien 服虔

"Fu Ch'ing-chu shih-lüeh" 傅青主事略

Fu Hsi 伏羲

Fu Shan 傅山

Fu Sheng 伏勝

"Fu-tzu cheng-yüeh lun" 夫子正樂論

Hai-kuo t'u-chih 海國圖志

Han 韓

Han-hsüeh shang-tui 漢學商兌

Han Ing 韓嬰

Han-ju t'ung-i 漢儒通義

Han-shih wai-chuan 韓詩外傳

Han Yü 韓愈

Hang Shih-chün 杭世駿

heng-ch'ao 橫超

Hengyang 衡陽
Ho Cho 何焯
Ho Hsiu 何休
Ho Shen 和坤
Ho-t'u 河圖
Ho-t'u yüan-ts'uan p'ien 河圖原舛篇
Hou-Han-shu pu-chu 後漢書補注
Hou-kuan 侯官
Hsi-chai chi-yü wei-chui chi hsü 習齋記餘未墜集序
Hsi-ch'iao shan 西樵山
hsi hsiang yüan 習相遠
Hsia Sui-ch'ing 夏穗卿
Hsia Tseng-yu 夏曾佑
Hsiang Hung-cha 項鴻祚
Hsiang-tsung lo-so 相宗絡索
hsiao-ch'en 爻辰
(Hsiao) Hsia-hou Chien 小夏侯建
Hsiao-hsüeh 小學
(Hsiao) Tai Sheng 小戴聖
Hsiao-tu-shu-chai ssu-lu 曉讀書齋四錄
Hsin-hsiao-shuo 新小說
Hsin-hsüeh wei-ching k'ao 新學偽經考
Hsin-hui 新會
Hsin-min ts'ung-pao 新民叢報
Hsin-yün p'u 新韻譜
hsing hsiang chin 性相近
Hsing-ming ku-hsün 性命古訓
hsing pen shan 性本善
Hsiung Hsi-ling 熊希齡
Hsü Hsia-k'e, see Hsü Hung-tsu
Hsü Hsing 許行
Hsü Hung-tsu 徐宏祖 (Hsü Hsia-k'e 徐霞客)
Hsü Kuang-ch'i 徐光啟
Hsü-san-t'ung 續三通
Hsü Shen 許慎
Hsü t'ien-wen-lüeh 續天文略
Hsü Yen 徐彥
Hsüeh-hai-t'ang 學海堂
Hsüeh-hai-t'ang ching-chieh 學海堂經解
"Hsüeh pien" 學辯
"Hsüeh-wen p'ien" 學問篇
Hsün Hsü 荀諝
hsün-ku 訓詁
Hu-mu Sheng 胡毋生
Hu Shih 胡適
Hu T'ien-yu 胡天游
Hu Wei 胡渭
Huai 淮
Huang-ch'ao san-t'ung 皇朝三通
Huang-Ch'ing ching-chieh 皇清經解
"Huang Li-chou hsien-sheng shen-tao-pei" 黃梨洲先生神道碑
Huang Tsun-hsien 黃遵憲

Huang Tsung-hsi 黄宗羲

"Huang Tsung-hsi chuan" 黄宗羲傳

Huang Tsung-yen 黄宗炎

Hui Shih-ch'i 惠士奇

Hui Tung 惠棟

Hung-fan cheng-lun 洪範正論

Hung-fan wu-hsin chuan 洪範五行傳

Hung Liang-chi 洪亮吉

Hung Liang-p'in 洪良品

Hung-lou-meng 紅樓夢

Hung Pang 洪榜

Hung Sheng 洪昇

I-chiao p'ien 易教篇

I-chiao ts'ung-pien 翼教叢編

I-chuan shih-i 易傳十翼

I-Han-hsüeh 易漢學

I-heng-kuan 藝衡館

I-hsüeh hsiang-shu lun 易學象數論

I-Men tu-shu-chi 義門讀書記

I-t'u ming-pien 易圖明辨

I-t'ung-chih 一統志

I Yin 伊尹

jen chih ch'u 人之初

Jen-hsüeh 仁學

Jen-shih 人史

Jen Ta-ch'ün 任大椿

Jih-chih-lu 日知錄

Juan Yüan 阮元

Kai-tsao tsa-chih 改造雜誌

Kai-yü ts'ung-k'ao 陔餘叢考

kan-chih 干支

Kan-shan 憨山

Kan-yü p'ien 感遇篇

K'ang-hsi 康熙

K'ang Yu-wei 康有為

Kao T'ang-sheng 高堂生

k'ao-cheng hsüeh 考證學

Kou-ku ke-huan chi 句股割圜記

Ku-chin wei-shu k'ao 古今偽書考

Ku-li k'ao 古曆考

Ku-liang fei-chi 穀梁廢疾

Ku-shu i-i chü-li 古書疑義舉例

Ku Tsu-yü 顧祖禹

Ku-wen Shang-shu k'ao 古文尚書考

Ku-wen Shang-shu yüan-tz'u 古文尚書冤詞

Ku Yen-wu 顧炎武

Kuaichi 會稽

Kuang-fu Hui 光復會

Kuang-ya su-cheng 廣雅疏證

Kuang-yang tsa-chi 廣陽雜記

k'uang-ch'an 狂禪

k'uang-chung 匡衷

Kuei-ssu lui kao 癸巳類稿

Kuei-ssu ts'un-kao 癸巳存稿

Kuei Yu-kuang 歸有光

k'un 坤

Kung An-kuo 孔安國

"Kung-ch'e shang-shu" 公車上書

Kung Tzu-chen 龔自珍

Kung-yang ch'ien 公羊箋

Kung-yang chuan 公羊傳

Kung-yang chuan-chu tzu-hsü 公羊傳注自序

Kung-yang mo-shou 公羊墨守

K'ung Kuang-sen 孔廣森

K'ung Shang-jen 孔尚任

K'ung-tzu kai-chih k'ao 孔子改制考

K'ung Ying-ta 孔穎達

Kunshan 崑山

Kuo Chan-po 郭湛波

Kuo-ch'ao ch'i-hsien lei-cheng 國朝耆獻類徵

Kuo-ch'ao Han-hsüeh shih-ch'eng-chi 國朝漢學師承記

Kuo-ch'ao hsüeh-an hsiao-shih 國朝學案小識

Kuo-ch'ao liu-ju sung 國朝六儒頌

Kuo-feng 國風

Kuo-feng pao 國風報

Kuo-ku lün-heng 國故論衡

Kuo-t'ing-lu 過庭錄

Kuo-yü 國語

Lao-tzu 老子

Lao-tzu yen 老子衍

li 理

li 禮

Li Chao-lo 李兆洛

Li Chien 黎簡

Li Chih-ts'ai 李之才

Li Chih-tsao 李之藻

Li Chung-fu 李中孚

li-hsüeh 理學

Li Kuang-ti 李光地

Li Kung 李塨

Li Ping-huan 李炳寰

Li Shan-lan 李善蘭

Li-shuo 禮說

Li Ting-i 李定一

Li-wen 曆問

Li Yü 李漁

Li Yün 禮運

Liang Ch'i-ch'ao 梁啟超

liang-chih 良知

Liang-ch'iu Ho 梁丘賀

Liang Yü-sheng 梁玉繩

Liao P'ing 廖平

Lien-tz'u 蓮池

Lin Chih-chün 林志鈞

Lin Kuei 林圭

Lin Shu 林紓

Ling-hsien 令嫺

Ling T'ing-k'an 凌廷堪

Liu Chih-chi 劉知幾
"Liu-ch'u-shih mu-piao" 劉處士墓表
Liu Feng-lu 劉逢祿
Liu Hsien-t'ing 劉獻廷
Liu Hsin 劉歆
liu-jih ch'i-fen 六日七分
Liu-li-ch'ang 琉璃廠
Liu-shu yin-yün piao 六書音韵表
Liu Ta-k'uei 劉大櫆
Liu T'ai-kung 劉台拱
Liu Tsung-chou 劉宗周
Liuyang 瀏陽
Lo-shu 洛書
Lo Yu-kao 羅有高
Lu 魯
Lu Chi-lu 陸繼輅
Lu Hsiang-shan 陸象山
Lu Lung-ch'i 陸隴其
Lu Shih-i 陸世儀
Lu Te-ming 陸德明
Lu Wen-chao 盧文弨
Lü-lü hsin-i 律呂新義
Lü-shih Ch'ün-ch'iu 呂氏春秋
"Lun chiang-hsüeh" 論講學
Lung-ch'eng cha-chi 龍城札記
ma-fa 瑪法
Ma Kuo-han 馬國翰
Ma Yung 馬融
Mao-chuan 毛傳
Mao Ch'i-ling 毛奇齡
Mao Kung 毛公
"Mei-ting-chiu-cheng-chün chuan" 梅定九徵君傳
Mei Wen-t'ing 梅文鼎
Meng Hsi 孟喜
Meng-ku t'u-chih 蒙古圖志
Meng-tzu tzu-yi su-cheng 孟子字義疏證
ming-chiao 名教
"Ming-Ch'ing chih-chi Hsi-hsüeh shu-ju Chung-kuo k'ao-lüeh" 明清之際西學輸入中國考略
Ming-i-tai-fang-lu 明夷待訪錄
Ming-ju hsüeh-an 明儒學案
Ming-t'ang ta-tao lu 明堂大道錄
Mourao Ioannes 穆經遠
Mu-piao yin 墓表引
na-chia 納甲
Na-lan-hsing-te 納蘭性德
Ou-chou wen-i fu-hsing shih-tai shih, tzu-hsü 歐洲文藝復興時代史，自序
Ou-yang Hsiu 歐陽修
Ou-yang Sheng 歐陽生
Pan Ku 班固
Pao T'ing-po 鮑廷博

Pei-feng 邶風

P'eng Shao-sheng 彭紹升

Pi Yüan 畢沅

Pieh-chi 瞥記

Pien-fa t'ung-i 變法通議

p'ien-wen 駢文

po-shih 博士

Po-yeh 博野

Po-yüeh p'ien 博約篇

p'u-hsüeh 樸學

Pu-jen tsa-chih 不忍雜誌

Saddharmapundarika 法華

San-chia-shih i-shuo k'ao 三家詩遺說考

San-chia-shih i-wen su-cheng 三家詩異文疏證

San-tsang fa-shih pa-shih kuei-chü-lun tsan 三藏法師八識規矩論贊

San-tzu-ching 三字經

Shang-shu ku-wen su-cheng 尚書古文疏證

Shang-shu Ou-yang Hsia-hou i-shuo k'ao 尚書歐陽夏侯遺說考

Shao Ch'i-t'ao 邵齊燾

Shao I-ch'en 邵懿辰

Shao Yung 邵雍

Shen Kung 申公

Shen T'ung 沈彤

Sheng-che hua-hsiang tsan 聖哲畫像贊

sheng-chiang 升降

Sheng-lei piao 聲類表

Sheng-yün k'ao 聲韵考

Shih-chi 史記

Shih-chi t'an-yüan 史記探原

Shih-chia-chai yang-hsin-lu 十駕齋養新錄

Shih-chiao p'ien 詩教篇

Shih ku-wei 詩古微

shih-kuei 世軌

Shih-san ching chu-shu 十三經注疏

Shih Shou-wen 釋守溫

Shih-tai 石埭

Shih Ts'ou 施讐

Shih-wen 釋文

Shih-wu hsüeh-t'ang 時務學堂

Shih-wu pao 時務報

shih-ying 世應

Shou-shu sui-pi 授書隨筆

Shu-an wen-ch'ao 述庵文鈔

Shu ku-wei 書古微

Shu-tzu chi 叔子集

Shu Wei 舒位

Shui-ching-chu shih 水經注釋

Shui-ti chi 水地記

Shun 舜

Shun-chih 順治

Shuo-lin p'ien 說林篇

Shuo-wen chieh-tzu chu 說文解字注

Siuning 休寧

Ssu-chieh 俟解

Ssu-i-kuan ching-hsüeh ts'ung-shu 四益館經學叢書

Ssu-k'u ch'üan-shu 四庫全書

ssu-k'ung ch'eng-tan 司空城旦

Ssu-ma Ch'ien 司馬遷

Sun Ch'i-feng 孫奇逢

Sun Chih-tsu 孫志祖

Sun Hsing-yen 孫星衍

Sun I-jang 孫詒讓

Sun Yat-sen 孫逸仙

Sung Hsiang-feng 宋翔鳳

Sung-lun 宋論

Sung Ying-hsing 宋應星

Sung-Yüan hsüeh-an 宋元學案

Süancheng 宣城

"Ta Cheng Yung-mu shu" 答鄭用牧書

(Ta) Hsia-hou Sheng 大夏侯勝

Ta-hsing 大興

Ta-ssu-t'u 大司徒

(Ta) Tai Te 大戴德

Ta-t'ung shu 大同書

"Ta yu-jen lun-hsüeh shu" 答友人論學書

Tai Chen 戴震

"Tai Chen chuan" 戴震傳

Tai-shih i-shu, chiu, fu-lu 戴氏遺書，九，附錄

Tai Tung-yüan chi, chuan-shou 戴東原集，卷首

"Tai Tung-yüan hsien-sheng shih-lüeh" 戴東原先生事略

"Tai Tung-yüan mu-chih-ming" 戴東原墓志銘

Taiyüan 太原

T'ai-chi t'u-shuo i-i 太極圖說遺議

T'ai-p'ing yü-lan 太平御覽

T'an Hsien 譚獻

T'an Ssu-t'ung 譚嗣同

T'ang Chien 唐鑑

T'ang Pin 湯斌

T'ang Ts'ai-ch'ang 唐才常

Tao-Han-wei-yen 菿漢微言

Tao-ku-t'ang chi 道古堂集

Tao-kuang 道光

Tao-te-ching 道德經

T'ao-hua-shan 桃花扇

Tehtsing 德清

Tiao Pao 刁包

T'ien Ho 田何

T'ien-hsia chün-kuo li-ping shu 天下郡國利病書

T'ien-hsia p'ien 天下篇

T'ien-i ko 天一閣

T'ien-kung k'ai-wu 天公開物

Ting Ching-li 丁敬禮

Ting I 丁廙

T'ing-lin hsien-sheng shen-tao-piao yin 亭林先生神道表引

T'ing-lin wen-chi 亭林文集

Ts'ai Ao 蔡鍔

Tsang Lin 臧琳

Tsang Yung 臧庸

Ts'ao Chih 曹植

Tse-fang-kuang-yü 職方廣輿

Ts'e-suan 策算

Tseng Kung 曾鞏

Tseng Kuo-fan 曾國藩

Tso-shih Ch'ün-ch'iu 左氏春秋

Tso-shih Ch'un-ch'iu k'ao-cheng 左氏春秋考證

Tso-shih kao-mang 左氏膏肓

Ts'ui Shih 崔適

Ts'un-hsüeh pien 存學編

"Tu-shih fang-yü chi-yao hsü" 讀史方輿紀要敘

Tu-shu tsa-chih 讀書雜志

Tu-shu ts'o-lu 讀書脞錄

Tu T'ung-chien lun 讀通鑑論

Tu Yü 杜預

T'u-shu pien-ho 圖書辨惑

Tuan Yü-ts'ai 段玉裁

"Tuan Yü-ts'ai hsü-yin" 段玉裁序引

Tung Chung-shu 董仲舒

tung-hsiao 動爻

Tung-lai 東萊

Tung-lin 東林

Tung-shu tu-shu-chi 東塾讀書記

Tung Yu-ch'eng 董祐誠

Tung-yüan chi 東原集

Tung-yüan wen-chi 東原文集

T'ung-ch'eng 桐城

T'ung-i tang 統一黨

T'ung-li 通禮

T'ung-meng Hui 同盟會

Tunghai 東海

Tzu-chih t'ung chien 資治通鑑

tz'u 詞

Tz'u-yüan 辭源

Vijnānāmātra 唯識宗

"Wan Chi-yeh hsien-sheng chuan" 萬季野先生傳

Wan-i 萬一

Wan-mu ts'ao-t'ang 萬木草堂

Wan Ssu-t'ung 萬斯同

Wang Ch'ang 王昶

Wang Chung 汪中

Wang Fu-chih 王夫之

Wang Fu-ssu 王輔嗣

Wang Hsi-ch'an 王錫闡
Wang I-fu, see Wang Yen
"Wang Jung-fu mu-chih-ming" 汪容甫墓志銘
Wang K'ai-yün 王闓運
Wang Mang 王莽
Wang Ming-sheng 王鳴盛
Wang Nien-sun 王念孫
Wang P'eng-yün 王鵬運
Wang Pi 王弼
Wang Shih-chen 王士禎
Wang Su 王肅
Wang T'an 王曇
Wang Yang-ming 王陽明
Wang Yen 王衍 (Wang I-fu 王夷甫)
Wang Yin-chih 王引之
Wang Ying-lin 王應麟
Wang Yüan 王源
Wei-ching k'ao 偽經考
Wei Chung-hsien 魏忠賢
Wei Hsi 魏禧
Wei Hsiang-shu 魏象樞
Wen-hsüan 文選
Wei I-chieh 魏裔介
Wei ku-wen shang-shu 偽古文尚書
Wei Yüan 魏源
Wen-li p'ien 文理篇
Wen-lu 文錄
Wen-shih 文始
Wu-chin 武進
Wu Ch'ung-yao 伍崇曜
Wu Hsiang-feng 吳翔鳳
Wu Kuang 吳廣
Wu-liang-shou-ching hui-i 無量壽經會譯
Wu Wei-yeh 吳偉業
Wusih 無錫
Yang-chou shih-jih chi 楊州十日記
Yang Hsüan-kan 楊玄感
Yang-hu 陽湖
Yang Wen-hui 楊文會
Yao 堯
Yao Chi-heng 姚際恒
Yao-chiang 姚江
Yao Fan 姚範
Yao Nai 姚鼐
Yeh Te-hui 葉德輝
Yen An-lo 顏安樂
Yen Fu 嚴復
Yen Hsi-chai hsien-sheng nien-p'u 顏習齋先生年譜
Yen Hsi-chai yen-hsing-lu 顏習齋言行錄
Yen Jo-chü 閻若璩
Yen-kung p'ien 言公篇
Yen P'eng-tsu 嚴彭祖
Yen-tzu Ch'ün-ch'iu 晏子春秋
Yen Yüan 顏元
Yi Li 儀禮

Yü Yüeh 俞樾

Yüan-chün 原君

Yüan-fa 原法

Yüan-ho 元和

Yüan-hsiang 原象

Yüan Ku 轅固

Yüan Mei 袁枚

Yüan-shan 原善

Yüan-tao p'ien 原道篇

Yüeh-ya-t'ang ts'ung-shu 粵雅堂叢書

Yühang 餘杭

Yün Ching 惲敬

Yüyao 餘姚

Yin-chen 胤禛

Yin-hsüeh wu-shu 音學五書

Yin-lun 音論

Yin-ssu 胤禩

Yoga 瑜伽

Yung-cheng 雍正

Yung-li 永曆

Yung-lo 永樂

Yü Cheng-hsien 俞正燮

"Yü-ch'in ya-yen hsü yin" 娛親雅言序引

"Yü chu t'ung-chih lun chiao-shu chih nan" 與諸同志論校書之難

Yü Fan 虞翻

"Yü Fang Hsi-yüan shu" 與方希原書

Yü-han shan-fang chi-i shu 玉函山房輯佚書

Yü Hsiao-k'e 余蕭客

Yü-kung chui-chih 禹貢錐指

"Yü-mou shu" 與某書

"Yü mou yu-jen shu" 與某友人書

Yü T'ing-ts'an 余廷燦

"Yü Yao Chi-chuan shu" 與姚姬傳書

"Yü yu-jen lun men-jen shu" 與友人論門人書

"Yü yu-jen shu, erh" 與友人書，二

"Yü yu-jen shu, shih" 與友人書，十